"Michael S. Lewis, M.D.'s book distills the metabolized experience of some of the world's legendary wise humans in a way that motivates all of us to cultivate and harvest our wisdom for the common good."

Chip Conley, NY Times bestselling author and founder and CEO of the Modern Elder Academy.

"Michael S. Lewis, M.D. has given us a book with inspiring examples of how the best get better."

Scott Barry Kaufman, author of *Transcend: The New Science of Self-Actualization*, and host of *The Psychology Podcast*, rated number one psychology podcast in the world.

"In Getting Wiser, Dr. Michael Lewis has captured many of the inspirational moments we shared when we worked together with the Chicago Bulls in the 1990s. You won't find as good a collection of real-life advice from celebrities, athletes, artists, scientists, CEOs, and politicians together in one place. This book is filled with "smarts' for getting through life."

Bill Wennington, former Chicago Bulls center and three-time NBA Champion.

"Life is a blessing frequently missed by people until they are exposed to some unanticipated event – good or bad – which suddenly arouses awareness and appreciation of how magnificent and fleeting a life can be. Michael's book, Getting Wiser will help each person reading it to enjoy life's fullness every day."

Thomas Kirk, retired colonel in the U. S. Air Force. Former Vice Commander of all Special Forces in Europe. Former prisoner of war at the "Hanoi Hilton" North Vietnamese prison camp for almost six years.

"I am pleased to be included in Michael's book. But even had I not been a participant, I would still be recommending Getting Wiser. His insights into human behavior, losses, and successes make this an invaluable addition to anyone's bookshelf."

Dolores Kohl, founder of the Kohl Children's Museum. Initiator of the Kohl McCormick Early Childhood Teaching Awards and Story Bus, a traveling pre-literacy skills develop-

ment exhibit. Former member, Board of Trustees, Brandeis University.

"If you read Getting Wiser, you will find practical wisdom you can use today, and all of the profits go to the Himalayan Cataract Project, to help cure preventable blindness."
Carmen Terzic, M.D., PhD., professor and chairman of the Department of Physical Medicine and Rehabilitation at Mayo Clinic. Former member of the Venezuelan National Fencing Team.

"If you are looking for an inspiring book you can learn from, you won't do better than Dr. Michael Lewis's Getting Wiser. It is filled with personal stories of real people who have overcome challenges, achieved great things, or suffered significant losses. They tell you how they did it and what they have learned."
Stephen Jones, former member of the U. S. Delegation to NATO. Former chief of staff for U. S. Representative Paul Findley. Former candidate for the U. S. Senate from Oklahoma.

"Michael S. Lewis, M.D.'s talent for drawing out the very best in people is evident on every page of this inspiring book."
David Berg, founding partner of Berg & Androphy Law Firm. Author of *The Trial Lawyer: What it Takes to Win* and *Run, Brother, Run: A Memoir of a Murder in My Family*.

"The lessons Dr. Michael Lewis has learned from working with professional athletes will benefit young competitors in any arena."
Wilbur Wood, Chicago White Sox pitcher, 1967 – 1978, three-time All-Star.

"It is an honor to be included among the profiles in Michael's book. I have the greatest respect for him not only as a medical professional but as a skilled writer who recognizes the gift of wisdom others have to offer. This book will enable you to address challenging times."
Robert A. Bensman, founder and CEO of The Bensman Group.

"Learn why four contributors to Michael Lewis's latest book, Getting Wiser, mention the same high school debate coach in their essays, and why she taught them the survival of a democratic society requires citizens who can listen to, critically analyze and persuasively express their views on public issues."
Tom Broussard, former general tax counsel of Atlantic Richfield. Former vice president and general counsel of Technicolor, Inc.

"This book is life-affirming, optimistic, graceful, and joyful."
Gary Greenberg, managing director, Feldman Advisors venture capital firm.

GETTING
WISER

---

101 Essential Life Lessons
and Inspiring Stories

MICHAEL S. LEWIS, M.D.

xxx

GETTING WISER:
101 Essential Life Lessons And Inspiring Stories

First Edition
Copyright © 2022 by Michael S. Lewis
Published by
Munn Avenue Press
300 Main Street, Ste 21
Madison, NJ 07940
MunnAvenuePress.com

ISBN: 979-8-9861680-3-6

Printed in the United States of America

Profiles in Heroism

Overcoming Adversity

Moving Past a Challenging Childhood

Adapting to Change

Changing Perspective

Humility, Courage, and Integrity: Character Counts

Inquiring Minds

Giving More Than Expected

Focusing on Excellence

Serving Others

The Challenge and Honor of Public Service

The Value of Our Relationships

Parents, Siblings, and Children

Spiritual Journeys

The Fragility of Our Lives

This book is dedicated to the remarkable people whose wisdom created this book.

May you continue to enrich the lives of your families, friends, and future generations.

Introduction

*"Once in a while it really hits people
that they don't have to experience life
in the way they have been told to."*
Alan Knightly

*"All any man can do is add his fragment to the whole....
What he leaves is stones for others to step on or stones to
avoid."*
Robert Henri

Getting Wiser

101 Essential Life Lessons and Inspiring Stories for Today

"We are drowning in information while starving for wisdom."
E. O. Wilson

Poet Mary Oliver asks, "What do you plan to do with your one wild and precious life?" This question urges us to reply. My response has been to ask 101 of the most accomplished people I know to answer one of the following questions:

- If you could pass on one life lesson to the next generation, what would it be?
- What adversity have you overcome?
- Which causes are you passionate about and why?

The questions seem to have struck a chord for many of the contributors. They offered their raw materials — their ideas, attitudes, values, experiences — and released an outpouring of thought-provoking essays filled with practical wisdom.

My initial goal was to produce a small volume of life lessons for my family. It was to be titled, *What I Learned After I Thought I Knew Something.* I wanted to follow physicist Richard Feynman's advice: "Teach your children early what you learned late in life." But the book could not be so easily contained. It kept expanding and grew richer and more useful.

Getting Wiser interweaves the contributions of others with what I have learned. I have (or have had) a personal relationship with each participant, the nature of which is mentioned in the section at the end of the book, titled 'The Remarkable People Whose Wisdom Created This Book.' Many of the individuals in the book have died, including Sir John Charnley, David Halberstam, Jerry Krause, Mollie Martin, Abraham Maslow, Bill Veeck, and Elie Wiesel. In each case, I enjoyed lengthy conversations with them and observed them for long periods of time. In my opinion, this enabled me to understand how they would have answered the above questions.

Other people mentioned in the book, including Michael Jordan, Phil Jackson, and Dennis Rodman, are still very much alive. Although I have not recently spoken with them, I feel that I knew each of them well enough to share the wisdom I learned from them.

This book explores different perspectives on how to measure success. The contributors come from diverse backgrounds. Some have known formidable hardships. Others have made significant contributions after starting from a position of privilege. As civil rights leader Booker T. Washington stated, "Success is not measured by where you are in life, but by the obstacles which you have overcome."

To make this book as user friendly as possible, I divided it into short chapters, each not exceeding both sides of one page. You can dip in anywhere, starting at whatever chapter interests you the most.

Quotations have always given me delight and inspiration, and it was a joy finding applicable ones to accompany both the introduction of each chapter and the beginning of the individual contributions.

In this book, I have endeavored to follow Mary Oliver's dictum: "Pay attention. Be astonished. Tell about it." A common idea expressed in my family is, "If you can't be a genius, be a genius appreciator." This especially applies to the remarkable people whose insights created this book. They generously shared their wisdom, and my life has greatly benefitted by knowing each of them. I can only hope that their stories of hope and inspiration do the same for the reader.

Seeking Creativity

Art is doing anything well.
When the artist is alive in any person,
whatever his kind of work may be,
he becomes inventive, searching, daring,
self-expressing, creative.
Robert Henri

Every now and then, a man's mind is stretched
by a new idea or sensation
and never shrinks back to its former dimensions.
Oliver Wendell Holmes

Abraham Maslow, Joseph Werlin

Tapping Into Our Creative Capacity

"Let the beauty we love be what we do.
There are hundreds of ways to kneel and kiss the ground."
Rumi

I ONCE THOUGHT creativity was destiny's rare gift visited upon a select few. However, Abraham Maslow, a psychology professor at Brandeis University, expanded my definition. He stated, "A first-rate soup is better than a second-rate poem." I then realized that although most of us won't become artists in the traditional sense, such as opera singers, actors, or professional photographers, each of us can still be creative.

Now I see creativity everywhere. Chicago Bulls player Michael Jordan had plenty of talent, but he also constantly responded to situations creatively. I watched him night after night on the basketball court. It was like watching an improvised ballet. He adapted his game to meet the needs of the team and generated wondrous moves to outmaneuver his opponents.

Pablo Picasso said, "Every child is an artist. The problem is how to remain an artist once he or she grows up." Creativity is not just a gift, but a skill that can be developed. Inventiveness is a building block of creativity. Thus, fostering a child's imagination and playful spirit is essential. I love the story of the four-year-old girl who tells her teacher that she is drawing a picture of God. Her teacher responds that nobody knows what God looks like. The girl answers, "They will, in a minute."

One never knows how significantly a small word or deed can encourage a child. For example, when I was six years old, my Uncle Joseph Werlin, a university professor, would take students on summer tours of Europe. When he returned, he brought coins from the countries he visited and distributed them to my cousins and me. I would roll them over and over in my hands. The coins ignited my imagination, and I dreamed of visiting exotic places, such as Greek temples or royal castles in England. This prompted a life-long interest in travel.

Creativity is at the very foundation of who we are as humans, and who we can become. The contributors to this chapter, John Charnley, Art Shay, Tom Sewell, Yuan-Quig Yu, and Bud Frazier share with us ideas to enable us to increase our own imaginative thinking. They demonstrate how, when combining talent with hard work, individuals can perform at the highest levels in medical research, photography, art, and music. This will result in enhancing the lives of uncounted thousands.

Albert Einstein said, "Logic will take you from A to B. Imagination will take you everywhere."

Sir John Charnley

A Surgical Pioneer

"In the training of young surgeons, I believe that fostering the questioning of accepted beliefs ought to start from the earliest moment."
Sir John Charnley

IT IS fair to say that I was overwhelmed with excitement when I found out that I had the opportunity to spend time with Mr. John Charnley (surgeons in Britain are addressed as "Mr."). I met him in the early 1970s, when he was performing surgery and working in his laboratory at his surgical and research Center at Wrightington Hospital near Manchester. He was working on a new procedure, namely hip replacement, a radical and exciting advance in orthopedic surgery.

John Charnley became a Fellow of the Royal College of Surgeons when he was 25 years old, the youngest physician to receive that honor. In 1939, he volunteered for the Royal Army Medical Corps and attended wounded soldiers who had been evacuated from Dunkirk, in France.

Throughout his orthopedic career, he continued inventing surgical appliances and instruments. Prior to the invention of hip replacements, people with failing hip joints had to live with unbearable pain, and the early surgical procedures to treat the condition were inadequate.

The first prosthesis was implanted on November 22, 1962. That day could be considered the beginning of modern artificial joint replacement, certainly one of the greatest orthopedic advances of the 20th century. In addition to inventing and perfecting the procedure in the 1960s, Charnley pioneered the development of knee replacements in the 1970s.

In addition to developing the artificial joint itself, to decrease the possibility of infection, Charnley invented an air filtration system to improve the passage of clean air in the operating room, as well as a full body gown incorporating an exhaust system.

John Charnley's passion for innovation was intense. For years he constantly refined his techniques and tested numerous different surgical implants before finding one that worked to his satisfaction. Thomas Edison said, "When working on inventing the light bulb, I did not keep failing. I have just found 10,000 ways that didn't work."

Joint replacement surgery now includes hips, knees, shoulders, elbows, fingers, toes, ankles, and wrists. John Charnley was knighted by Queen Elizabeth II in 1977.

He was a living legend, and surgeons from all over the world came to observe him. He took a personal interest in many of his visitors. Even though I was by far the lowest man on the totem pole among his vast entourage, he took time to give me a personal tour of his laboratory and even invited me for dinner. Everyone felt honored to be in his presence.

Sir John Charnley was a strict and demanding teacher. He stated, "In the training of young surgeons, I believe that fostering the questioning of accepted beliefs ought to start from the earliest moment." With enthusiasm and dedication, he never stopped practicing what he preached.

As a result of his inquiring mind and his persistence, the lives of millions of patients have been transformed. In the history of medicine, few individuals have had such an impact.

Art Shay

An Unquenchable Zest for Life

"Look for the picture that hits you in the guts."
Art Shay

ART SHAY WAS A WORLD-CLASS PHOTOGRAPHER, whose images appeared
on the covers of *Life, Time, Sports Illustrated,* and *Fortune* magazines. He
photographed seven U.S. presidents and dozens of the luminaries of his time,
including Marlon Brando, Elizabeth Taylor, Muhammad Ali, Jimmy Hoffa,
Judy Garland, Eleanor Roosevelt, and Senator Joseph R. McCarthy.

Art's personal photographs were just as powerful. He published a tribute
to his wife Florence, titled, *My Florence: A 70-Year Love Story.* It is filled with
seven decades of achingly beautiful images of her and his reminiscences about
their life together.

Art was a mentor to me and would critique my photographs. At times, his
criticism was often intense, and I would like to think that my images improved
as a result. George Lucas said, "Mentors have a way of seeing more of our
faults than we would like. It's the only way we grow." When he eventually
told me he was proud of his influence on my work, especially given his reputation for being parsimonious with compliments, he greatly boosted my
confidence.

There were so many facets to Art Shay's personality. He raged against
pretension. He raged against hypocrisy. He raged against injustice. Yet, no
one better captured the joy, the humor, the elation of everyday life than Art
Shay. He was courageous, competitive, combustible, learned, loyal and
lovable.

He was an excellent storyteller with an abundance of memorable stories
to share. For example, Art was photographing the New York Yankees in 1951.
The diminutive shortstop, Phil Rizzuto, 5'6" tall and 150 pounds, was lifted
up by Joe DiMaggio. At that point, "Joltin' Joe" turned to Art Shay and said,
"Hey Kid, can you enlarge this in your darkroom?"

Playboy founder Hugh Hefner, called Art "the best photojournalist I
know." Great writers have waxed eloquent about his photographs. Studs
Terkel said Shay was "one of our truest photographers...[he] captures the
beauty, humor, and pathos of America." Film critic Roger Ebert said, "Art

Shay's photography shakes you up, sets you down quietly, pats you on the head, and then kicks you in the ass."

Art was a Renaissance man. He was an outstanding writer. He wrote five plays, two of which were performed on the stage. In addition to being a photographer and a writer, a husband and a father, he was a warrior who flew more than thirty missions as a lead navigator in World War II. He witnessed D-Day from his Liberator bomber. This is how he captured that experience: "A thousand ships sit in the dirty Thames without a Helen. Now we are of the countless men who left England on brave purpose. Little boys with man-hearts. This is the day we spit in Hitler's eye."

The following are among his indelible photographic lessons:

Photography forces you to take a point of view. The life of a photographer can never be one of indifference.

You can't just wait until something happens.

You have to be tuned in and turned on all the time; then things happen.

Find your own voice.

Look for the picture that hits you in the guts.

Say something so well that it can't be said in another way.

We had many discussions related to the philosophy of photography. He inspired me to articulate some of my own thoughts related to what I try to achieve when photographing:

Get out of your comfort zone. Try new things. If you never fail, you are not trying hard enough.

Isolate, simplify, distill the essence of a photograph. Hear a single note.

Look for photographs with a meditative quality, those with intimacy, harmony, and serenity.

There are no boring places, only boring ways to look at them.

Strive for photographs that ask questions.

When assessing your images, if you are not your own severest critic, then you are your own worst enemy.

Photography is an act of love. The eye is the servant of the heart.

Tom Sewell

Seeing What Others Don't See

"My middle name is serendipity. I wake up in the morning and wonder what miracle is going to happen today."
Tom Sewell

Actress Selma Hayek states, "People often say that beauty is in the eye of the beholder, and I say what's the most liberating thing about beauty is realizing that you are the beholder. This empowers us to find beauty where others have not dared to look, including inside of ourselves."

While visiting Tom Sewell's warehouse-sized studio in an abandoned sugar mill on Maui, I was awestruck by the dozens of huge metal sculptures he had created from discarded found objects, each work unique and fascinating. When Tom looks at rusted machine parts, or sheets of flat and corrugated metal, he can envision something entirely new and then weld, pierce, paint, assemble, and combine those objects into interesting and beautiful sculptures, many of which require a crane to lift. Where others see trash, Tom Sewell sees potential.

The home page of Tom Sewell's website announces that he creates "Objets Trouvés, Photography and Sculpture." Which doesn't begin to do justice to this polymath's artistic and business accomplishments.

Tom lives on Maui, and he has turned his property into a fascinating retreat and vacation spot and an art center that houses the Sewell Archive, a collection of over 100,000 images and archival films documenting the "artists, architecture and eccentrics of Venice, Los Angeles, and Santa Monica in the 1960s, 70s, and 80s."

Tom's photographs, which range from the exotic to the documentary, have appeared in the *New York Times* and the *Wall Street Journal*.

Before moving to Maui, Tom lived in Venice, California. He had the vision to purchase and repurpose old industrial buildings into design centers with boutique shops.

Tom names as his mentors such acclaimed artists as Marcel Duchamp and David Hockney, as well as Poet Laureate W.S. Merwin. Add to that list real estate executives and Columbia Records President Goddard Lieberson, and you get a sense of the range of Tom's interests.

9

Tom never hesitates to take artistic risks. He says, "One can't be afraid to make a mistake. It's part of the creative process." An essential part of Tom's creativity emanates from his openness to new ideas, opportunities, and people. His friends say, "Tom is never the life of the party. He is the party." As he stated to me, "My middle name is serendipity. I wake up in the morning and think, "'What miracle is going to happen today?'"

Songwriter Leonard Cohen wrote, "Forget your perfect offering. There is a crack in everything. That's how the light gets in." Tom Sewell reminds us that creative thinking involves imagining things in a new light.

Yuan-Qing Yu

Music as an Act of Love

**"It's not enough to just play a piece,
you need to put yourself into the music."
Yuan-Qing Yu**

VIOLINIST YUAN-QING YU IS A SOLOIST, chamber musician, teacher and, since 1995, assistant concertmaster of the Chicago Symphony Orchestra.

Born in Shanghai during the Cultural Revolution, Yu was recruited as a violinist by Southern Methodist University. She emigrated to Texas, alone, in her early 20s. When I asked her how she found the courage to move from Shanghai to Texas, she explained that her father, an independent thinker, was insistent that she try new things and not just conform to current fads and trends. She was awarded a master's degree in music from SMU in 1994. She initially assumed that Texas was a microcosm of the entire United States. "I thought barbeque was normal," she joked.

Yuan-Quig's father also taught her not to worry about the other contestants. He told her that she is only competing against herself. "When you go to a competition as prepared as you can be, you are more likely to be able to rise to the occasion, to accept the challenges you will face."

"In China," she said, "children start playing at a young age and the competition is intense. For example, hundreds applied for a place at the Shanghai Conservatory in the violin." (She was one of only five accepted).

"You didn't have a choice," she said. "The system was very selective. You had to devote your life to music."

Yuan-Qing Yu, a professor at Northwestern and Roosevelt universities, mentors her own students. I asked her what qualities and skills helped her to achieve success as a professional musician and how she conveys to her students what it takes to thrive in this field.

She responded, "There is no quick way out. You must do the hard work. You also must work smart. If something isn't right in a piece, you must figure out why before you move on.

Music, she teaches her students, is not just an abstract exercise that relies solely on mastering the technical aspects. She says, "It is not enough just to play a piece. You must love the music and put yourself into it. If you are

11

playing Mozart, you have to be Mozart. The connection between the music and the composer and the musician is critical."

She loves showing her students how much joy music can bring to others. As an example, in 2011, she, with several colleagues, founded the non-profit organization Civitas Ensemble; she serves on its board and as its president. She explained, "One of the reasons I created Civitas Ensemble was to bring music to people who have limited access to live performances, so it performs outreach concerts at hospitals, schools, and senior-living facilities."

Yuan-Qing continued, "To be successful, passion for the work is essential. You must give everything you have to the work, and you must enjoy the process of practicing. In addition, music must be part of the student's core identity. He or she must be able to say to themselves, 'I am a musician,' rather than simply, 'I am someone who plays the violin.' You must do that knowing that not everyone will be able to become a professional musician."

When asked if she is successful, Yuan-Quin modestly replied, "I continue to think of myself as a work in progress."

O. H. "Bud" Frazier

Heartfelt Commitment

"One cannot be creative or innovative looking backwards."
Bud Frazier

CARDIAC SURGEON BUD FRAZIER shared with me the following story of his journey to create a total artificial heart:

"I began working with Dr. Michael DeBakey on artificial hearts by accident. In 1963, I was a first-year medical student at Baylor College of Medicine in Houston, and at that time, every medical student was required to have a yearly research project. I had been a History/English major in college with little interest in science. However, after reading powerful portrayals of doctors by Anton Chekhov – who himself was a doctor -- I decided medicine would be a good calling.

"Frank Polk, a classmate at Baylor, was an intense student, always ahead of me academically. We had until November 1st to submit our research subject. On October 30th Frank asked about my project. I replied that I had another day to think about it! Frank laughed, and he said he had already signed me up to work with him on Artificial Heart Development with Dr. Michael DeBakey and Domingo Liotta, who later built the first implanted artificial heart. Unfortunately, Frank had to leave our project. So, by sheer accident, I began my artificial heart research."

I would add that Dr Michael DeBakey, perhaps the world's best known heart surgeon at that time, had developed a technique for correcting aortic aneurysms with a graft and was among the first to perform coronary artery bypass surgery.

Bud continued, "I enjoyed this research and continued it throughout medical school. In 1968 I was drafted into the U.S. Army and was assigned to a combat Assault Helicopter Company in the Central Highlands of Vietnam. During that time, Dr. Denton Cooley implanted the pump I had worked on as a medical student. Dr. DeBakey felt that Dr. Cooley had purloined the artificial heart from his laboratory and dismissed him from Baylor College of Medicine. My classmates later told me that I might have been safer in combat in Vietnam than in Houston!

"Of course, I was not in a safer place in Vietnam. After seeing so much violence and so many lives wasted there, I was determined to spend the rest of my career working to save lives, which was clearly the right thing for me to do. So, I decided to continue to pursue artificial heart research during my cardiac surgery training. I moved to Dr. Cooley's Texas Heart Institute, where I had access to a first-class research lab. I had great respect for both Drs. DeBakey and Cooley, but felt I had more opportunity to contribute to Dr. Cooley's laboratory. I also continued work on the development of pulsatile cardiac pumps, which mimicked a pumping heart. The main problem with these pulsatile pumps was durability. The human heart beats 100,000 times every 24 hours. A pulsatile pump doing this work would usually last 18 to 24 months. Therefore, it was a temporary solution because the pump was only useful while the patient waited for a heart transplant, and there was a limited number of donor hearts available.

"Because of this limitation, in 1985, I began working on a small continuous flow, pulseless heart pump. My contemporaries in Cardiac Surgery did not believe this could work. It was assumed that mammalian physiology dictated the presence of a pulse. However, I knew for sure that at the capillary level, where nutrients and oxygen go from the blood to the cell, the blood flow does not depend on a pulse, and that the only organ that needs a pulse is the heart itself. So, I followed fellow Texan Davy Crockett's mantra, "Be sure you are right, then go ahead."

When Bud couldn't get support to develop his pulseless pump, he funded the project himself!

"So, after fifteen years, with much patience and persistence, various perceived problems/barriers were overcome, and in 2000, I implanted the first permanent pulseless, continuous flow ventricular assist heart pump. To date, over 50,000 of these pumps have been implanted world-wide in patients facing imminent death. All these pumps were developed under my direction in my lab at the Texas Heart Institute. I am extremely grateful for the opportunity to have played a part in the development of this life-saving technology."

Bud is currently working on a total heart replacement. If successful, thanks to his daring imagination, this device could save the lives of countless grateful patients. John Eliot said, "History shows us that the people who end up changing the world – the political, scientific, and artistic revolutionaries – are always nuts until they are right, and then they are geniuses."

Leading The Way

Average leaders raise the bar on themselves.
Good leaders raise the bar for others.
Great leaders inspire others to raise their own bar.
Orrin Woodward

If your actions inspire others to dream more, learn more, do
more, and become more, you are a leader.
John Quincy Adams

Phil Jackson

Leading by Example

**"Be in the moment. Feel the joy of the dance.
This is not a rehearsal. This is your life."
Phil Jackson**

WHAT QUALITIES ARE necessary for leadership? The contributors to this chapter share how they were able to lead at the highest levels in their chosen fields.

In 1997 and 1998, during the last two Chicago Bulls basketball team's championship seasons, when Phil Jackson was the coach and I was an orthopedic consultant, I observed him closely to determine what qualities made him successful.

Phil had credibility. He had paid his dues not only by playing in the NBA for 12 years, including winning two championship rings with the New York Knicks, but also by being an assistant coach for many years. This enabled him to earn the respect of his players. And Phil respected them. In his book *Eleven Rings: The Soul of Success,* Phil said, "You can't force your will on people. You meet them where they are and lead them. Listen without judgment. If you want them to act differently, you need to inspire them to change themselves."

Other leadership principles he embedded in pithy sayings, such as "The grass won't grow faster by pulling on it." I found this quotation especially helpful at times when I needed more patience, especially in raising children.

Phil was the master at finding the right balance between being a disciplinarian and acting as a kindly father figure, knowing when to be firm and when to show tolerance for his players' quirks. In private medical meetings, for example, he would talk about giving a player, who needed an emotional boost, additional playing time.

Another of Phil's favorite techniques was to talk about the team as both a wolfpack and a tribe. He said, "Good teams become great teams when the members trust each other enough to surrender the Me for the We." Adam Grant, in his book *Think Again,* discusses a variation on the theme: psychological safety. His study at Google demonstrated that the most successful teams create a "climate of respect, trust, and openness."

Credibility, listening with an open mind, understanding that each player needed to be motivated differently: Phil's carefully crafted multi-strategy approach to leadership took the Bulls to six NBA championships.

There are many unique styles of leadership, as demonstrated by the other contributors to this section, including Carmen Terzic, Chris Miller, Richard S. Strong, Brenda Langstraat, Albert Madansky, and Jack Gould.

Carmen Terzic

Taking Leadership to Heart

"It is essential for a leader to empower team members, to help them find their strengths, and then to support them in developing those strengths."
Carmen Terzic

CARMEN M. TERZIC, M.D., Ph.D., has worked and taught at the Mayo Clinic since the early 90s. One of her main research interests is investigating the use of stem cells to regenerate damaged hearts. Not surprising for, in a way, her life is about the heart.

Carmen states, "When she was growing up in Venezuela, connections of the heart were much more important than material possessions. When a stranger would move into your neighborhood, you didn't ask, "Where are you from," but instead, "What can I do to help?" Writer Isabel Allende described this as "carefree generosity." Cousins were like immediate family and neighbors like extended family."

She said, "In Venezuela, if you have children, you know you will always be taken care of. You will not be put in a nursing home. It is a matter of responsibility and respect." Carmen illustrates the idea with the following delightful story: When Carmen's daughter was nine, she told her mother, "Mind your own business." She quickly realized that was the wrong thing to say. Carmen replied, "You are my business, forever!"

In Venezuela, Carmen was on the national fencing team from 1978 to 1992, and the most important lesson she learned as an athlete was the importance of being a team player, of being supportive of her teammates materially, physically, and emotionally.

She credits her current success as an administrator and teacher to her emphasis on the team approach. She says, "It means putting yourself on the same level as your associates, even if you are the leader. That means not telling people what to do, but coordinating the team effort, empowering other people, helping the team members find their strengths and then supporting them in developing those strengths into a useful skill set through education, encouragement, extra training, or whatever else they need. I use this team approach in every aspect of my profession."

Carmen would agree with the philosophy that you don't inspire your colleagues by showing them how amazing you are. You inspire them by showing them how amazing they are. She loves to enable others to express their own gifts.

Other people cite her honesty and transparency as qualities that make her a good leader, not doing things for personal gain but always being part of the team. She also knows the importance of asking for help. In Venezuela, she explained, people are never shy about knocking on someone's door and asking for help or advice, and she is not bashful about doing that at Mayo Clinic.

Her early mentors included her father and her fencing coach. When she came to the U.S., her mentor was Andre Terzic, who helped her learn to navigate life in the United States and at Mayo Clinic. Apparently, he was an excellent mentor, because later they married and had a child.

Carmen and I share a love of teaching. She says, "I try to teach my students that being a doctor is largely a matter of the heart; to be a doctor you must love the work and take joy in it." Her clinical field is rehabilitation, and often she deals with patients who have significant disabilities, such as the after-effects of stroke, or a brain injury, or cancer. "My main message is to encourage them to adjust to a new normal and appreciate what they have. I am an optimistic person and I try to communicate my optimism to them, to love and support them and to help them have meaningful lives."

Chris Miller

Listen Up

"In every facet of life, listening is key."
Chris Miller

MY WIFE and I met Chris Miller and his family in a most unusual fashion. Just before Chicago was shut down because of Covid, my wife and I and another couple were dining at a downtown restaurant. The restaurant was normally packed but that evening, it was almost empty. In a random act of kindness, a total stranger paid our bill. We were shocked. Chris later explained that he had felt sorry for the servers, who had so few tables, and assumed, correctly, that we would leave an extra-large tip.

We naturally went over to his table to thank this mysterious benefactor. We exchanged contact information, and he subsequently bought my books from my website. He was so inspired by the Himalayan Cataract Project, which receives the proceeds from my books, that he gave a generous donation to the organization. He later bought a large number of my books and donated them to the Chicago Public Library Foundation to be distributed in under-served areas.

When I later asked Chris, a successful businessman, to what does he attribute his success, he replied that in business, listening is often the most difficult and usually the most important thing to do. With a degree in business administration and management from Lewis University, Chris was a young salesperson selling electrical products to USX Steel company when his company came up with a new product that he was sure could save USX time and money. The customer listened to Chris's pitch, loved the product, and said he would be in touch.

Waiting for the orders to roll in, Chris heard that another company had won the contract. He asked the customer why, and received this reply: "I love the product and what it can do for us. But you didn't hear what we needed. I needed a product that we could get quickly. The longer the mill is down, the more it costs. This includes workers, product, shipping, and everything else. You said we couldn't get the product for six weeks. I don't care how good it is, I can't wait." Chris learned a very valuable lesson that day about listening to what the customer needs.

A few years later, Chris joined his brothers in a new venture, making security and hurricane shutters; QMI Security Solutions was born. Chris remembered and implemented the lesson about listening. As a result, QMI's company list includes Wal-Mart, Walgreens, Rite Aid, CVS, AT&T, T-Mobile, Verizon, Best Buy, Luxottica Retail and JP Morgan. Its 100+ employees have provided security for more than 35,000 retail locations. In 35 years, QMI has never lost a major customer.

"Because we listened to what they needed, not what we wanted to sell them, they came back to QMI for other products again and again. Because we listened to one customer, we found that other customers were having the same problems and could use our solution too," said Chris. After thirty years, a survey done by an independent assessment firm found, "QMI's scores on Key Performance Metrics, along with the engagement and loyalty of these customers, are the highest scores in our history; 100% of the customers interviewed are truly loyal."

"That is because QMI learned how important listening is," said Chris. Further, the survey reported, "The vast majority of customers we spoke with had QMI providing 100% of their product needs, or very close to that percentage." Chris shared some of the Key Performance Metrics used by the independent firm to grade QMI. "They are all listening-related," said Chris.

Among the survey questions were: Matters a lot if could not purchase from QMI; Likelihood to continue purchasing from QMI; Cares about customer; Trustworthy/Reliable/Consistent; Available when needed; Effectively communicates with your organization. All categories were rated 100%!

"The three that I am most proud of are 'Cares about customer,' 'Available when needed,' and 'Trustworthy,'" said Chris. QMI had a 100% rating on those three metrics. "This is just one example," said Chris. "In every facet of your life, listening is key; spouses, children, business associates and friends all just want to be heard - Thanks for listening to me!"

The Dalai Lama stated, "When you talk, you are only repeating what you already know; but when you listen, you may learn something new."

Richard S. Strong

Teaming Up for Success

**"Three things are critical to success in any field:
teamwork, encouraging your colleagues,
and surrounding yourself with good people."
Richard Strong**

RICHARD S. STRONG has created world class financial institutions. These include Baraboo Growth, LLC., which he formed in 2003. An integral part of the company's culture is an emphasis on teamwork, and one way Dick fosters that idea is to provide education and development opportunities for the firm's associates. He offers them trips to various parts of the world for education and training, and he hosts a monthly speaker's series for which he brings world-class speakers to his company's headquarters in Milwaukee. I met Dick at a conference he sponsored several years ago, and although these programs are primarily for the benefit of his associates and their spouses, he generously has added me to the guest list.

Dick explained to me that his experience as a basketball player formed the basis of his commitment to the personal and professional development of his associates.

He stated that when he was in third grade, his father took him to a basketball game to see the 6'10" center George Mikan, who during his professional career scored 11,764 points. Dick lived in Wahpeton, North Dakota, a town of fewer than 8,000 people even today. That a player from the Minnesota Lakers would come to play in his small town, 40 miles from Fargo, made a big impression on the youngster.

When Dick was in sixth grade, the family moved to the town of Stillwater, near St. Paul, Minnesota. He loved going to basketball games with his father, who on occasion would even let him go to games by himself, armed with a cowbell to ring when the other team's players were taking free throws!

Dick's parents allowed him to follow his passion, which was to play basketball. He played in high school and in college. At the end of his senior year in high school, he was named to the all-conference team by his conference's coaches. But he did not win the Most Valuable Player award on his own team. It was selected by the players. He remembers not being so bothered by this at the time, but clearly it left a scar. He concluded this meant people did not like or respect him, so he set out to figure out why. He didn't like what he saw – a self-centered young man.

After college, he was in a summer league in Ohio, when it finally clicked. He made the winning shot in a game, and another player called out, "Great shot!" Dick had an epiphany! It was then Dick understood that it was not just about him. Encouraging other people was the way to go. It was then that he embraced the concept of a team.

Dick earned his B.A. in history from Baldwin Wallace College in 1963 and his MBA in finance from the University of Wisconsin-Madison in 1966. He decided to make a career in business. In thinking about what he'd learned from basketball, he figured out that three things were critical to success in any field: teamwork; encouraging your colleagues; and surrounding yourself with good people.

Running his own business, Dick hires people right out of college, always the best and the brightest. He advises them to follow their passion. "Find out what you're really good at because then you'll love what you are doing." He likes to find people who have been in competition, because they know how to be self-disciplined and have learned the importance of teamwork. His formula works. Many of his associates have been with him for more than 30 years.

Dick told me that whenever he faces a major challenge and thinks, "No one can get out of this mess," he returns to when he was seventeen years old on the basketball court, when he always found a way out of difficult situations. So even today he reaches back to that seventeen-year-old basketball player to give him the confidence to go forward! When I asked Chicago Bulls center Bill Wennington how he coped with the pressure of the NBA finals, he said that he also imagines being on a schoolyard playground!

There appears to be no limit to Dick's appetite for new ideas. He is interested in everything and everybody. Dick's ability to communicate his excitement inspires his associates, and his passion is seeing them love what they are doing, being productive, and growing in the job. That brings him great joy.

Brenda Langstraat

Fundraising Is a Value Proposition

**"An essential part of leadership is preparing
an organization for its next phase."**
Brenda Langstraat

BRENDA LANGSTRAAT IS President and CEO of the Chicago Public Library Foundation. She shares the following adventures which occurred along her impressive professional journey:

"When I was young and someone asked what I wanted to be when I grew up, my response was "an NFL coach." Both of my parents were educators, and my father was a high school football coach. I loved football, still do, and there was something about being a coach that captured my imagination. Turns out, building a team is an important part of leadership.

"In the fall of 1992, I was a freshman at Wheaton College. An older student had a car. A few of us piled into it, and we headed to downtown Chicago for the Jazz Festival. I'll never forget that drive on the inbound Eisenhower, with the skyline framing the city. I felt an electric charge as the expressway turned toward Congress, and we slipped under the old post office. What I didn't know then, that I see clearly now, is that this small-town, born-and-raised-in-Iowa girl had found her new home. Every time I drive into the city, that charge remains, like butterflies with a life-long love.

"In the late 1990s I was in graduate school at University of Illinois-Chicago in the master's program for English. My plan was to complete the program, carry on earning a Ph.D. and then to write and teach. But soon I discovered an internship opportunity with the Chicago Humanities Festival. I fell in love with the work immediately. The hustle was constant, and the team fueled each other, motivated by our common mission.

"It was at the Chicago Humanities Festival that I found my calling in development work. I began to recognize two fundamental aspects of leadership. The first was development and fundraising as a value proposition, not an ask for money. My draw to development was the value exchange between donor, mission, and impact. The second was the understanding of the power of team-based mentorship. There was no formal mentorship structure. Rather, we were all both mentors and mentees. We were entrepreneurs. We were creating systems and programs, and fundraising models in real time.

"This experience opened the door to Parkways Foundation, a philanthropic partner of the Chicago Park District. It is where I began to understand the impact of private funding in the public sector. When I took a position at Working in the Schools (WITS), one of the most important leadership lessons I learned at WITS was to build teams around complementary skill sets and strengths. This sharpened my instincts in hiring and building teams. I learned to hire leaders smarter than I. It was at WITS that I understood how the main part of leadership is to prepare an organization for its next phase.

"When I was at Parkways, I looked to the Chicago Public Library Foundation as the best practices model for public/private partnership. Even then, it became my dream job. I'll never forget walking out of the interview with the Foundation board. I was charged, ready, just like driving on the inbound Eisenhower. Joining the Foundation felt less like a new job and more like a homecoming. Leading the Foundation is truly the culmination of all that I've gathered along the way from the humanities to the parks, to the schools and now...all roads lead to the library.

"Visiting the library is part of my DNA; it is a life-charge. My most vivid and constant memory of childhood is standing at the front door of our house in Indianola, Iowa, with a heavy stack of books piled in my arms, excitedly waiting for my mom to take me to that magical place, the public library. Then I would show my card with pride, return my stack, explore, reload, devour every page, and then do it all again.

"Now I work closely with the library leadership, staff, and partners. I see up-close all the library does for all our seventy-seven neighborhoods and how, through private and public support, our library system thrives. For me, this is certainly a full-circle homecoming."

Andrew Carnegie said, "A library outranks any other one thing a community can do to benefit its people. It is a never-failing spring in the desert."

Albert Madansky, Jack Gould

Words from the Wise

"You will have to work hard for whatever success you will have. You don't have it coming to you."
Chana Rachel Madansky

ALBERT MADANSKY and Jack Gould worked together for years at the University of Chicago Booth School of Business. Al served as associate dean for Ph.D. studies, and deputy dean for faculty.

Al understands that success is never a single factor, but rather a combination of talent, work, luck, and environment. His mother, Chana Rachel Madansky, told him that he would have to work for whatever success he would have. She would say to him in Yiddish, "Es kumpt dir nisht" (You don't have it coming to you). As author Malcolm Gladwell says, "Working really hard is what successful people do."

Al would add that the qualities of persistence and patience are essential for success. He elaborated, "Not everything can be accomplished quickly. Some things take time to get done. My lesson to all is to sit still and develop a habit of a stick-to-it-iveness."

One of the primary lessons he teaches his grandchildren revolves around humility. Its importance is epitomized by verses from Deuteronomy 8, which he always keeps in mind:

"Then your heart be lifted up (i.e. you become haughty), and you forget the Lord your God,

"And you say in your heart, My power and the might of my hand has gotten me this position.

"And you shall remember the Lord your God; for He is Who gives you power to get this position.

"[No one] should think it is THEY who are in control of things. Each person's skill is so by the grace of God."

Another lesson that his life surely exemplifies is what he learned from Phil Wolfe, a Ph.D. mathematician at RAND: "Use more of yourself." "Everyone has multiple potential abilities," says Madansky. "You have multiple talents, and you are short changing yourself and the world by not exploring them and using as many of them as possible." This explains why Al has worn so many different hats in the academic and business worlds. Many in his position would have remained exclusively on a prestigious faculty, but Al wished to push his intellectual and creative limits. He branched out into consultant positions for the Department of Defense and the RAND Corporation, and became president of Madansky and Associates, Inc.

Jack Gould served as Dean of the University of Chicago Graduate School of Business. His colleague Al Madansky describes what it was like working with Jack: "Not only was he an outstanding dean, but he was such an asset to the community that [University President] Hanna Gray also made him a Vice President of the University. He managed to do both jobs simultaneously and well."

Al continued, "As a faculty member, he was always generous with his time and attention. When a prior business school dean decided to put together a 'swat team' of editors to improve the reputation of the *Journal of Business,* he appointed Jack editor-in-chief. His combined skills of organization and savvy made him superb at that job. I've watched Jack crack tough problems and marveled at how his mind worked. Jack also revised a standard introductory college textbook, *Microeconomic Theory.*"

When I asked Jack what qualities he possesses that have resulted in his success, he responded, "My initial reaction was to think that it is more about luck than any special quality I may possess. The luck I refer to includes the good fortune to have had exceptional mentors throughout my life and career, such as George Shultz, Hanna Gray, and Merton Miller and Myron Scholes, (both were winners of the Nobel Prize in Economics).

"Early in my career I learned that it is important to listen and compromise when necessary, so that all parties feel satisfied, or at least that they were heard and respected. Missteps I have made usually result from not giving sufficient weight to this important fact. I share the view that economics is not always a zero-sum game and that talented groups of people can work together to find meaningful approaches to significant problems or opportunities."

Jack concluded, "Looking back, perhaps the one quality that helped me succeed was the willingness to listen and learn from others and not think I had all the answers."

Inspiring Teachers And Mentors

*When the untapped potential of the student
meets the liberating art of the teacher, a miracle unfolds.
Mary Hatwood Futrell*

*I have come to believe that a great teacher is a great artist,
and that there are as few as there are any other great artists.
Teaching might even be the greatest of the arts,
since the medium is the human mind and spirit.
John Steinbeck*

William Meltzer, Morrie Kaplan

Those Who Light the Flame

"Great teachers, coaches, and mentors
allow you to see the hope inside yourself."
Oprah Winfrey

THERE IS much overlap in the roles of teachers, coaches, and mentors in helping us to learn about ourselves. Each discovers potential within us that we didn't realize was there. As physician, theologian, and Nobel Peace Prize recipient Albert Schweitzer said, "Each of us has cause to think with deep gratitude of those who have lighted the flame within us."

In 1975, I joined William Meltzer in the practice of orthopedic surgery. He was my mentor for the almost 40 years we were in practice together. Bill was a superstar. He was first in his class in high school, college, and medical school. Imagine, never being anything but number one! It wasn't easy being in his shadow. He was a master surgeon and was one of the first to perform hip replacement surgery in this country. Bill and I were the orthopedic consultants with the Chicago White Sox baseball team. My diagnostic and surgical skills improved dramatically under his mentorship, although, in retrospect, I probably relied for too long on his judgment instead of forming my own independent opinions.

I learned so much from him. Like the finest athletes, Bill brought his A-game every day. No one could tell if he wasn't feeling well or was concerned about a family problem. And he always did more than his share of the work.

Morrie Kaplan was the whole package: curious, imaginative, kind, a good listener, and passionately dedicated to making the world better. Morrie, whom I discuss at greater length in the chapter Profiles in Heroism, also was a friend and mentor to me.

Morrie didn't pull any punches when critiquing my behavior. For example, once I was complaining about a problem to Morrie. At the time, I was in my late 60s and he was in his early 90s. His response: "Stop acting like an old fogey and join the 21st century."

Although Morrie passed away several years ago, still today I find it helpful when I am faced with a difficult decision to ask myself, "What would Morrie do?"

Michael S. Lewis, M.D.

The other contributors to this chapter include Mollie Martin, Abraham Maslow, Henry Mankin, Jr., Tom Broussard, and Ken Krimstein. Mentorship is a two-way street and must be important to both participants. It depends on the fit between the mentee's aspirations and the mentor's lived experience. I am convinced that the potential importance of having a mentor is greatly underappreciated in our society.

Mollie Martin

There's More than One Side to Every Issue

"You need to be able to understand and articulate the arguments your opponents will make better than they can."
Mollie Martin

MOLLIE MARTIN, my speech and debate teacher in high school, was my first mentor. She was a wisp of a person, 5 feet, 2 inches tall, weighing all of 100 pounds. But when she reproached you, she appeared to be a 10-foot-tall colossus. She set high standards and was exceedingly demanding, both academically and behaviorally. At debate tournaments, we wore jackets and ties, looked people in the eye when we shook their hands, and said "sir" and "ma'am" to everyone.

Mollie imparted a strong foundation for what we needed to know to be citizens in a democratic society. She made us realize the necessity of going beyond our comfort zone and challenging our own ideas to sharpen and refine our thinking. Under her wing, I learned how to dissect an argument by looking for logical fallacies and evaluating the quality of evidence. These are essential skills, especially in this era of "fake news."

Mollie taught us how to see both sides of an issue. She said, "You need to be able to understand and articulate the arguments your opponents will make better than they can." She instructed us to seek out information that goes against our views. She trained us to listen and try to understand what the other person was thinking and feeling, to take the other person's thoughts, feelings, and arguments seriously, and to talk *to* each other, not *at* each other.

At college, I was amazed at how many intelligent people didn't have those skills. During a discussion or argument, fellow students would paint themselves into a corner and not know how to get out of it. I was shocked. I had assumed any intelligent person would be able to see both sides of a question, but that was not the case. Our inability to see and respect another person's point of view is a significant problem today.

Mollie Martin understood that to be a citizen, to know how to make the changes in the world we want, we need to be able to talk to each other with understanding and respect. She didn't care which side of a question we argued, or even if we agreed with the side we were assigned to defend. She encouraged us to think carefully about the issue and prepare strong, logical arguments, and that we present those arguments persuasively and politely.

Mollie intensely disliked dogmatism. She stated, "If your opinions on one subject can be predicted from your opinions on another, you may be in the grip of ideology. You must think for yourself."

Several of her students went on to do great things, but she remained humble and modest, never taking any more credit than saying she gave us a push in the right direction. That's what mentors do — quietly (or not so quietly, in Mollie's case!) working behind the scenes to make their students the best possible version of themselves.

Mollie not only pushed us to work harder, but also told us that everyone can accomplish more than he or she thinks they can. She changed our horizons, our awareness of who we might become. We could feel our intellectual and emotional capacities expanding. Mollie didn't just make us better debaters, but also better human beings.

Abraham Maslow

Revolutionary Psychologist

"I believe in you' is maybe more important than 'I love you."
Mike Krzyzewski

AT BRANDEIS UNIVERSITY, professor of psychology Abraham Maslow was my mentor. For more than sixty years, he has continued to capture my imagination, immeasurably expanding, and enriching my world.

In the summer of 1960, I arrived as a freshman at Brandeis in Waltham, Massachusetts, nine miles west of Boston. Most of the students were from metro New York or the New England area. Houston, Texas, in the 1950s was by comparison the Wild West. I felt like a hick surrounded by sophisticated Yankees. Eventually I realized that almost everyone was just as scared as I was, and also was overwhelmed by the quantity and difficulty of their classroom assignments. But, in those first few months, I felt alone and troubled.

Of all my classes, the one that excited me the most was Abraham Maslow's class on self-actualization. In the 1950s and early '60s, he revolutionized the field of psychology. Instead of focusing his work on people who were struggling, and often failing, to cope with life's challenges, Maslow chose instead to study people who were leading successful, healthy, relatively satisfying lives. He tried to discover how they got that way. He called these people "self-actualized."

Suddenly, I had an answer to my frustrating and painful attempts to find a direction in life: Discover what self-actualized people are like, and try, if possible, to emulate their qualities. What an electrifying idea! I felt as though I had found the Holy Grail.

Qualities that Maslow attributes to self-actualization are an accurate perception of reality, acceptance of self, a sense of purpose, a capacity for humor and celebration, curiosity, a creative spirit, being in the moment with a continued freshness of appreciation, and a strong capacity for love and friendship.

Many of Maslow's students were too intimidated to take advantage of his office hours, but I wasn't going to miss the opportunity. I took an ancient Chinese proverb literally: "Teachers open doors, but you must enter by yourself."

Abraham Maslow became a mentor. I developed a close personal relationship with him. Like all the best teachers, he continually expected more and insisted on greater effort. It was in his cramped office, piled with books and papers on every surface, that one of my rare, life-changing epiphanies occurred. It happened during my junior year, on Wednesday, March 13.

Maslow had a round face, large nose, and bushy mustache. He always wore a tweed jacket, white shirt, and tie. He had a permanent twinkle in his eye, but for a moment he looked at me solemnly and said, "Someone is going to make significant contributions in the field. Why shouldn't it be you?" Hearing those words from the master, I was immediately struck in the chest by a thunderbolt of energy that surged through my body. The future of psychology could be in my hands!

It has been more than sixty years since that day, and I can still feel the deep-seated jolt of confidence those words conveyed. Boosting one's self-assurance and courage, at a particularly vulnerable moment, from someone we respect, can change one's life. On some level I'm still trying to fulfill the promise he saw in me, and this book is part of that attempt.

Henry Mankin, Jr.

A Higher Standard

"When you make a mistake,
there are only three things you should ever do about it:
1. Admit it. 2. Learn from it. 3. Don't repeat it."
Paul "Bear" Bryant

HENRY MANKIN, Jr., M.D., was chief of my orthopedic residency program at Hospital for Joint Diseases in New York City. He was a kind and compassionate caregiver and an accomplished physician and educator who had done groundbreaking research in osteoarthritis and musculoskeletal tumors. He published numerous papers, maintained a busy clinical practice, and lectured worldwide.

He was imposing, both physically and intellectually. He had a Falstaffian frame, broad face, balding crown, thick horn-rimmed glasses, and a full jet-black mustache. He often had a wry smile, but if he was displeased with a resident's performance, he rapidly turned irascible.

He had breathtakingly high academic and ethical standards. He was the epitome of leadership by example. He worked harder than anyone else; he would even make house calls, highly unusual in New York City at that time. Typically, we orthopedic residents arrived at the hospital at 5 a.m., but no matter how early we got there, he was already in his office. Dr. Mankin emphasized the importance of making and keeping commitments and to be willing to do things that others cannot be bothered to do.

Medicine is a lifelong process of self-improvement. Part of this experience is learning to react positively when being criticized, acknowledging mistakes, and figuring out how they might be corrected. One morning while it was still dark outside, I was making rounds and tending to a patient who was complaining that his arm hurt where his IV had been inserted. I thought I'd examined his arm properly, but I didn't realize that the IV was not still in his vein, and the solution was slowly infiltrating the surrounding tissues. I missed the diagnosis. Fortunately, it wasn't a serious error, but all the same, it caused some increased swelling in the arm and unnecessary discomfort for the patient.

As luck would have it, the patient was Dr. Mankin's, and he saw the man later that morning. When he questioned me about the IV, I tried to make an excuse. I said, "I couldn't see properly in the dark and when I felt the arm, I thought the IV was in place." This explanation didn't go down well. Dr. Mankin didn't scream or yell, but he made it abundantly clear that my response – making an excuse -- was not acceptable.

Henry Mankin, Jr. had the same philosophy as my high school track coach, Ora Middleton, who had an answer for all of life's traumas, from a hamstring muscle strain, to the trials and tribulations of teenage love. It was always the same answer: tape it up and run it out. In other words, don't feel sorry for yourself, and don't make excuses.

I thought that I had learned this valuable lesson in high school, but I had to relearn it from Henry Mankin, Jr. Dating from the time of that experience during my first year as a resident, I never, to my knowledge, made an excuse again.

Author Steve Maraboli said, "Your life begins to change the day you take responsibility for it."

Tom Broussard

A Most Magnificent Mentor

**"No bubble is so iridescent or floats longer than
that blown by the successful teacher."
Sir William Osler**

MOLLIE MARTIN, my high school debate coach, had a profound impact on the lives of her students. This was especially true for Tom Broussard. He shares some of his own reflections about Mollie, including the dramatic evolution of their relationship:

"As a freshman at Bellaire High School in 1958, I enrolled in a Speech Class and signed up for the Debate Team, not thinking that it would forever influence my life. My teacher and debate coach was Mollie Martin.

"In the fall of 1951, at age 20, a year before she graduated from Oklahoma Central State College, summa cum laude, she began teaching at the public high school in Purcell, Oklahoma. There she began her career as a serial mentor. To recruit Joe, her leading debater, who was alleged to have burglarized a local men's haberdashery, she persuaded the judge to suspend prosecution and parole him in her custody, with her promise that he would help the school win the State Debate Championship. Since Joe's mother supported the family by taking in laundry, Mollie got many teachers to give their laundry business to Joe's mother, so he wouldn't have to work after school. She persuaded the owner of the burglarized haberdashery to donate clothes for Joe to wear to debate.

"Joe won the State Debate Championship and a scholarship to the University of Oklahoma. Mollie entered him in every state speaking contest that had a cash prize to win extra money for college. Joe became a judge on a District Circuit Court of Appeals in Texas. His debate colleague, Don Beck, the first in his family to attend college, became a university professor and a cofounder of Spiral Dynamics, a model of the evolutionary development of individuals, organizations, and societies.

"In 1955, Mollie moved to Bellaire, Texas. By 1959, her high school debate teams won two consecutive Sweepstake's Trophies at the National Forensic League tournament. She was named Coach of the Year twice. No coach's students ever won more rounds of national competition. She was

39

posthumously elected to the National Speech and Debate Association Hall of Fame. Mollie was dedicated to her students and spent as many hours outside of the classroom as within, not only teaching us but mentoring us.

"Mollie's mentoring extended beyond her students. After she moved to New York City, Michael Ledwidge, a porter in her apartment building, asked Mollie to read the draft of his first novel. She encouraged him to continue and introduced him to the author Malachi Martin, who helped him find a literary agent. After publishing three novels of his own, Ledwidge co-authored 14 books with James Patterson, and now has just completed his 6th novel.

"At Charles De Gaulle airport, Net Ramjee, an immigrant from Mauritius, who pushed wheelchairs part-time, assisted Mollie. Impressed with his service, and depressed that five years' worth of tips paid for one family weekend vacation, Mollie enthusiastically explained the French word "entrepreneur," and urged him to start his own business. When she returned to Paris and found Net had not started his business, she called him "lazy." On her next trip, Net boarded the plane, presented her with flowers, and escorted her to a new wheelchair with two attendants. NET Services is now the largest Meet and Greet service in France.

"It is easy to forget that every action we take can have a significant impact on the lives of those around us.

"I learned more in three years from Mollie, than three years at the Harvard Law School, about how to think logically and critically, how to research the pros and cons of any issue, and how to stand on my feet and speak clearly, confidently, and persuasively. I was taught how to disagree with persons expressing opposing positions, and to dissect and refute their arguments in a logical, respectful, and courteous manner so as not to antagonize a judge or my opponent.

"The most important use of the persuasive speaking skills I learned from Mollie was that, after graduating from law school in 1967, I persuaded her to marry me. For the next 50 years she continued to mentor me in talking my way up corporate ladders, and establishing a successful law practice using the analytical skills and powers of persuasion she taught me."

Ken Krimstein

Who Cares?

"It's all about the other person. How will you make them care?
How will you make them feel?"
Ken Krimstein

Ken Krimstein has written ads for American Express and Coca-Cola, drawn cartoons and graphic narrative for *The New Yorker Magazine* and *The New York Times Book Review,* and created three-non-fiction graphic "novels." When I asked Ken about a mentor who had influenced him, this is what he shared:

"Who cares?

"Two little words that change my life every single day. When I told my dad Jordie, I was thinking of going to graduate school after completing my history degree at Grinnell College, he said, 'You should call this Don Schultz fellow I met at Northwestern's Medill School of Journalism.'

"While I wasn't necessarily thinking of going into the "family business" of advertising, this was, after all, my father talking. It was the least I could do. Some forty years (!) after that fateful encounter in Schultz's crowded office, I can truly say I'm still trying to catch up to everything that was going on in Don Schultz's peripatetic mind. And what a mind, and the larger-than-life character that came along with it, which impacts my own mind several times every day.

"Although Schultz passed away in 2020, whenever I face a tough problem, or (a lot less frequently), manage to achieve a breakthrough — I hear Schultz's laconic (but pointed) Oklahoma drawl from on high (he stretched well over six feet) as he utters his inimitable "Who cares?"

"When spoken by Don, those two words contained universes. With his wife, Heidi, he revolutionized global marketing by inventing the thing we've come to know as Integrated Marketing Communication — the paradigm-shifting discovery that everything communicates.

"And in Don's brave new world where everything communicates, he saw that the key to making that communication effective was caring.

"To put a finer point on it, when it comes to communication or to connecting, you've got to get out of your own head (or navel, or whatever other body part you may care to conjure). It's all about the other person. Where are they coming from? How will this thing you're making, make it through the barricades they have erected, intentionally or unintentionally, against paying attention to what you have to say?

"How will you make them care? How will you make them feel? Who cares???

"And beyond that, there was so much more I learned from the man: He taught me to be bold, bolder than I ever imagined. After all, this was a guy who, when I'd meet him in some far-flung corner of the planet over the course of my career in advertising, whether it was drinks in Hong Kong, lunch in New York, or dinner in Los Angeles or London, would regale me with tales of how he had just told the board of the Leo Burnett Company that they were 'being ripped off' for relinquishing their intellectual property, or how he'd counseled media giants that they needed to streamline their offerings. He didn't just see around corners; he saw around entire city blocks, even around countries.

"He mentored generations of students, clients, and, as I was to learn, Schultz family members all over the country and the world. He showed up. Wherever I was on my journey from a wet-behind-the-ears cub copywriter at Ogilvy & Mather in New York to a graphic novelist, cartoonist, and historian, he was there at the drop of a hat — with ideas, provocations, queries, and that nuclear-powered couplet of his — 'Who cares?'

"This pointed, distilled, Southern-accent-inflected challenge has guided me every day - from each of my professional activities to raising my kids, getting along with my wife, my friends, and even, I hope, my world. Show up, be bolder than you ever imagined, figure out how to make the other person care. All that from a little, 'Maybe you should give this guy a call?'"

Profiles In Heroism

*True heroism is not the urge
to surpass all others at whatever cost,
but the urge to serve others at whatever cost.*
Arthur Ashe

*If you have at hand an example of good character
from whom you will have learned the lessons
by which you can live your own life, you are blessed.
Make the most of it.*
John McCain

Julius Tabin

A Self-Effacing Visionary

"The greatest gifts you can give your children are the roots of responsibility and the wings of independence."
Denis Waitley

HEROES INSPIRE us and enrich our lives by showing us the best of what we can be.

Julius Tabin studied experimental physics and cosmic ray research at the University of Chicago. Enrico Fermi asked Julius to join him on the Manhattan Project in Los Alamos, New Mexico. Julius, along with Robert Oppenheimer, Edward Teller, Neils Bohr, and other world-class scientists, was responsible for inventing the atomic bomb. Later in life as an attorney, Julius subsequently played an important role in establishing peaceful uses of atomic energy in medicine and energy production.

Julius shared many stories with me from his days with the Manhattan Project. He painted vivid portraits of his fellow scientists. One of my favorites was the story of his first ski lesson. He had never skied before, but his friends said that they would teach him. First, they hiked up a steep mountain. (There were no ski lifts at that time). When they reached the top, the lesson consisted of them saying, "See you at the bottom."

At Los Alamos, Julius was exposed to a high dose of radiation when he volunteered to collect surface samples at ground zero, the point on the earth's surface closest to where the atomic bomb detonated. He was advised never to have children. Julius and his wife Johanna didn't listen and had two sons, who are now changing the world. Elder son Cliff is chairman of the Department of Genetics at Harvard Medical School. Younger son Geoffrey is co-founder and chairman of the Himalayan Cataract Project, which has helped to cure preventable blindness around the world. Rarely has ignoring medical advice paid richer dividends!

Following Los Alamos, Julius, while teaching physics at MIT, "thought it would be fun" to get a law degree from Harvard Law School. He subsequently became a patent attorney and became the confidant and advisor to CEOs of several large corporations, including General Dynamics and Kimberly Clark.

Julius inspired love and devotion from his children and extended family. It would have been easy for Julius's sons to be intimidated by their father's extraordinary accomplishments, but he didn't overwhelm them with his own ego, thus giving them plenty of room to pursue their own destinies. Julius, one of the finest men I have ever met, was as humble and unassuming as he was gifted and accomplished.

Each of the individuals in this chapter, Thomas Kirk, Elie Wiesel, William Levine, Marjorie Benton, and Morrie Kaplan have affected the lives of thousands, both from their contributions to the common good and from the personal qualities they have exemplified. Each of them combined a vision of how to create a better world with a commitment to making it happen.

Thomas Kirk

On Heroism and Forgiveness

***"The hero shows us what we ought to be, and we make him a
hero because we wish to be what he is."***
Richard C. Crepeau

THOMAS KIRK WAS a fighter pilot for 28 years. He flew 50 bombing missions
during the Korean War and then 66 bombing missions in the Vietnam War.
On his 67th mission when he was leading 24 planes in the largest fighter
bomber mission in that war, he was shot down over North Vietnam. Tom
became a prisoner of war, held at the notoriously brutal "Hanoi Hilton," for
almost six years, from 1967 until 1973.

He was tortured, with his arms and legs bound behind his back and a rope
around his neck. Eaten by mosquitos, deprived of food, he was forced to kneel
on a small stool. He prayed, "Give me the strength to endure." He lasted ten
days, then he passed out.

Tom told me he was sustained by his belief that the war would end some-
time, while still acknowledging the reality he was enduring. The ones who
were in psychological trouble, he told me, were the pure optimists, those who
expected release at a particular date, such as Christmas, which, of course,
rarely happened.

While in solitary confinement for two years, he spoke to no one. For two
hours of his day, he practiced playing an imaginary flute. Sleeping on a
concrete floor led to pressure sores. His weight dropped from 180 pounds to
100 pounds.

He later was imprisoned in a cell with John McCain, who would become
a U.S. senator, and Vice Admiral James Stockdale, the most senior Naval
officer imprisoned in Hanoi.

Tom told me that from his prisoner of war experience he learned how
important attitude was in how he lived each day. He stated, "You can hurt me
and cause me great pain, but you cannot change my attitude toward life and
its blessings. The only control I had was over my heart, my will to live, and my
mind." When I asked him how long it took him to return to "normal life," I
assumed he would say, "Never," but he answered, "About 24 hours."

I am convinced that part of his remarkable psychological and physical endurance came from his belief in forgiveness. He immediately forgave his captors. As he stated, "I did not hold any bitterness. They were fighting a war they believed in, as was I." Tyler Perry said, "It's not an easy journey, to get to a place where you forgive people. But it is such a powerful place, because it frees you."

After his release, Thomas Kirk became Vice Commander of all Special Forces in Europe. He eventually returned to Vietnam to help rebuild the country's farming industry.

Although he has received the Air Force Cross, four Silver Stars, two Distinguished Flying Crosses, and two Purple Hearts, Thomas Kirk is as modest and humble as anyone I have ever met.

When he was in his 80s, he became a ski instructor in Vail, Colorado, and played saxophone in a band! Today, in his 90s, he states, "Every day I seek not to give in to age or weariness, but to grow spiritually and intellectually."

Bob Dylan said, "I think of a hero as someone who understands the degree of responsibility that comes with his freedom."

Elie Wiesel

Scholar, Storyteller, Social Reformer

**"The greatest crime is to do nothing because we feel we can
only do a little."**
Elie Wiesel

IN 1944, at just 15 years old, Elie Wiesel and his family were deported to Auschwitz-Birkenau. Only Elie and his two older sisters survived.

Elie made it his life's work to make sure the Holocaust was never forgotten. In *Night*, his account of his time in the death camps, he wrote, "For the survivor who chooses to testify, it is clear: his duty is to bear witness for the dead and for the living. He has no right to deprive future generations of a past that belongs to our collective memory. To forget would be not only dangerous but offensive; to forget the dead would be akin to killing them a second time."

And bear witness he did, first teaching Judaic studies at the City University of New York in the 1970s, and then teaching humanities at Boston University for more than four decades. He gave lectures, interacted with world leaders, traveled to countries where injustice reigned, and wrote more than 40 books.

For one weekend a year for twenty-five years, Elie Wiesel visited our synagogue in the Chicago area. My wife was always in charge of selling his books. This entailed meeting with him so that he could sign them. Frequently we would drive him to the synagogue, which gave us the precious opportunity to have private time with him.

As well as being a scholar and an educator, Elie was a storyteller who viewed human beings through the novelist's lens. He said that God made man because God loved stories.

One of my favorites was Elie's Hasidic tale about the Tzaddik of Nemerov. He had a way of disappearing during the time of Rosh Hashanah. Everyone knew that it was because he went to heaven at that time — to take care of a few things. One member of the congregation was skeptical and was determined to follow the rebbe.

The congregant observed that the rebbe arose early, dressed like a peasant, chopped down a tree and split it into logs. Then, disguised as a seller of wood, he went to the home of a poor, sick widow. She told him that she could

49

not afford his wood, but he proceeded to light the fire and told her that he would trust her for the money. After observing all of this, the congregant became the rebbe's most devoted follower. When asked if the rebbe went to heaven during the high holidays, the congregant no longer sneered, but answered, "To heaven? No, higher."

Elie spoke truth to power. He told President Ronald Reagan that it was not appropriate for him to attend Bitburg Cemetery in Germany, where members of the Nazi SS were buried. He stated, "This is no proper place for you, Mr. President. Your place is with the victims of the SS."

He won the Nobel Peace Prize in 1986. The Nobel Committee said he was awarded the prize "for being a messenger to mankind: his message is one of peace, atonement and dignity." In his acceptance speech, Elie said, "There may be times when we are powerless to prevent injustice, but there must never be a time when we fail to protest."

Elie continuously confronted hatred without regard to race or religion. He continued, "We must remember the suffering of my people, as we must remember that of the Ethiopians, the Cambodians, the boat people, Palestinians, the Mesquite Indians, the Argentinian *"desaparecidos"* – the list seems endless."

Elie Wiesel had a great sensitivity to human suffering. He said, "We must always take sides. The opposite of love is not hate — it is indifference."

William P. Levine

A Legacy of Leadership

"You lifted me up into your hands, and you took care of me."
Maurice Pirot

MAJOR GENERAL WILLIAM P. Levine was drafted as a private into the U. S. Army in 1942. He attended Officer's Training School, and during World War II, his unit participated in the D-Day invasion on Utah Beach in Normandy, France. He was among the first Allied Forces to enter the Dachau concentration camp in Germany.

I recently interviewed his widow, Rhoda Levine, now in her 90s. She said, "When then Captain Levine entered Dachau concentration camp on April 29, 1945, conditions were so terrible that he refused to speak about them. For more than forty years, he never spoke of his experiences, even to his family.

"Eventually he was convinced that the most effective way to prevent another Holocaust was to educate people. The first time he spoke about his experiences publicly, which took place at a local high school, he cried uncontrollably."

In 1985, General Levine spoke at Yad Vashem, The World Holocaust Remembrance Center, in Jerusalem. A man named Maurice Pirot, a Belgian Jew, recognized him. He said, "When you came into Dachau, I was lying in the agony of death, and you lifted me up into your hands and you took care of me."

After the war, Levine worked for the resettlement of more than 5,000 Holocaust survivors.

Rhoda described an emotional meeting which took place in the late 1980s between her husband and Holocaust survivor, Elie Wiesel. She quoted Elie: "I want to thank you for all your efforts to save me and my fellow concentration camp survivors."

After the war, Will joined the Army Reserves and rose to be a Major General. Even though he did not have an engineering background, imagine how talented he must have been for the Army to have sent him to school to acquire the skills to command a company of engineers. He commanded several infantry training divisions, typically comprised of more than 2500 soldiers.

After retiring from the military in 1975, he used his construction and engineering skills gained in the army to be a construction project manager for building a Jewish Day School and two synagogues. "He asked the right questions and expected the right answers," said Phil Kupritz, the architect on these projects. "He knew the names of every person who worked on his job site. I once observed him in his late 80s, high on a ladder, wearing his hard hat, supervising several construction workers. He took no money for any of his work."

General Levine passed away in 2013, at the age of 97.

Rhoda described her husband as family oriented and extremely giving. She continued, "He had great wisdom, and a marvelous sense of humor." General Levine was awarded the Legion of Merit and Distinguished Service Medal. His son John said, "For someone who achieved as much as he did, he was remarkably humble."

Rhoda Levine concluded, "Several soldiers told me that he led by example and set high standards and worked as hard as anyone else in the organization. He expected nothing but excellence. He went out of his way to encourage and support the soldiers in his unit and their families. They loved serving with him."

Marjorie Craig Benton

An Uncommon Advocate for the Common Good

"Every act of compassion is important as we move forward
together towards creating a better world."
Robert Alan Silverstein

ALL HER LIFE, Marjorie Benton has worked unceasingly for the common good. After joining the board of Partners in Health, founded by the late Paul Farmer, she chose to work in Haiti, where she helped build a women's clinic in Lascahobas, a small hospital in La Colline, and a major teaching hospital in Mirebalais.

In 2010, a magnitude 7.0 earthquake struck Haiti. It destroyed the capital, Port-au-Prince. An estimated 220,000 people were killed, 300,000 were injured, and 1.5 million were left homeless. Within hours, Marjorie organized four planeloads of supplies to be airlifted to the victims.

In 2012, Marjorie visited the new Mirebalais National Teaching Hospital, a 320-bed, state-of-the-art facility just 30 miles from Port-au-Prince, built by Partners in Health. Marjorie had been deeply involved in the project for two years. Like the late Paul Farmer, she doesn't just dream; rather her vision is accompanied by practical experience of how to get things done.

In an interview with *Foundation News* magazine, Benton said this about her international philanthropic work: "After working in Ethiopia during the famine, it was shocking to go to a restaurant here in the U.S. and watch people turn food away because they thought it wasn't cooked properly. It's an entirely different way of looking at resources, stewardship, your family, and friends. You find out how fragile life is. Things definitely get put in perspective."

In addition to Partners in Health, Marjorie is trustee of the Benton Institute for Broadband and Society, which works to ensure that media and telecommunications serve the public interest and enhance democracy. She is proud of the fact that the family tradition of public service is being carried on by her daughter, Adrianne Benton Furniss, who serves as executive director of the organization.

Statuesque and always elegant in appearance, she is invariably gracious in a social setting. At the same time, she is disciplined and tenacious when it comes to applying her imaginative ideas for the benefit of several organizations, for which she continues to work 16-hour days. She is acutely aware of the shocking numbers around the world who do not have access to essential health care. However, she remains optimistic that Paul Farmer's vision of improved health care for all can be realized.

Her perspective is that a life devoted to serving others, especially women and children, is a life well spent. Her standards are impossibly high for herself. She has improved the lives of hundreds of thousands and inspires those around her to reach higher.

Marjorie reminds me of the idea of a Bodhisattva in Buddhism – that we are all connected, and we should strive not just for our own enlightenment, but also to be able to help others.

Marjorie Benton has an indomitable belief in a better future, a vision of how to achieve it, and the exceptional ability to facilitate it.

Morrie Kaplan

Connecting with a Noble Soul

"The day you stop learning is the day you stop living."
Morrie Kaplan

MORRIE KAPLAN WAS ALWAYS a game changer. He was smart, well-informed, well-read, caring, wise, and imaginative. Morrie's innovative philanthropic, business, and educational projects changed the lives of thousands. Bobby Kennedy said, "There are those who look at things the way they are and ask why? I dream of things that never were and ask why not?"

Morrie had a lively mind. He was instrumental in the development of the Sealy Posturepedic Mattress and was chairman, president, and CEO of Sealy when it was the foremost mattress company in the United States. But his interests were wide-ranging. He was a life member of the Board of Trustees of Northwestern University, the Chicago Symphony Orchestra, the Ravinia Festival Association, and the Chicago Council on Global Affairs.

Morrie created the Morris and Alice Kaplan Chair of Ethics and Decision in Management at Northwestern University's Kellogg Graduate School of Management. For 50 years he served the Mayer and Morris Kaplan Family Foundation, a multi-generational foundation inspired by the tradition of Tzedakah, a Jewish concept, which is an ethical obligation to help others and encourage justice. The foundation is dedicated to advancing educational opportunities for young people and fostering sustainability in our natural environment.

For me, the sum of Morrie's accomplishments doesn't begin to capture his essence. Morrie had a noble soul. Your race, politics, or religion were not important to Morrie. He always gave you one hundred percent of his attention and made you feel like you were the only important person in his world.

For me, Morrie was that unique combination of friend, mentor, and hero.

Morrie had perfect moral pitch. The right thing to do seemed to emerge effortlessly from him. One could feel his presence elevating those around him to a higher plane. You knew that he always had your best interests in mind. He frequently reminded us that, as often as possible, we should tell those we love how much they mean to us.

He was filled with a childlike sense of wonder and joy and was always in the moment. He was full of creative ideas, like the summer camp he established at his home for his grandchildren. There was only one rule: no parents allowed!

Morrie was always elegant in appearance, with the wiry body of an athlete, even in his late 90s. He frequently said, "It's important to learn every day. The day you stop learning is the day you stop living." When Morrie was 95 years old, I asked him what his reading plans were. His response: "I feel guilty that I don't know more about George Washington. I'm going to read several books about him."

Overcoming Adversity

There are uses to adversity,
and they don't reveal themselves until tested.
Whether it's serious illness, financial hardship,
or the simple constraint of parents who speak limited English,
difficulty can tap unexpected strengths.
Sonia Sotomayor

The most beautiful people we have known are those who have
known defeat, known suffering, known loss,
and have found their way out of the depths.
These people have an appreciation of life
that fills them with compassion, and a deep loving concern.
Beautiful people do not just happen.
Elisabeth Kubler-Ross

Bill Wennington, Jimmy Piersall

Overcoming Adversity

"The true test of a person's character is not how they act when things are going well, but how they cope when facing hardships."
Stoic Philosophy

How WE FACE our challenges and how we handle adversity are, in large measure, how we define who we are.

Take, for example, Chicago Bulls center Bill Wennington. At the end of a game with the New Jersey Nets in 1997, Bill felt a pop in his left foot that caused him pain so sudden and so severe that he was unable to bear any weight on that leg. For a professional athlete, the timing of his injury could not have been worse. As his treating orthopedic surgeon, it fell to me to deliver the news that he would not be able to participate in the upcoming playoffs.

Few of us would have been able to turn on a dime and deal with the situation as positively as Bill did. He acknowledged that he was terribly disappointed, especially since at that moment he did not know if he would ever play in the National Basketball Association (NBA) again, but responded, "I have been lucky in my career. NBA players average six years in the league, and I have already played for ten years. I have had a good run." Bill's example was inspiring.

Shizuka Arakawa is a retired Japanese figure skater who won an Olympic gold medal in 2006. It was estimated that during her many years of training, she fell 20,000 times. What is important is that she got up 20,000 times. As writer William Ward said, "Adversity causes some people to break, others to break records."

Jimmy Piersall, who had been an All-Star for the Boston Red Sox in the 1950s, overcame another kind of adversity. He was the radio and TV announcer when we both worked for the Chicago White Sox baseball team from 1977 to 1981. He told me that in the past he had been plagued by self-doubt, anxiety, and panic attacks. In 1955 he published his memoir, *Fear Strikes Out: The Jimmy Piersall Story*. In 1957, it was made into a movie starring Anthony Perkins and Karl Malden.

Jimmy was willing to ask for the help he needed. He recovered, and became an All-Star baseball player and a charismatic, first-rate baseball announcer. Psychiatrists said that Jimmy's describing his struggles with bipolar disorder inspired others to seek treatment.

In this chapter, other contributors, including Tom Herskovits, Gary Greenberg, Michael Golden, and David Berg describe how they have dealt with overwhelming challenges. As Rabbi Harold Kushner stated, "Bad things happen to good people." The challenge is to find the inner resources, the faith, the intelligence, and the support of friends and family to help us survive devastating events.

Oprah Winfrey said, "Turn your wounds into wisdom."

Tom Herskovits

Escape to Opportunity

**"You don't need to see the whole staircase,
just take the first step."
Martin Luther King, Jr.**

Tom Herskovits, when asked what important life lesson he wished to share, responded with the following astonishing story:

"September 7, 1950. The Hungarian-Austrian border. I was a 3-year-old, with a runny nose and soggy clothes, firmly planted in the cold mud. My 1-year-old sister was next to me sobbing. My mother, usually a meticulously outfitted beauty, was in shambles. Her clothes were soaked in the blackish mud that seemed to be everywhere and tears were running down her face. A burly Russian border guard mumbled in broken Hungarian that if she turned toward her kids, he would shoot her and her children. My mother will not see her children for the next three years as she will be incarcerated in the infamous "no visitors" jail for those caught trying to escape. A few yards away lies my father, lifeless from the Russian bullets that pierced his body. The family's escape attempt from Hungary was a disaster.

"For me, this situation was not adversity; it was calamity. The first 6 months, I spent in an orphanage where I learned to hate force-fed spinach, and fish from a polluted nearby lake. The days were long, the chores were tough, and sleep was difficult in a one-space bed occupied by two. The dream of America seemed far away.

"Fast forward to 1954. Mom is out of jail and just married, and my sister is cute and loved by all. I am in an accelerated program and being groomed to be on the under-12 national chess team. The family is living well by Hungarian standards, but the dream of America still burns bright.

"December 7, 1956. The Hungarian-Austrian border. Did we learn from adversity? Are we really trying another escape from Hungary a mere 6 years from the disaster of 1950? The brave woman, who endured 3 years of hell in a jail cell, declared, "We must go. I want a better life for my children."

"The border had an eerie likeness to 1950—a light rain, mud all over and lots of Russian soldiers. Rockets lit the skies to try to spot escapees. After one of these episodes, my mom and I somehow got separated from our group. It was difficult to determine the right path in the middle of a pitch-black night. I overruled my mother on direction, avoiding a potential disaster. We rejoined the group and after about 8 more hours slogging in the mud, we were safely in Austria.

"March 6, 1957, Camp Kilmer, New Jersey. Miracles do happen. On this day, my mother, pregnant with future brother Mark, my stepdad Nathan, my sister Judy and I disembarked from the USS Douglas McArthur onto American soil. From there it was on to Brooklyn, and then Clifton, NJ, where the focus was on basketball and academics. Syracuse University provided a BS in architecture and finance and an MBA.

"June 1971, a Procter & Gamble Brand Management position—a very prestigious starting job. While a lot was learned about business, the highlight of the 10 years at P&G was meeting, courting, and marrying the love of my life, Rita. This incredible person has made the last more than forty years a total joy. Credit must go to my boss at P&G, Peg Wyant, who persevered in getting her sister-in-law Rita and me together. We have also been blessed by two amazing children Kathryn and David -- who tragically passed away at age 38 from a heart attack.

"After P&G, I became President of the General Foods Breakfast Foods division, and subsequently President of Kraft Dairy and Frozen products in Chicago. In 1993 I became CEO of Specialty Foods, a $2 billion+ food company. In 1996, I formed Herskovits Enterprises that helped start and manage a dozen businesses. As for my siblings, my brother Mark has been a very successful insurance agent, and my sister Judy was a highly respected federal judge who spent 33 years on the bench. My mom and dad both lived to be 94 and very much enjoyed the success of their children and their 6 grandchildren. America offered even more opportunities than any of us could imagine.

"The lesson I would highlight in my family's experience is fairly simple and obvious. If you have a goal or a dream and do not succeed at first, don't give up."

Tom finished his remarkable story by saying, "If there is an America waiting for you -- don't quit until you get there."

Michael Golden

Golden's Rule

"Deep human connection is the purpose and the result of a
meaningful life – and it will inspire the most amazing acts of
love, generosity, and humanity."
Melinda Gates

MICHAEL GOLDEN IS the author of *Write Or Die: Negotiating Life – One Column At A Time.* He has battled depression and anxiety for many years. He shares with me some of his most personal, vulnerable moments in the hopes that others will benefit from his experience:

"Standing in my mother's kitchen, I could feel a totally irrational fear taking hold of my nerves. It was the realization that I might not have the mental capacity to drive my car to my home that night. My mind and my body had finally hit bottom. The twin devils of depression and anxiety that I'd been experiencing for weeks, now had me fully in their grip.

"I knew how hard it was for my mom to hear my fear. And I realized in that moment that I might just be suffering a nervous breakdown. Observing this fact — as it's happening to you — is positively surreal. What's worse is that you feel powerless to reprogram your mind. My next panicked thought was wondering how I would be able to continue teaching at Arizona State for the next six weeks. If I couldn't drive 20 minutes home, how would I make the 45-minute trek to campus and function in front of 100 students? Pacing the kitchen, I called my teaching mentor at Arizona State University, Jack Crittenden, and asked him what happens when a professor can't finish a semester?

"Jack listened patiently as I described my dilemma. Then he said: "My God, Michael. You must be terrified." My friend could hear it. And he was right.

"I did end up driving my car home that night. I was shaky, but I knew I just had to. I also ended up finishing the semester. Each class session was mentally and physically exhausting, and there were times when I thought I would literally collapse. But being amongst those young people, talking to them and listening to them, was the first time I realized the full power of connection.

"During those brutally painful months of depression, at the age of 51, I let my mother take care of me. We connected in a wholly different way, and we became closer. My friends Dana and Laurie would push me to climb out of my bedroom dungeon and meet them for a meditation class or a slice of pizza. I didn't want to, but as soon as I was out of my dark pit and amongst other people, the hurt would start to ease a bit.

"Human connection, be it in the form of love, friendship, collegiality — or talking to a stranger at a bus stop — feeds and fuels our hearts and our heads.

"A few years later, when a similar episode visited me, a newer friend of mine named Tracy Thirion — whom I've still never met in person — nursed my frantic psyche over a phone line from Scotland. We spoke for hour after hour, and when I wondered aloud why she was doing this, Tracy said: "This is how it works. So many of us have been through it. And then when we get to help someone else, that's part of our purpose."

"To me, that sense of "purpose" — a dedication to a cause greater than oneself — is the second essential key to navigating this often confusing journey. After that second episode, I published my second book. *Write Or Die* is a collection of columns — including a few, like this one, about mental health.

"One reader reached out and asked if I would talk to a friend whose daughter had recently tried to take her life. I was on the phone with him that night. And then with her. We quickly became fast friends and talked for hours over several weeks. She faced all her pain head-on, and now she is feeling a whole lot better. In a beautifully written card I received from my new friend, she included this sentence: "I only hope that I can touch someone's life the way you have touched mine." She will. And that's the whole point.

"To be clear, the right medication and the right therapist can make a huge difference for anyone battling mental health issues. Trust me. But human connection and meaningful purpose have the power to sustain us. And more often than not, that connection with other people — who struggle just like us — is our purpose. We are here for each other."

Gary Greenberg

The Solution to Adversity? Friends and Family

"Show me someone who has done something worthwhile, and I'll show you someone who has overcome adversity."
Lou Holtz

GARY GREENBERG GREW up in a middle-class Chicago neighborhood, but in an effort to be "tough," he found a group of troublemakers with whom to hang out. He ended up being arrested several times, which devastated his parents. Recognizing their son's athletic ability and hoping to disrupt his delinquent behavior, Gary's parents enrolled him in Camp Ojibwa, an overnight sports camp in northern Wisconsin. He got off to a rough start. The camp owners pulled him aside the first day and said, "Greenberg, you have a bad reputation. One wrong move and we will send you back to Chicago."

He quickly got his act together and excelled as an athlete. "Many of the camp counselors became my mentors, and those mentors saved my life. But for them, I might have wound up in prison," he said. Gary returned to Camp Ojibwa for several years and developed friendships that have lasted a lifetime, and have seen him through his own tragedies.

In 1965, Gary enrolled at the University of Oklahoma. There he made good friends and was elected president of his fraternity in 1968. "But then my lifelong goal to become a college baseball player was ended when I was struck by a random bullet. The bullet lodged in my heart. Months of medical care bankrupted my parents. I finished college without a clue as to what career I could possibly follow."

However, two fathers of campers at Ojibwa introduced him to the owners of a company, Pronto Food Corporation. He was hired as a sales trainee. There he met the young man who would be his business partner for 30 years. By the time he was 38, Gary was president of Sage Foods, Inc., in charge of more than 450 employees. Gary said, "I was admitted to the Young Presidents' Organization (YPO), and through my company business relationships and membership in the YPO, I developed relationships that changed the trajectory of my life and helped me grow personally and professionally."

Then came the tragedy of 9/11. Sage Foods floundered. "Our business was tied to the airline industry, and we were crushed. The company had to shut its doors and more than 250 people, including my business partner and me, lost their jobs. At age 55, with a family to support, I had to reinvent myself in some type of new career. The relationships I developed at Ojibwa, YPO, and my country club helped me find a new path. Today, because of them, I am a partner in a boutique investment firm in Chicago."

In 2020, tragedy struck again. "In late August, in the middle of the Covid pandemic, my wife of 44 years was diagnosed with an incurable brain disease that ended her life six weeks later. I felt unable to move forward without her. My amazing daughters, sons-in-law, and other close friends helped me survive the loss of my wife."

Gary continued, "After my wife passed away, I worked on putting my life back together. The strength of so many relationships aided my recovery in countless ways that are impossible for me to articulate. Today I still receive emotional support from many of these same people. The life lesson I want to leave with you is that family and friends are what life is about. Without those incredible relationships, I would not be where I am today. I am slowly making headway. I have recently entered a relationship with a wonderful woman. How lucky can I be!"

David Berg

I Am My Brother's Memory Keeper

"*Kid, there is nothing you can't accomplish.*"
Alan Berg

THIS IS David Berg's response to the question, "What adversity have you overcome?"

"On May 28, 1968, Charles Harrelson, a Texas pimp and hit man, and his girlfriend, kidnapped my brother at gunpoint and drove him to a remote location outside of Houston. There, Harrelson shot him through his temple and when Alan would not die, dragged him by his necktie to choke him to death. Then they drove to a distant county and dumped his body. From the moment Alan's wife called me around 5 a.m. the next morning, asking if I knew where my brother was, and for the following six months, until his remains were found, no one knew the answer to that question except the murderer and his girlfriend.

"The six months he was missing were excruciating. The Houston police refused to investigate, telling us that "husbands run off all the time." Nor would the FBI, until then-Congressman George H.W. Bush got involved. Starting from the day Alan went missing, Dad and I tracked down every halfway credible lead, even to Mexico City, but to no avail. Finally, Dad spent his last dime on a lead that proved true. I awoke on a Sunday morning to a front-page picture in the *Houston Post* with a deputy sheriff holding Alan's skull for the camera.

"There is no way to describe how close we were. Alan, six years older, was my father-figure, protector, and cheerleader. "Kid," he would say, "there is nothing you can't accomplish." If I ever bemoaned the competition, as when I faced a tough team in a high school debate tournament, he would remind me, somewhat less elegantly, "Kid, remember, even Queen Elizabeth breaks wind." Yet, for all our closeness, the movie I played on a loop in my head of Alan's tortured last hour, blotted out almost everything that we had said and done together, and would for years to come. A violent death can do that, can obscure the most treasured memories.

"In 1970, a jury in the rural, redneck county where Alan's body was found acquitted Harrelson. It came as no surprise. Harrelson's lawyer was famous for his stable of "reserve witnesses," individuals in his debt who took the stand to swear the accused was with them at the time of the crime. That was what happened in Harrelson's trial; three men put Harrelson hundreds of miles away at the time of Alan's murder. Under Texas law, the indictment against the man who hired Harrelson—an ex-employee in my father's and brother's carpet business, whom Dad had caught stealing and fired, and who had left threatening to kill both of them —was dismissed.

"For twenty-six years, except for an essay on gun control, I never spoke about Alan's murder, embarrassed not only by the squalid newspaper and magazine articles that follow all murder cases but also, worst of all, that a hit man murdered him, as if we were some Mafia family in Queens.

"During that time, I plunged headlong into my practice, committed to winning every case I tried, and damn near did, including a life-changing victory in the United States Supreme Court less than two years into my practice. Then, years later, I read the novella, A River Runs Through It, a memoir disguised as fiction about the murder of the author's brother, who was pistol-whipped to death over a gambling debt. Deeply moved, I began to talk about Alan, and could not stop, as memories came rushing back. In 2013, Scribner published my memoir, Run, Brother, Run: A Memoir of a Murder in My Family, to wonderful reviews and wide recognition of what a remarkable, and remarkably complicated, man my brother was.

"The question posed is how I overcame adversity. The answer is, I am not certain. I know I felt some degree of vindication when Harrelson was later convicted of two other murders-for-hire, one the assassination of a federal judge that resulted in his being confined to a Supermax prison until he died 26 years later.

"I know I never once asked, "Why me?" or sought the sad eyes and sympathy of friends. I knew implicitly that "closure" was nonsense, as if I could simply move on, Alan's murder a distant memory. But I did have dreams and direction, fanned by my brother, that never died, that have pushed me to accomplish far more than I could have hoped had he not lived and loved me."

Moving Past A Challenging Childhood

Your struggles develop your strengths.
When you go through hardships and decide not to surrender,
that is strength.
Mahatma Gandhi

Winning doesn't mean being first.
Winning means you're doing better than you've done before.
Bonnie Blair

Ron LeFlore

A Second Chance at Bat

"The moment you take 100 percent responsibility for everything in your life is the same moment you claim your power to change anything in your life."
Hal Elrod

RON LEFLORE GREW up in one of the most dangerous neighborhoods in Detroit. "While other kids were in school studying algebra and geography, I was standing on the corner drinking wine, smoking grass, and selling speed and stolen clothes to prostitutes and pimps. That was the way I grew up," he said in the book he wrote with Jim Hawkins, *One in a Million: The Ron LeFlore Story*.

Both of his parents worked hard at low-paying jobs to support their children, and so didn't have much time to spend with them. Nevertheless, Ron felt that they loved him unconditionally and that they tried to do their best for him and his three brothers.

LeFlore was smart and resourceful, and, by his own acknowledgment, a really good liar. Soon he was stealing whatever he wanted. He thought he could get away with anything. The only choices he saw for himself when he grew up were to be a thief or a drug dealer. In 1967, when he was 19 years old, he and some friends wanted heroin. To get the money to pay for it, they decided to rob a bar. A friend lent them a .22 rifle.

Ron was the leader of the group. The robbery got them $35,000, but the police soon caught them. Because he carried a rifle, he was sentenced to 5 to 15 years at a maximum-security prison. "At that moment, my whole life seemed over," he recalled.

LeFlore stopped using heroin in prison. "I quit using hard drugs not because I had to — there were plenty of drugs around — but because I didn't want the hassles drugs caused.... I even joined Narcotics Anonymous because I knew it would look good on my record when I came up for parole."

Ron played his first baseball game in prison, and he met a baseball scout. "He kept telling me I had the ability to play professional baseball. I began believing that maybe I could play professional ball when I got out of prison, so I began watching games on TV, trying to learn as much as possible."

71

The Detroit Tigers subsequently sent their own scouts to see him in prison. The Tigers were impressed enough so that when he was released from prison, his father drove him directly to the ballpark where he was put into the custody of the ball club. He signed a contract with $5000 in bonus money.

Just three years later, he was playing in an All-Star game. During his career, he played for the Detroit Tigers, Montreal Expos and Chicago White Sox. His career batting average was .288 and he hit 59 home runs. He also stole 455 bases, which seems almost foreordained.

Ron LeFlore's story is that of a young man who got off to a terrible start, partly because of the poor choices he made. But then he made different choices, which turned his life around. We developed a good relationship when he played for the Chicago White Sox and I was an orthopedic consultant for the team. He always treated me with great respect. I had the feeling that every day he realized how fortunate he was.

In this chapter, Ronald "Mark" Booker, Alyssa Webb Royle, and Charles Levin dramatically share their attempts to overcome a challenging childhood.

Mark Booker

Fighting Fire with Fire

"Man is nothing else but what he makes of himself."
Jean-Paul Sartre

RONALD "MARK" Booker, Jr. and my son-in-law Richie Campus were firefighters together. When I asked Mark how he negotiated a challenging start in life to become a professional firefighter, and responsible husband and father, this was his response:

"I grew up in Southern California. I was basically raised by women — my mother and my grandmother. My father wasn't in the picture much. He was in and out of prison, and my mother was the sole provider for me and my two sisters. A respiratory therapist, she always stressed the importance of having a profession, not just a job.

"Growing up in the late 80s and early 90s was nothing like the movies depict. My mother worked really hard; however, she was unable to provide me with what I thought I needed as a teenager growing up in LA in the 90s. My friends and I recognized early that we would have to do something different to get the things we thought we deserved.

"Ages 11 to 17 were a steep learning curve. I often felt ashamed that I had no money. At the age of twelve, I took the money my mother gave me and along with a friend bought some crack cocaine wholesale to sell. My life truly changed at that point.

"I became heavily involved in gang life. Although a lot of people look at gangs as negative, for me they provided my first true exposure to teamwork. In the "real world" you are often judged by your contemporaries, and gang life was the same. You are vetted by a group of your peers (also known as being jumped in), which means getting beatdown by the kids you grew up with to prove you have what it takes to fight the world around you.

"This was the crack cocaine era, and although I never did crack or any other dope, my parents and a lot of people close to me fell victim to the drug.

"At age thirteen, I caught my first charge — sales of a controlled substance: crack cocaine. Two assault charges followed. My involvement with selling crack quickly evolved to selling guns. By the time I was seventeen, I was

73

labeled an "active gang member." Then I got caught in a robbery and was committed for six years to the California Youth Authority.

"This was a wakeup call for me. Because of good behavior, I was allowed to participate in a program at the Fire Camp at the El Paso de Robles School for Boys. I learned a lot about myself. A firefighter became a mentor to me. I cannot imagine what my life would be like if I hadn't been given this opportunity. It is so important that rehabilitation programs exist to give people like me a second chance.

"When I was released in 1994, I was a grown man with a new outlook on life and three years of wildland firefighting experience. I had no adult record even though I had committed a violent felony. I came home to a racial war in my city. This was one of the most challenging times for me. I had a huge target on my back -- members of other gangs were out to get me. To the police I was simply someone who had committed a felony, and I lost a lot of friends and family.

"Fortunately, I was offered a job with the U.S. Forest Service as a wildland firefighter. Wildland firefighting changed my life. I had a child on the way. I moved to the Sierra Nevada mountains where I raised my first son, Myles. I mended my relationship with my parents. They both ultimately became drug-free. Today I am a loving father of three and married to the most amazing woman in the world."

Now Mark has achieved the highest levels in firefighting and currently works for the federal government as an Air Tactical Group Supervisor, coordinating air traffic and ground personnel in fighting wildfires.

Mark summarizes, "I try to be the best man that I can be. My life lesson is to pace yourself. Things take time. You can turn your life around. Understand that you can change."

Alyssa Webb Royle

Unpacking Her Memories

**"My mother filled my suitcase with memories to remind me
that my father loved me the best he could."**
Alyssa Webb Royle

ALYSSA WEBB ROYLE is an elementary school teacher and tutor in the
United Kingdom. She shares the following story:

"It was a child's suitcase: thick, pinkish red, with a red plastic handle and
a slot for a small umbrella that spanned diagonally across one side. It was
nothing special at first glance, but it meant the world to me because, at the age
of seven, I would pack that little red suitcase every Thursday evening before
bed. Friday was the day my father would be coming to collect me for the
weekend. At least, he was meant to come...

"Before the age of seven, I lived in a home with two parents. They were
by no means perfect people — both had their flaws and had made their fair
share of mistakes; however, life as a family made sense. My mother asked my
father to leave because of duplicitous wheelings and dealings that she knew
were not conducive to a healthy family situation. I wanted my father in my
life. Weekends were HIS time with me, and I wanted those moments. Thus
began my Thursday night packing ritual: I'd carefully take down my little red
suitcase from the top of my closet, insert two changes of clothes, whatever
books I was reading and my homework. I'd put the carefully packed case by
the front door to be ready for Dad after school.

"Unfortunately, I spent Friday afternoon after Friday afternoon standing
on a step stool, peering through the peephole, and watching for my father's
burgundy Lincoln Town Car to pull up in the driveway. He rarely came. My
mother could have torn him to shreds by telling me that he wasn't going to
show and destroying my belief that my father did indeed love me. But instead,
she conjured up white lie after white lie to protect my young and impression-
able mind from the fact that my father put his work and his new social life
ahead of me.

"The weekends I did spend with my father were not characterized by
trips to the zoo or to the park, but rather by me watching my father watch
baseball games on television. I'd pretend to watch alongside, but really, I was

watching him because he was a mystery to me. As the years passed, I began to understand why my mother covered for him because she could not bear to watch me cry myself to sleep nearly every Friday night.

"Seeing my father so sporadically did more harm than good in the end: he was relegated to stranger status, and I began to accept that I was a girl without a dad. And into my teen years, that disappointment morphed into anger — rage, even. I began to believe that I was unworthy of being loved.

"Decades later — long after my father passed — we lost my mother, and I had the task of clearing out my childhood home. In my closet, on the top shelf, I found that little red suitcase. I wasn't sure what to expect upon opening it. I took in a deep breath and separated the zippers; I closed my eyes as I slowly opened the case. When I opened my eyes, I saw something that changed everything from that moment onwards: that little red suitcase was filled with everything dad-related that my mother had collected over the years — photographs I'd never seen, every letter he'd ever written to me at summer camp, the purple unicorn candle he'd given to me on my tenth birthday. And most touching of all were the birthday cards addressed to me, stacked in chronological order from every year starting on my 7th birthday.

"My mother had collected these items and placed them into the one vessel that she knew I would associate with my father. Like the little lies she told to cover for him, this was her way of protecting me — of assuring me that he did love me in his own way. She filled that little red suitcase with memories to remind me that he loved me the best that he could; the instant I zipped it shut, I forgave him for all those times he had made me wait."

Alyssa states, "From that experience I learned not to make assumptions about those you love, that time will often reveal the truth. Also, as often as possible, it is essential to let family and friends know how much I love them."

Charles Levin

What His Mother Left Him

"It may take a lifetime to understand the complexity and grace of another person's life, if we can do it at all, but it's worth an ever-loving effort."
Charles Levin

CHARLES LEVIN SHARES this poignant memory of his mother:

"While cleaning out my crazily cluttered attic, filled with 38 years of things my wife, Amy, and I don't need but couldn't part with — broken chairs, ancient computers, '80s vintage suitcases— I stumbled across one particularly meaningful artifact, a permission slip from my mother:

> To whom it may concern,
> My son Charles Levin has my permission to play "Pocket Billiards."
> Very truly yours,
> Mrs. Yvonne B. Levin, 377 So. Harrison St., East Orange, N.J., OR6-5432

"The pool hall I wanted to frequent required customers to be at least sixteen, and I was just fourteen. The note, the permission slip, seems straightforward enough, but as I examined it more closely, I discovered it contains clues to my mother's life story, a snapshot of the 1960s, and a hint of my relationship with my mother.

"First, there's the actual content of the note. For her to have written this note, I must have asked her to let her youngest child hang around, unsupervised, at a seedy, smoke-filled pool hall. Why would she agree to that? I'd like to think it was because she trusted me, but that might only be part of the reason. I think that she also was worn out after losing two husbands who died young, the first at 29 and the second, my father, at 49, and working full time to raise three kids. My sister is thirteen years older and my brother nine years older than I. So, by the time she got to me, it was pretty much anything goes. A current expression may capture it best. With this note, I think she was saying, "Whatever...(sigh)."

"At the bottom of the note, there is another clue to my mother's life:

"Warner, Jennings, Mandel & Longstreth," a stock brokerage firm. She worked there as the first female stockbroker ever in New Jersey.

"My mother's world turned upside down when my father died. At age forty, she had to go to work to support the family. At first, she didn't know what she would do. In the '50s, men worked, and women stayed home with the kids, and she had three young ones.

"As unlikely as it seems, when she was a teenager, my mother used to hang out at the local stock brokerage office, watching the ticker tape of the stock prices being posted and erased, posted and erased, on a big chalkboard. Being a numbers person, she just loved it. That's what she had always wanted to be when she grew up, but there were no women stockbrokers. With a little encouragement from a friend, she studied, took her exams, passed, and got a job with a room full of men in Newark, New Jersey. Soon she was the top producer in the office. She could sell, really sell. She was rightfully proud of her new career.

"Warner, Jennings, and its successors were eventually bought out by Thompson McKinnon, where they promoted her to vice president. In 1984, at age 72, she had her best career year ever. She was a force of nature. Unfortunately, the following year Prudential bought out Thompson and because of her age, they made my mom retire. It was the end for her. Husbands gone, kids gone, and the job that filled her days with challenging joy, gone.

"Then one awful day in 1989, I got a call from my sister. "I can't reach Mom." We both rushed to her apartment in East Orange. Mom had taken an overdose of pills. The sight of her barely breathing, prone on the floor with the empty bottle of pills beside her, haunts me to this day. She lasted two days in the hospital and then she left us.

"Before mom died, I carried this note, the permission slip, around in my wallet for many years. She passed away more than 30 years ago. Still, I think I'll put the note back in my wallet — the date is blank, so it should be good anytime. 'Cause you never know when you might need a permission slip."

Adapting To Change

The art of life lies in a constant readjustment to our surroundings.
Okakura Kakuzo

When facing a new challenge, one should not ask,
"Why me?" but instead,
"What am I supposed to learn from this?"
Chip Conley

Richie Campas, Eldee Young

The Courage to Reinvent Yourself

"Change is the only constant in life. One's ability to adapt to those changes will determine your success in life."
Benjamin Franklin

RICHIE CAMPAS WAS A SMOKEJUMPER, a select group of people who parachute into remote wildland fires. Among the skills necessary to fight fires are parachute jumping, water landing, climbing trees and using chainsaws. The physical requirements include hiking with full gear packs weighing 115 pounds. Many candidates do not make it through the five-week training period.

Richie loved the work, and he was good at it. Smokejumpers work six months during the fire season and then have six months off. During one of his breaks, Richie met my daughter in Maui. He is now my son-in-law, and I am the proud grandfather of two beautiful grandsons.

Despite his expertise and his love of smoke jumping, Richie realized he could not be a good father to young children if he was away for six months every year. Richie stated, "I had to let go of my ego. I was at the top of my game as a smoke jumper. But I couldn't bear the thought of missing out on seeing my boys grow up."

Richie, who exudes strength and determination, had the confidence that he had other skills that would enable him to change careers. He loves the outdoors. Initially he became an arborist. However, an arborist's work is also very hazardous. So, he got his boat captain's license, then he earned his contractor's license. Richie adapted by making dramatic career changes.

Eldee Young, a professional singer and base player, late in his career also figured out a way to adapt to changing circumstances. He was able to help support his family while keeping music at the center of his life.

One of my most memorable times with Eldee occurred when I was performing an operation on his hand under local anesthesia. As I began, I heard him sing in a soft, beautiful voice the words, "The very thought of you and I forgot to do...." I spontaneously added, "The little ordinary things that everyone ought to do." Then together we sang, "I'm living in a kind of

81

daydream; I'm happy as a king...." Singing with Eldee Young was my one shining moment in show business!

Eldee was always debonaire with an infectious smile. He was one of eight children, and an older brother taught him to play the guitar when he was 10. He was playing the upright bass professionally by the time he was 13.

He co-founded the Ramsey Lewis Trio, one of the most important jazz bands of that era. The trio's reputation grew through the 1950s and early 1960s. They played a sold-out concert in Carnegie Hall. In 1966 they recorded the hit jazz single "The In Crowd." Suddenly they were famous, and they were making a lot of money.

Then it was over. Young told the *Chicago Tribune,* "We had worked so hard on our music together, and when the group broke up, it was like a family breakup. I took it very hard."

Musicians have to play wherever people will listen. As a result, in the 1980s, Young took his music to Singapore, Vietnam, India, Malaysia, and Thailand, where it was especially appreciated, as evidenced by his being asked to perform for three months at a time in each of these locations.

Eldee would quote to me George Gershwin's saying, "Life is a lot like jazz.... it's best when you improvise." Tragically, in 2007, Eldee passed away of a cardiac arrest while performing in Thailand.

Most young people today will have more than one job over the course of their working lives. Like Richie Campas and Eldee Young, they will be called upon to set new priorities and to learn new coping skills.

Sometimes change is expected, sometimes it is unpredictable and cataclysmic. Contributors to this chapter, including Scottie Pippin, Robert Bensman, Gordon Green, Rachel Merriman Frazier, Brian Ralston, and Kimmie Ouchi, describe how they handled unexpected circumstances.

Richard Branson said, "Every success story is a tale of constant adaptation, revision and change."

Scottie Pippin

Responding to Change

**"It is not the strongest of the species that survives.
It is the one that is most adaptable to change."**
Charles Darwin

SCOTTIE PIPPEN WAS BORN in Hamburg, Arkansas, in 1965, the youngest of twelve children. Scottie arrived at the University of Central Arkansas, without a scholarship, intending to play basketball. But at 6'1", he was not even a walk-on player, he was a walk-on *manager,* until a dramatic growth spurt. By the time he left the university as a senior, he was 6'8", and he had earned Consensus National Association of Intercollegiate Athletics All-American honors.

In 1987, Scottie began his NBA career with the Chicago Bulls. From his challenging beginnings, Scottie transformed himself into one of the greatest defenders ever to play the game, making the NBA All-Defensive Team ten consecutive years. He played 17 seasons in the NBA, winning six championships with the Bulls.

Assistant coach Tex Winter told me how he respected Scottie for his intense work ethic and his unselfishness on the court. Bill Wennington shared how he felt about his teammate in his book, *Tales from the Chicago Bulls Locker Room:* "Scottie Pippen is my favorite Bull. I loved Michael [Jordan] as a person and a teammate. I just appreciated Scottie more.... Scottie is a passionate person. He was driven like Michael to succeed.... Other than Michael, Scottie was head and shoulders above all the outstanding players I had previously played with – in terms of leadership and what he stood for as a team player. You have to have drive, desire, and leadership qualities within you to make it work the way Scottie did."

Many analysts considered Scottie to be the second-best player in the league, after Michael Jordan. Michael and Scottie were teammates for parts of ten seasons, winning six championships. Neither of them won a championship without the other.

On most other teams, Scottie would have been the face of the franchise. Many athletes would have found it difficult to sublimate their game and ego to accommodate an even more talented teammate. People, relationships, and perspectives may change over time, but the Scottie Pippin I saw when I was with the Bulls in the 1990s was an inspiring example of putting what's best for the team first.

I observed Scottie adjust to changing circumstances necessary not only to survive in the highly competitive NBA but to thrive. Scottie's willingness to do whatever was necessary to help his team win, was an essential part of his greatness.

Robert A. Bensman

Your Power is in the Question

"Asking the 'why and what' and 'is this really working'
questions and answering from your heart can yield outcomes
beyond your wildest dreams."
Robert A. Bensman

WHEN BOB BENSMAN, family friend and advisor, was 60, he decided to enter his first triathlon. To achieve his goals, which others may consider merely pipe dreams, Bob values asking the right questions over having all the answers.

He reflects on how to achieve one's goals: "Having never swum or run before, it was a challenge to think about competing against experienced and driven athletes. Particularly challenging were the subconscious effects of the memory that I had almost drowned in a swimming pool as a child."

"After engaging a terrific coach, Marcia Cleveland, a world-class swimmer, I realized what I needed to do to overcome my fears and to prove to myself that I could compete. As a result of this understanding, and committed training with a great coach, I finished sixth in my age group and was in the best shape of my life."

Bob goes on to say, "I have found that two types of unasked questions prevent us from reaching our potential. The first type generally has to do with the "what and why" of the goal we need or want to achieve.

"We may believe that achievements are measured by defined outcomes — a financial milestone, the best time in a race, a game with the lowest or highest score. These outcomes may in themselves be very worthwhile and recognized as wonderful achievements. But identifying a meaningful purpose, the 'inner goal,' will make it much easier to determine what the next steps are. Understanding 'the why' of the goal you wish to achieve will support your efforts and help others to support you. It will help you to focus and give that 'extra effort' required to become the best you can be when 'the going gets tough, and the tough get going.'"

"The second type of question is often the most difficult, and it may take many years to develop the courage to confront it. The toughest question, 'Is this really working?' requires a 'gut honest' answer.

"For many years, when I was asked by friends, family, and clients, 'How are things going?' I would respond with truthful, relevant answers that were considered normal, such as, 'family's great,' 'business is growing,' and so on. Yet deep down, I did not want to admit that my marriage was not what I wanted, nor did I feel good about it. Since I had committed to 'until death do us part,' I continued to remain stuck and unhappy. Yet, at the same time, my wife was feeling the same way, and she had the courage to articulate our mutual unhappiness. After numerous counseling sessions, hours of introspection, and support from professionals and friends, we have each gone our own way.

"Two years after we parted, I had the great fortune to meet Olga, and we were married five years later. In my wildest dreams, I could not have found a more loving, wise, supportive person. The opportunity to share my life with her would never have occurred if I had not asked the question, 'In spite of my trying everything to make it work, should my wife and I continue in the marriage?' The answer to that question gave me the courage and conviction to move forward.

"Ultimately, asking the tough questions continues to empower me, resulting in relationships with like-minded souls."

Shannon L. Adler said, "Courage doesn't happen when you have all the answers. It happens when you are ready to face the questions you have been avoiding your whole life."

Gordon Green

Hope for Simplicity, Plan for Complexity

"Plans are worthless, but planning is everything."
Winston Churchill

GORDON GREEN WAS a classmate of mine at University of Texas Southwestern Medical School. When asked if he has one life lesson to pass on to the next generation, he responded, "What's my motto? Probably not so much a motto, but more of a pervasive Law of the Universe, governing all actions and interactions.

"It goes as follows: 'Nothing is simple.' I humbly refer to this Formulation as "Green's Law." (This is not to be confused with George Green's law regarding the propagation of gravity waves, or his mathematical theorem.)

"Any situation, any pathway, any plan of action you approach may initially appear to be a straightforward course of action or a simple decision. However, it is not always so. This underlying Law of the Universe will prevail, and the entire situation will turn into a can of worms.

"Just recall the last time you realized that you were thirsty. You found yourself stirring from your comfy chair in search of a serviceable water faucet. But then you had to rummage through various cabinets, looking for a glass, a cup, or a laboratory beaker. Oh, good! Here it is! But it does look dirty. Now where did you put that dishwashing soap? Well, no matter: you can use the only product available at hand, a bar of Lava hand soap. Mmm, will the water taste gritty?

"And so on.

"An example from my own practice: what should have been straightforward antibiotic and respiratory care for an infant boy with an infection in his lungs quickly ballooned in complexity when we learned that the patient was, in fact, the Prince of the Gypsies in that part of the United States. Caravans of roving Romani camped out on our hospital lawn. We enjoyed uninterrupted attention from the concerned families for three days, until the baby could be discharged from the hospital.

"This transmogrification of a homely, uncomplicated Law into real, complicated life is unavoidable and inevitable. Just when you think you have matters well in hand, Green's Law works its magic, and you will have a tangled web of circumstances which you never anticipated. Good luck!"

Gordon Green concludes, "Nothing Is Simple." Please note that the only exception to The Law is The Law itself."

A variation on Green's theme is the term "Black swan," popularized by author and investor Nassim Nicholas Taleb. It is the occurrence of an unpredicted event that is beyond what is normally expected of a situation.

Green's Law reminds me of the rather indelicate boxing maxim, "Everyone has a plan until they get punched in the mouth." Or, as Murphy's Law states, "Anything that can go wrong will go wrong, so expect the unexpected."

Rachel Merriman Frazier

Fortitude on the Homefront

"I hope my new son learns the joys of achievements and derives pleasure from discovering the world around him."
Bud Frazier

WHEN I ASKED Rachel Frazier how she was able to cope with the challenge of giving birth to her first child while not knowing if her husband was going to survive combat in the Vietnam war, this was her response:

"The year was 1968. My husband, Bud, and I had been married four years. Bud was immersed in his General Surgery Internship, and I was busy teaching second and third grades and Head Start in the summer. Our career paths were off to a good beginning: I had received the Outstanding Young Educator Award from Houston Independent School District, and Bud received the coveted DeBakey Surgery Award for being his outstanding intern. We were both seriously committed to our career paths until a most unexpected thing happened.

"Bud was inducted into the United States Army and was assigned to the Republic of Vietnam. At first, we took the patriotic position: It would be a challenging year, but he was going to fight against communism. However, as the time of his departure grew nearer, I became pregnant with our first child and was informed by the school district that I could not continue teaching if I was *"expecting"* before school started. We had depended on my teaching salary to help support me for the year Bud was gone, but suddenly that was out of the question. Now our world was even more challenged. Where would I live? How could I pay for living expenses if I couldn't teach school? This is when *"angels"* came to my rescue. Both Bud's and my entire family opened their arms and their hearts and gave me their abounding love, a place to live, and much needed moral support. I definitely needed it.

"Of course, in 1968 there were no cellphones or computers for Bud and me to use for communication, so I had to wait patiently for each letter from him. There were days, and sometimes weeks, when I didn't know if he was alive or not. He was assigned to be the physician to an Assault Helicopter

Unit. It consisted of three hundred men; the average age was eighteen. Bud, at age 28, must have seemed ancient. They called him dad!

"Bud went on all the combat missions with the helicopter pilots into Vietcong territory. I learned that on two occasions, the helicopter he was in was shot down in the jungle. This was often a death sentence. In between combat missions, Bud set up outdoor clinics in nearby villages to treat the sick. The Vietcong were often nearby, and on most nights mortared his camp. He cared for countless wounded and had to identify numerous dead soldiers.

"I didn't know from one letter to the next if Bud was going to make it home to see his new son who was born on June 22, 1969. After Bud received a telegram from me announcing the birth of our son, this is what he wrote in his diary:

"*I hope the boy will have a good life. It seems so easy for things to go otherwise, now. I hope he never has to risk his life in a brutal, raw, vicious war. I hope he learns the joys of achievements and derives pleasure from discovering the world around him. I know he could never ask for a more loving and devoted mother.*"

"There are no words to adequately describe the challenges we faced that year. For the entire time, I was terribly afraid for Bud's life. Of course, I realize that those same feelings were shared by thousands of other families affected by that war. Bud did make it home alive, and we three were reunited as a family. We are forever thankful for the loving support of our families, our friends, and a very loving God. In times of fear and dread, they gave us strength, reassurance, and hope.

"What life lessons emerged from that year? First, we can't control events, but we can control our reaction to events. Specifically, Bud decided that because he had seen so many lives lost, he wanted to dedicate the rest of his to saving as many people as possible. And I learned never to take anything for granted, to accept the help of family and friends, and never to miss an opportunity to let them know how much I appreciate and love them."

Brian Ralston

Wisdom of the Stoics

**"Accept what you cannot control, and focus resources and
creativity on what is in your control."**
Brian Ralston

IN OCTOBER 2002, Brian's Ralston's house caught on fire. No one was hurt,
but the house was badly damaged, leaving him without most of his material
possessions. I asked Brian, a physician, educator, and author, what he had
learned from this devastating event.

Brian said that to cope with such an immense and sudden loss and make
decisions about how to move forward, he relied on the Serenity Prayer, once
popular on bumper stickers, having been adopted by the group Alcoholics
Anonymous: *"God, grant me the serenity to accept the things I cannot change,
the courage to change the things I can, and the wisdom to know the difference."*

Brian explained that this is a version of a prayer written by the Protestant
theologian Reinhold Niebuhr in the 1940s. "But its message can be traced
back even further, to Epictetus, the Greek Stoic philosopher. The very first
sentence in *The Enchiridion*, a collection of Epictetus' teachings, reads (translated) 'Some things are in our control, and others are not.'"

As the last of the flames were being extinguished, the best Brian could
come up with in the moment was to ask one of the firefighters if he wouldn't
mind watering some of the bushes! Then, when there was clearly nothing left
to do at his home, he got a hotel room, bought some clothing, and contacted
his insurance company.

Brian said, "I learned many things from the experience, including, 1) life
really *does* throw curve balls; 2) most of our material possessions aren't that
important; 3) "Good Hands" is just a slogan, and if you have the means, it's
worthwhile to pay for better insurance; and 4) Stoic philosophy is very
practical!"

He told me that while there are many idioms intended to help us accept
loss, such as "Don't cry over spilled milk," "Take your medicine," and "If you
are in a hole, stop digging," it's one thing to understand the message, and
another thing to make it a habit.

"When applied to day-to-day decision-making, this Stoic practice can provide clarity and calm, even in complex and changing circumstances. The Covid pandemic is a good case in point," he said. "At the start of the pandemic, I saw the images on television from Italy, where medical systems were overwhelmed with critically ill patients. Certainly, the same could happen in my community. So, I took what seemed the next logical step: learning to manage ventilators. I hadn't worked with ventilators since my ICU rotations 30 years earlier, this normally being the domain of specialists in intensive care, pulmonary disease, and anesthesia. But if enough people were sick, including some of these doctors, I thought I might be called upon to keep patients alive. Also, I would be in the best position possible to save lives in an unprecedented global medical emergency."

"The Chicago-area medical system was not so overwhelmed that I needed to put these new skills to use. Instead, I have focused on the diagnosis and treatment of Covid-19 hospital patients. Despite our best efforts, I have lost several of my patients to Covid, most either before vaccines were available, or, sadly, some who chose not to be protected. Speaking with patients who are anti-vaxers or on the fence, has been an urgent and continuing priority."

Brian concludes, "I recommend practicing the simple but profound wisdom of the Stoics: identify and accept what is out of your control and focus resources and creativity on what is within your control. This reduces anxiety and distractions, and decisions become easier."

Kimmie Ouchi, M.D.

Self-Compassion Strategies that Work

**"Self-compassion is the sustainable energy
that allows us to stay fueled and engaged."
*Kelly McGonigal***

DR. KIMMIE OUCHI is a family medicine practitioner in Hawaii. She is active in Health and Wellness for physicians and their patients at the regional and inter-regional levels. Like so many medical professionals, Dr. Ouchi has been on the frontlines of caring for Covid patients. I asked her what strategies she had discovered for preserving mental health for herself, her colleagues, and her patients. Here is her response:

"As a practicing front-line primary care physician during Covid-19, I have witnessed a significant uptick in depression and anxiety among my patients. I have seen an unprecedented level of emotional exhaustion and a sense of social isolation everywhere. With it comes burnout, and burnout brings decreased empathy and an impaired ability to connect with self and others. For medical practitioners, burnout is especially imperiling. If we as healthcare providers are unwell, it affects our ability to care for others.

"In my role as a physician wellness leader, I have pondered ways to combat burnout. In October 2017, I attended the inaugural American Conference on Physician Health in San Francisco and heard a talk by Dr. Kelly McGonigal, health psychologist and lecturer at Stanford University, who spoke on the importance of self-compassion. She proposed that self-compassion is the sustainable energy that allows us to stay fueled and engaged.

"I have presented her principles of self-compassion at the local and regional level, and I have used these principles as guidance in sustaining my own wellness.

"So how might we strengthen our own self-compassion? Dr. McGonigal spoke of five practices that can help. These are guideposts each of us can use. I have taken these principles to heart in nurturing my own self-care.

"Mindful self-connection — Take a pause to connect to something personally meaningful. I absolutely love my morning ritual of enjoying a cup of espresso with whipped soy milk, which helps me to create space for self-evaluation. Consider a morning ritual to spark daily self-reflection.

"Celebrate self-care — Choose what brings you joy. I recently took the day off for my birthday. I didn't plan anything and let the day guide me moment by moment, as I intentionally chose what would bring joy. It worked! Live everyday like it's your birthday and celebrate!

"Common humanity — We are all human and all vulnerable in times of stress. I have been involved with creating evidence-based camaraderie groups within my organization at the regional and inter-regional levels, to build social community and connection. Such groups have been shown to decrease burnout and promote meaning in work. Look for opportunities (or create opportunities) for shared experience. We are all in this together.

"Compassion satisfaction rituals — Seek out moments of caring by serving others. This can decrease depression and foster hope. I often reflect upon the great privilege it is to be a primary care physician, partnering with my patients to achieve optimal health and to thrive. Consider engagement in a community service project or reflect on things you may already be doing to help others.

"Gratitude — Count blessings. I have learned to look for the positives and the silver lining. I find the more I do that, the more positivity miraculously appears in my day-to-day. Consider keeping a gratitude journal or writing a gratitude letter to someone you love.

"The practice of self-compassion has helped me to look at life with a more balanced view. Self-compassionate people exhibit more happiness and optimism and have more social connections than others. Let self-compassion be the fuel that helps us all to increase our connection to self and others... and to remain engaged in the things that matter most."

Changing Perspective

Between stimulus and response there is a space.
In that space is our power to choose our response.
In our response lies our growth and our freedom.
Viktor E. Frankl

No one will live my life for me,
no one will think my thoughts for me or dream my dreams.
Abraham Joshua Heschel

Dennis Rodman, Dewitt Jones

Change Perspective; Expand Possibilities

"Life is 10% what happens to you
and 90% how you react to it."
Charles R. Swindoll

CHICAGO SUN-TIMES COLUMNIST Rick Telander said when Dennis Rodman joined the Chicago Bulls, "They've acquired a 6 foot, 8-inch man-child who could mess with the chemistry of the team the way vinegar can mess with baking soda."

April 1997, Chicago, Illinois. I was treating Dennis Rodman for an injury he had sustained. Dennis was paying precious little attention to my recommendations. However, a fortuitous conversation changed all that.

In the training room where the Chicago Bulls practiced, I heard Dennis talking to his teammate Steve Kerr about the popular rock-and-roll, soul, and blues singer Janis Joplin. I interjected that in 1969, during my internship year in San Francisco, I had heard Janis perform in concert. I added that during that year, I had seen many of rock-and-roll's greats, including the Grateful Dead, Jefferson Airplane, and Creedence Clearwater Revival.

Dennis seemed to be impressed. I could see the wheels turning in his head. If I had been tuned in enough to hear Janis Joplin in person, perhaps my medical advice at least was worth considering. He pulled me aside and whispered, "Doc, what's up with my leg?" It seemed as if my medical IQ had suddenly and unexpectedly risen.

He subsequently made an excellent recovery, in time to make important contributions in the playoffs leading to the Bulls fifth NBA championship. His simple change of attitude had significant implications for Dennis and his team.

Recently, I spent a day with *National Geographic* photographer Dewitt Jones on the remote island of Molokai, where he lives. He has been a long-time mentor and supporter of my own photography. Through his work, Dewitt has thought a lot about creating one's own reality. In his TED Talk, "Celebrate What's Right with the World," he explains that "our vision controls our perception, and our perception becomes our reality." How we look at the world, whether we see "a world based on fear and scarcity and

97

competition," or a world of "incredible beauty and possibility," determines what we experience in our lives.

Dewitt's viewpoint is that there is more than one lens through which to view the world and ourselves. In fact, changing lenses – altering how we react to the world around us – is something we do without even realizing it. When I stop to think from how many perspectives I view the world daily – husband, father, grandfather, son, teacher, mentor, orthopedic surgeon, athlete, friend, author, photographer, citizen – it is clear that each of us can come up with an extensive list.

Dewitt continues, "Look for what's right and celebrate it. Celebrating what's right is not a perspective that denies the very real pain and suffering that exists on this planet. Rather, it's a perspective that puts those problems into a larger, more balanced context – a context where we can see that there's far more right with the world than there is wrong with it. When I put on that lens of celebration, I really allow myself to see and to connect with the beauty of the world; I feel like I'm a cup that's so full it's just about to overflow. I feel like I'm falling in love. Celebrating what's right gives us the energy to find that next right answer."

Each of the following contributors to this chapter – In-Hei Han Mark Moffett, Melissa Wells, Llewellyn Miller, Scott Barry Kaufman, Bill Veeck, Steve Bennett, and Charles Levin – illustrate ways in which changing our perspective can change our lives.

In-Hei Hahn

Cherishing a Multicultural Upbringing

"My parents taught me, by their example, to embrace cultures old and new, and be open-minded, accepting, and non-judgmental."
In-Hei Hahn

IN-HEI HAHN IS an emergency medicine physician and medical toxicologist. She has traveled widely and delivered health care to indigenous people in the Amazon rainforest, ultramarathoners in the "Racing the Planet" series, and NASCAR drivers. As medical expedition officer for the department of pale-ontology at the Smithsonian Institute and the American Museum of Natural History, she has provided health care in places such as the Gobi Desert in China and Mongolia and the backcountry of Transylvania.

In-Hei described her own background: "My parents moved to America in the early 1960s from South Korea. They were quite old-school, with many Korean traditions. I didn't appreciate the difficulties they faced when they first moved to the United States in a very different and probably less tolerant world than today. That is, until I had a chance to live in Paris, France, by myself."

"In 1990–1991, I worked at the Institut Pasteur during a gap year before medical school. There, I was hit with a new language, new culture, no real friends, and no other support system — all this in a *sans* internet and cell-phone world. Life was initially glamorous, but then it quickly became quite isolating and lonely at times. My dad told me to get a television and watch the news, learn the language, and try to meet people and make friends, which was good advice. It was a reflective time for me. I spent a lot of time during this year abroad thinking about how I wanted to live my life and how to conduct myself in this world. To this day, I have been constantly rewriting myself as I mature and gain experience and try to be a better person."

She reflected on how different countries and cultures have different world views, and how those perspectives are sometimes reflected in their flags. Drawing on her personal background, she analyzed the symbolism of the flags of South Korea and the U.S.

"The Korean flag is called the Taegukgi, which means supreme or ultimate. The flag was adopted by South Korea as its national flag when it won its independence from Japan on August 15, 1945.

"Taegukgi has three parts: a white rectangular background, a red and blue Taegeuk [often called the yin-yang symbol] in the center, and four black trigrams, one in each corner," she explained. "The red and blue center symbol stands for the state of harmony of yin and yang, representing a balance in the universe. The white background of the flag symbolizes the purity of the Korean people and their peace-loving spirit. The flag is symbolic of the ideal of the Korean people that they are in harmony with the universe. The four trigrams at each corner of the flag represent the elements, the heavens, fire, water, and earth.

"In the American flag, the 50 stars represent the 50 separate states of the United States of America. The 13 stripes represent the 13 states that declared their independence from Great Britain in 1776.

"This is a radically different message from the one the Korean flag carries. The American flag symbolizes independence from the motherland, unlike the Korean flag, which signifies unity with the universe. I talk about both flags, because I try to incorporate the best from both traditions. As I get older, I realize how influential both of my Korean and American heritages are in the way I form my personal and professional relationships."

Actor Martin Henderson said, "I love new people, new ideas. I love cultural differences, and I'm fascinated by the truth – all the different versions of it."

Mark Moffett

A Life of Adventure

"Move forward – and don't be afraid to change your mind."
Mark Moffett

MARK MOFFETT, a one-time high school dropout, is a tropical biologist who earned a PhD in ecology and evolutionary biology at Harvard University. He has trekked across all the world's rainforests and ascended the tallest trees in their canopies. On the ground, he has earned a reputation for his extreme close-up photography documenting ant biology. His books include *The Human Swarm*, *Adventures Among Ants*, *Face to Face With Frogs*, and *The High Frontier*. Melissa Wells, Mark's wife and co-author, is in charge of videography during their explorations.

Melissa and Mark describe the love of their work in remote places: "The tropical rainforest canopy is a triumph of earthly life. There is more feasting, more famine, more courtship and sex, more tender care of the young and of home, more combat, and more cooperation in this arboreal realm than anyplace else on the globe. It has only begun to capture our imagination."

I asked Mark what life lessons he and Melissa learned while they were adventuring across the planet. His response:

"Keep moving forward if it seems right to you, even if you don't know everything about a particular situation.

If I had known the "right" way to go about my education and my work, I would have been too caught up in details, and less focused on the outcome. When I first met my future mentor, the revered biologist E.O. Wilson, I was an undergraduate from a small college visiting Harvard, and I had no idea I shouldn't treat him as "just another nature-loving guy," yet he was delighted with my attitude toward him and sat with me as if we were both kids telling stories about ants. Moving forward, even with incomplete knowledge, can yield amazing results: Many of the animal behaviors that I've documented in nature I was later told I should never have been able to see or photograph.

"Make something your own.

I realized early on that carving my own path meant working with more independence and less supervision. In graduate school, I was drawn to a previously-unstudied ant species that was unusual in having workers in a wide range of sizes. Understanding what those workers did, and documenting their complex activities firsthand, became my mission and eventually my doctoral thesis. Climbing trees to understand the life in their crowns became another mission of mine, resulting in my first book. I had known how to climb trees as a child, but I had to learn new techniques, using ropes and other methods, to ascend the huge ones I encountered as an adult.

"Be good at decision-making.

People expect you to know what you "want to do" when it concerns education and career. A better way to approach life choices is to become skilled at decision-making, which will serve you no matter what you do. Poker champion Annie Duke focuses on this topic quite a bit with her foundation, Alliance for Decision Making, which centers on teaching students skills they need for making better decisions. I like the challenge of changing course every few years, choosing new interests in science, writing, photojournalism, the creation of museum exhibits, or stage and TV appearances. What fascinates me is learning the possible ways forward that lead to success in each area.

"Involve others.

Acknowledge that your thinking or attitudes can limit you in one way or another; for that reason alone, involve people whom you trust — at least two of them — to have your best interests in mind when you are making significant decisions. Value their experience and hear them out.

"Change your mind.

Take advantage of the thoughts and behaviors that have served you well, but constantly be on the lookout for how they might impede you going forward. Indeed, taking breaks from those entrenched thoughts and behaviors is good for the brain. A favorite saying of mine is "true creative time is the time between things" — by which I mean those periods when the mind is free to roam, as happens often for me on rainy days in the rainforest. Emptying the mind is quite different from outright procrastination, which involves filling one's time with unproductive activities.

"Develop mental and physical endurance.

Don't underestimate the value of constantly testing your mental and physical endurance. The ability to persist at a goal beyond normal expectations is an essential tool."

Llewellyn Miller

Tips for Success: Before/During/After College

"Your college education can help you develop discipline and character to become a steady and balanced person able to organize your gifts and use your talents to make the world better."
Llewellyn Miller

LLEWELLYN MILLER, trained in engineering, economic systems, operations research, mathematics, and statistics, knows numbers and he knows business. Lew also knows people.

He was born in Harlem, New York City. Both of his parents had immigrated to the United States from Barbados. At a very early age, his mother warned him that as a Black man in America he would face persistent challenges to his abilities and qualifications. She suggested a focus on disciplines with "right answers" and acquiring the strongest possible credentials. He interpreted this as a call to major in math and science. He attended The Bronx School of Science and received a scholarship to Yale University.

Having been a minority student in high school and at university, he has a unique perspective in offering advice, especially to first-generation college applicants. However, his words of wisdom apply to everyone. I wish I had received them before I entered university.

In Lew's words: "A college education should not be so much to set you up for a career, but for you to develop discipline and character, to become a steady and balanced person able to organize your gifts and use your talents to make the world better."

His recommendations during college:

• Take some courses from famous professors. Pay attention to suggestions from juniors and seniors.
• Get into a study routine early and do not try to do everything yourself. As soon as you need help, ask for it from your professor. It's not a sign of inadequacy. It's a sign of self-knowledge.
• Sometimes a professor is a potential employer or a scout for one. Professors

look for brilliance. Employers look for reliability and professionalism. Try to show both.

After college:
• Don't use professors as your only career advisor. They typically do not know about fields outside their own.
• Talk to practitioners. Most of them love to talk about their work. If someone offers to help you learn about their job, they usually mean it. Helping you get a job is quite different. Don't confuse the two.
• Don't try to replicate other people's resumes. Professions are changing rapidly; career paths in the future will not necessarily look like those from the past.

Interviews (or interacting with professors):
• Look the interviewer in the eye early and often — but do not stare or you will look like a maniac.
• The first part of the response to a question should be a direct answer to make sure the interviewer knows you understand the question and are responsive. Sometimes it's all right to argue.
• Do not try to be "cool." It's interpreted as indifference.
Put yourself in the position of the interviewer, who wants to know, "Is this person listening?" "Are they really interested?"

Your boss:
• Your job is to make your boss's job easier. Sometimes that means getting good at the things the boss doesn't like to do.
• Presentation is important. Knowing the right answer isn't always enough. Things like proper grammar, spelling and layout are often underrated.
• Don't try to find problems without solutions. Prove how smart you are by solving problems, not just identifying new ones.

Having multiple sequential (or even simultaneous) careers now seems to be the norm. Therefore, his suggestions of how to put oneself in a position to make the world better are more essential than ever.

Scott Barry Kaufman

Validating Abraham Maslow's Theories

"Humans not only have a need for belonging and connection, but also have a need to feel as though they are having a positive impact in the lives of other people."
Scott Barry Kaufman

SCOTT BARRY KAUFMAN is a cognitive scientist and humanistic psychologist whose work focuses on realizing human potential. As a child, Scott had learning difficulties. A special education teacher took a particular interest in him and saw his hidden strengths. He learned first-hand the value of encouragement from a teacher, and apparently, the teacher's assessment was accurate. Scott received an undergraduate degree from Carnegie Mellon, an MPhil in experimental psychology from the University of Cambridge, and a Ph.D. in cognitive psychology from Yale University. He has taught at Yale, NYU, Columbia, and the University of Pennsylvania.

Scott is that rare person who is a big thinker and asks important questions, but also supports his conclusions with definitive scientific data. For example, one of Scott's recent books, *Transcend: The New Science of Self-Actualization,* clarifies and expands Abraham Maslow's most important ideas and validates his concepts related to self-actualization.

Abraham Maslow describes self-actualization as the ability to become the best version of oneself. Scott emphasizes that it is a direction, not a destination. The characteristics which distinguish self-actualized individuals include the importance of having deep and loving relationships with others based on giving, tolerance, kindness, humility, and forgiveness. As writer Robert Heinlein said, "Love is that condition in which the happiness of another person is essential to your own."

Further, Maslow says, "Self-actualizing people are, without one single exception, involved in a cause outside their own skin, in something outside of themselves. They are devoted to something very precious to them, which they love." Other qualities which Maslow found in self-actualizing people are a capacity to be in the moment and an ability to perceive and feel gratitude for the poetry and the sacredness in one's daily life. Additionally important is being able to accept life's ups and downs with grace and equanimity, and to possess a sense of humor.

105

Self-actualizing people tend to be independent and resourceful thinkers. Scott says, "Creative people are hubs of diverse interests, influences, behaviors, qualities, and ideas – and through their work, they find a way to bring these many disparate elements together." The range of Scott's curiosity and creativity is found not only in his books, but also in his podcasts, where his interviews range from philosophers and politicians to psychologists and prominent sports personalities.

Scott describes creative exploration, which takes several forms. Social exploration involves having a sincere interest in other people's lives and ideas. Cognitive or intellectual exploration includes being open to experiences and having the desire to learn, to grow, to overcome challenges, and to learn new skills. It is finding mystery attractive and challenging rather than frightening. As Scott says, "Creative people have a preference for complexity and ambiguity, and an ability to extract order from chaos and unconventionality, and a willingness to take risks."

In *Transcend*, Scott states, "The healthy personality constantly moves toward a life of freedom, responsibility, self-awareness, commitment, maturity, and change, rather than one that predominantly strives for status, achievement, or even happiness." Scott, along with co-author Jordyn H. Feingold, M.D., more recently has written a book titled *Choose Growth*, which demonstrates how to help one achieve this goal.

Choose Growth, in many ways, dovetails with Getting Wiser. For example, the authors discuss how to enhance one's character strengths and virtues, which include creativity, curiosity, perseverance, and kindness. The individuals in *Getting Wiser*, by their example, also demonstrate such qualities and how they have enriched their lives.

Choose Growth discusses how to find your Ikigai, the Japanese concept for "reason for being," by understanding what you love, and what you are good at with what the world needs. Finally, *Choose Growth* and *Getting Wiser* both demonstrate ways in which we can increase our capacity for savoring – using our thoughts, behaviors, and emotions to enhance our capacity for an enriched life.

Abraham Maslow's ideas have been criticized for having been generated with insufficient scientific evidence. Scott Barry Kaufman has now given empirical support to Maslow's characteristics of self-actualization. This enables us to understand to a greater degree how we can become the best version of ourselves.

Bill Veeck

Fun at the Old Ball Park

**"If you are going to start laughing about something in six
months, you might as well start now."
David and Daniel Hayes**

DURING MY PROFESSIONAL CAREER, I have worked with some unforgettable
personalities – Michael Jordan, Dennis Rodman, and Phil Jackson, to name
but three. But no one was more multifaceted and captivating than Bill Veeck.

Bill changed the world of baseball by the sheer force of his outlook and
personality. A great sense of humor, an inventive mind, and a thirst for knowledge helped. Bill read several books a week and was an author himself. His
autobiography, *Veeck As in Wreck: The Chaotic Career of Baseball's Incorri-
gible Maverick,* was a bestseller. He loved discussing literature, as well as
baseball trades, with the sportswriters covering the team.

Bill was a man positively brimming with creative energy, always thinking
of ways to bring more fun and excitement to the ballpark. He once showed me
hundreds of index cards on which he'd written ideas. One card said simply,
"Beer – 1000." He explained that it was more fun to give 1000 cans of beer to
one fan than one can of beer to 1000 fans. He established Fan Appreciation
Night, and on one of these occasions gave away orchids to all the young girls
and women attending the game. In the stadium, he created an atmosphere of a
never-ending festival, highlighted by such events as Mexican night, Greek
night, and German Oktoberfest.

He is also the guy who invented such traditions as fireworks exploding
from the scoreboard, players' curtain calls after hitting a home run, and having
Harry Carey sing "Take Me Out to the Ball Game" during the seventh inning
stretch.

He had been wounded in World War II, and after multiple surgeries, his
right leg had been amputated above the knee. Despite having a wooden leg,
Veeck loved to dance with abandon. He fully subscribed to the philosophy,
"Sing like no one is listening...dance like nobody's watching, and live like it is
heaven on earth." What a character he was! The first time I saw him use a
hole he had carved into his wooden leg as an ashtray, my eyes almost popped
out of my head!

107

Bill Veeck's fun-loving side never abandoned him. Among his classic pronouncements: "There are only two seasons —winter and baseball," and "Baseball is almost the only orderly thing in a very disorderly world. If you get three strikes, even the best lawyer in the world can't get you off."

Bill Veeck's creativity and his sense of humor were always obvious, but he exemplified something equally important. He always treated other people with respect, a quality I find almost universal in people who are comfortable with themselves.

Bill retained his sense of playfulness even in challenging times. He recounted a story from the period when he owned the St. Louis Browns in the early 1950s, when they had the lowest attendance in the league. It was not unusual for Veeck himself to pick up the phone when someone called the box office, so when a fan called asking for the start time for the Saturday game, Bill inquired, "How many in your party?" "Six," was the reply. Bill's response: "What time would be convenient for you?" That story has always resonated with me -- try hard, whenever possible, to find the humor in any situation.

Another example of using humor to keep challenges in perspective: Father-and-son team, David and Daniel Hayes wrote a book titled *My Old Man and the Sea*. They sailed around the world in a 25-foot boat, which they had built together. Because they were in each other's company 24/7, often in challenging circumstances, they established a basic ground rule. They wrote, "Our number one rule was that if you are going to start laughing about something in six months or a year, you might as well start now." I think about this a lot. It helps.

Bill Veeck, by his example, teaches us to treat everyone with respect, and every time you are able to find humor in a difficult situation, you win.

Steve Bennett

Expect the Unexpected

"If you swim through life with your eyes closed and attention elsewhere, you will miss the fish you'd truly love to catch."
Steve Bennett

STEVE BENNETT IS a lens-based visual artist whose practice includes traditional photography and abstract composites. His work has been juried into numerous exhibitions. In addition, he is president of a company that creates websites for authors.

He shares life lessons that he has learned from photography:

"Photography has played a vital role in my life for the past six decades. My father, a radiologist by day and an avid photographer all other times, practically raised me in our home darkroom. Ever since the first time I saw an image materialize in a tray of developer, I've been smitten by the very magic of capturing and preserving moments otherwise lost to time.

"Over the years, I've come to see how the lessons I've learned from photography track closely with life on the other side of the lens. Here are the takeaways that have been particularly important for me.

"*The fish that got away...is gone forever.* I used to keep a list of all the brilliant photo moments I missed on the street, because my gaze or mind was elsewhere. I thought the list -- which is still growing -- would be a good reminder to stay in the moment whenever I venture out with camera in hand (which is most of the time). There may be lots of fish in the sea, but if you swim through life unaware, with your eyes closed and attention elsewhere, you'll miss the ones you'd truly love to catch.

"*The open mind sees more light.* This is a corollary to the first lesson and it's the flip side of awareness: receptivity. Serendipity plays a huge role in photography. A fascinating person appears on the street at precisely the right moment...a sunbeam breaks through the clouds on the horizon...the wind tosses a feathery seed aloft, revealing nature's unmatched engineering prowess. It's one thing to be present and observant; it's another to expect the unexpected. Many great photos lie at the intersection of intention and accident. The same dynamic plays out in life.

"*The mundane is anything but mundane.* The most exciting subjects for

109

close-ups and found still life compositions are often the most prosaic. These gems—the extraordinary within the ordinary—are often hiding in plain sight. So it is in everyday life. A smile or a simple gesture of kindness reflect what matters most: our connections to each other and acknowledgement of our shared humanity.

"*One view does not fit all*. Taking good pictures is about making good decisions. When circumstances allow, slow down and look at the subject from different angles before you press the shutter button. Often, there's a better perspective, more pleasing light, or surprising hidden details, all of which result in a better photo. I think the same principle applies to making all manner of decisions in our daily lives. As in photography, when you pause, reconnoiter/reevaluate, and then commit, you might enjoy more winning outcomes.

"*Heed the law of diminishing returns*. I don't like admitting the number of times that I struggled to make an image work. In my mind's eye, I'd previsualized the scene exactly as I wanted to capture it. Everything in the viewfinder looked spot on. But back at the computer, where a lot of heavy lifting takes place, the image just didn't work. Maybe I miscalculated the exposure or misjudged the quality of the light. Some, but not all problems, can be fixed with software -- as Ansel Adams once proclaimed, "You don't take a photograph, you make it." It's taken me years to learn when it's time to turn to a trusted friend, the delete key. I think the same applies to most endeavors in life; it's invaluable to know when it's time to let go, move on, ready to seize the next opportunity.

"Finally, I'll return to the darkroom and the words of my father when I would ask when the picture was going to appear in the developer solution. 'Photography is first about light,' he'd say. 'But it's a lot about patience, too.' Good words to live by."

Charles Levin

Real-Life Lessons in the Cards

**"The game of poker has serious lessons
that just might improve the rest of your life."
Charles Levin**

CHARLES LEVIN HAS BEEN RANKED in the top 2% of poker players worldwide and has played in The World Series of Poker several times. He shared the life lessons he learned at the tables:

1. Follow the 40/70 Rule

Poker, like life, is a game of incomplete information. We don't know what cards the other players hold, what the next card will be, or what luck will do to support or upset our plans. But we must make decisions all the time with incomplete information. Former Secretary of State Colin Powell espoused the 40/70 Rule — if the action you are contemplating has between a 40% and a 70% chance of success, it's worth taking the risk. That's as opposed to waiting until you have 100% certainty and letting opportunity pass you by, or taking risks with a less than 40% chance of success and inviting failure. As an example, U.S. generals assessed the raid on Bin-Laden as a 50/50 risk. Therefore, they attacked and succeeded. Lean towards 70, but sometimes 40 is all you get.

2. Pick the Right Game and the Right Table

Table selection in poker cash games may be the player's most critical decision. It's putting yourself in a position to win before you even start the game. In life, similar decisions might be whom to marry or what job to take. In business, you might ask the question, "Who would I rather be — a good manager in a great industry or a great manager in a doomed industry?"

3. Position

Understanding your position relative to the other players in poker or in life is critical for a happy outcome. Marine Corps General David Shoup made this analogy: "The commonest mistake in history is underestimating your opponent; happens at the poker table all the time."

4. Know When to Hold'em . . .

One of the earliest poker/life lessons from the Texas road-gambler Amar-

111

Michael S. Lewis, M.D.

illo Slim: "It's not Results, it's Decisions." Huh? I had to think about that one. What he's saying is that if you make the right decisions consistently, even if you fail in the short run, you will succeed in the long run. You're keeping the odds in your favor, but there are no guarantees in any given hand and on any given day. But in the long run...

5. Study Your Game

If you want to be good at anything, you need to study. Would you want a brain surgeon who didn't study his game? No. By studying poker, it made me better than 98% of the other players. I recently donated 61 poker books to my local library (and kept ten). What's your game? Learn everything about it from its history to its strategy.

6. Pokernomics 101 - Manage Your Bankroll

The famous poker pro Stu Ungar won a million dollars one day in a tournament and blew it all at the craps table the same day. This is not good bankroll management. Knowing how to manage your money, avoiding unnecessary risks, and planning for the future will keep you in the game.

7. Avoid Going "On Tilt"

"Tilt" is a common word in poker; it means losing your cool when something bad happens. "Going on Tilt" usually leads to bad, emotional decisions. Meditate, go for a walk, sleep on it, talk to a friend, breathe. The lesson: never make important decisions when you're on tilt.

8. Learn from the Best

The most successful people have mentors. Who's your Yoda? How do you find one? She may find you. Be open to her when she appears.

9. Play Every Day

"Ninety percent of success is showing up." You must be in the game to win or to have that one lucky, serendipitous event that will change your life forever. Show up.

10. Be Ready to Go All-In

Be willing to commit when the time and circumstances are right, and the risk is low. We go all-in when we get married or start a new business or have a child. What happens if you lose, or it doesn't work out? Pick yourself up and start over. There's (almost) always another game.

Humility, Courage, Integrity: Character Counts

Angels can fly because they take themselves lightly.
G. K. Chesterton

Be brave. Without bravery, you will never know
the world as richly as it longs to be known.
Elizabeth Gilbert

I prefer to be true to myself,
even at the hazard of incurring the ridicule of others,
rather than to be false and incur my own abhorrence.
Frederick Douglass

Michael Jordan

A Cut Above

"Life is a long lesson in humility."
Sir James Barrie

MICHAEL JORDAN HAD many admirable qualities, several of which are discussed in the chapter on Focusing on Excellence. Although he was not known for his modesty, because of him on May 25, 1998, I received an unforgettable lesson in humility.

The Chicago Bulls were playing the Indiana Pacers in the Eastern Conference Finals in Indianapolis, Indiana. Early in the game, Michael Jordan and Pacers center Rik Smits went up for a rebound. On the way down Smits poked Michael near his right eye, opening a nasty cut on his eyelid. Blood was pouring down his cheek.

As Michael and I walked off the court toward the visitors' training room, my brain was racing between two options. One was to suture the eyelid laceration. This would mean injecting a local anesthetic, which would result in Michael's eye being closed. He wouldn't be able to return to the game. The other option was to apply strips of tape (called Steri-Strips) to the eyelid to stop the bleeding. Then he could play. However, the strips might not hold, and the blood might start flowing again.

Even though I had been in high-pressure situations before, I still experienced a massive adrenalin rush. Not only the game, but potentially the season, was at stake. Michael may have been the best basketball player in the world, but at that moment he was simply my patient, and I was simply his doctor. Easy to say now, but at the time, frankly, it took all my willpower not to feel intimidated by the situation.

I decided to recommend using the strips of tape instead of suturing the cut. This option would at least give Michael a chance to return to the game. The Steri-Strips in place, Michael went back out on the court. I didn't breathe for the rest of the game, but the strips held. The Bulls went on to defeat the Indiana Pacers in seven games and win their conference finals. They ultimately defeated the Utah Jazz to win their sixth NBA championship.

Of course, there are more serious matters than winning a basketball game. In the operating room I have had to make judgments with far more conse-

115

quential outcomes. At the same time, this decision could have negatively impacted the hopes and expectations of countless sports fans. It was a potent reminder that while I may have done everything right, the outcome might not have turned out well. It was a humbling experience. I felt fortunate indeed.

In this chapter, the qualities of humility, courage, and integrity are demonstrated by the following people: Wilbur Wood, Richard Strier, David Halberstam, Whiz Friedberg, Donald Duster, Jamie Malanowski

Wilbur Wood

A Major-League Mensch

"Humility is the surest sign of strength."
Thomas Merton

WILBUR WOOD WAS one of the great major league baseball pitchers of his era. His 17-year Major League career started in 1961 with the Boston Red Sox. In 1967 he joined the Chicago White Sox, where he finished his career in 1978. Early in his career, Wood had relied on his fastball and his curveball. He learned to throw the extremely difficult knuckleball because, he said, it was the only way he could prolong his career in the Major Leagues. While pitching for the Chicago White Sox against the Yankees on July 20, 1973, Wood started both ends of a doubleheader.

When I asked him how he had become such a successful pitcher, Wilbur credited other people, saying he was successful because he had such good teammates — good hitters and good outfielders. He loved pitching in Comiskey Park, because it had a big outfield that gave outfielders time to run under pop-up flies and catch them for an out. In Wilbur's words, "It gave you room for a mistake."

He is humility personified — an unassuming person who treats everyone with respect. He addressed me as Dr. Lewis when we worked together on the team, even though both of us were in our mid-thirties and he was a year older than I.

In appearance, Wilbur Wood was an unlikely athlete. He was portly and smoked cigars, pitched left-handed and batted right-handed. Sportswriter Roger Angell once described him as "having the physique of an accountant or pastry chef on a holiday." Wilbur would joke about his 39-inch waistline, saying that he needed all that weight in the middle to keep his balance.

On May 9, 1976, Wood was struck in the knee by a line drive off the bat of Ron LeFlore, Detroit's center fielder. My partner, Bill Meltzer, and I surgically repaired the shattered patella. When I talk with Wilbur these days, he recalls every detail of the surgery and his recovery as if it were yesterday.

It was a terrible injury from which many would not have returned. But Wilbur's grit and his diligent adherence to his rehabilitation program allowed him to pitch two more seasons. In 1978, after a Major League career that spanned almost two decades, he said, in his typical low-key way, "I guess all good things must come to an end."

When I asked Wilbur what I should tell my grandchildren (and myself) which life lessons participation in sports can teach us, he gave the following thoughtful response: "You learn how to handle adversity and failure. You learn discipline and the importance of consistency. You learn how to stay focused, to handle pressure, and to avoid distractions. You learn that it is essential to control your emotions and maintain a sense of humor. You learn to take responsibility for your actions and that there is no substitute for hard work."

Wilbur also emphasized the importance of grit. He continued, "Grit means putting in sustained effort over time. It means setting goals and having the patience, and perseverance to overcome whatever obstacles might get in your way."

Wilbur concluded, "And you learn how to win and how to lose. Many years ago a coach told me, 'When you win, don't crow, and when you lose, don't cry.' At the end of the day, winning is knowing that you gave your best effort."

Donald Duster

Carrying on a Legacy of Courage

**"Instead of complaining about a situation,
I ask, "How can I make it better?"**
Donald Duster

DONALD DUSTER WAS a business executive and community leader. He was a passionate man, whose family history inspired in him both pride and loyalty.

He was a grandson of the renowned Ida B. Wells. She was born into slavery during the Civil War and became a civil rights activist. She traveled throughout the eastern United States and Great Britain, speaking out about lynching. Don's grandfather, Ferdinand Barnett was a respected attorney and his mother, Alfreda Duster, was a University of Chicago educated social worker deeply committed to her community.

Don was not afraid of challenges, and he faced many. After his father died when Don was 13 years old, he grew up with a single mother in a southside Chicago neighborhood. Though he won a full scholarship to the University of Illinois, he still had to work his way through school by washing dishes and cleaning floors. As a Black student, he could not live on campus, but instead of being resentful in the face of this bigotry, he used it as a powerful motivation to succeed. His motto was, "Instead of complaining about a situation, how can I make it better?" He took advantage of his opportunities and was awarded a Bachelor of Science in Mathematics in 1953.

After graduating from college, Don served as a 2nd Lieutenant on active duty with the United States Army, stationed in Texas and Arizona. His daughter Michelle recounted, "Even in his uniform [when] he was with his white compadres, he was not welcome at many restaurants."

After his tour of duty with the army, Don earned his MBA from DePaul University in 1978. He quickly rose through the executive ranks for Commonwealth Edison, where he became responsible for equipment and material at two billion-dollar nuclear generating stations.

He took a leave of absence from ComEd when Governor James R. Thompson appointed him to be director of the Department of Business and Economic Development of the State of Illinois. Talk about challenges; the governor asked him to reopen closed factories, put the unemployed back to work, and convince companies either to expand or to relocate in Illinois.

Don was politically savvy and understood that politics was the art of the possible. At the same time, he never lost his idealism and his passion when it came to fighting for the rights of the underserved. From 1987 to 2007, Donald became the assistant executive director of Chicago Commons Association, a community-based nonprofit social service agency. He also served as a member of the United States-South Africa Leader Exchange Program.

Don had a clear sense of having an important part to play in continuing his family's history. He was a founder of the Ida B. Wells Memorial Foundation in Chicago in 1988, along with four of Ida's other grandchildren. The foundation supports "organizations, programs, and projects that focus on education, superior journalism, social justice, equality and integrity."

The high expectations his grandparents and parents had for him and his siblings were passed on to his children, David, Daniel, and Michelle. All three earned bachelor's degrees and two earned graduate degrees. David is now a member of our book club. He, in turn, carries on his family's tradition of having a deep concern for the well-being of others.

Donald Duster, a passionate man, was always respectful of other people and carried himself with a quiet dignity. Throughout his life, he resolutely accepted greater challenges.

Writer Anais Nin said, "Life shrinks or expands in proportion to one's courage."

Jamie Malanowski

The Many Forms of Courage

"Take chances, Be courageous. Help others to build confidence."
Jamie Malanowski

WHEN ASKED what the one life lesson writer and editor Jamie Malanowski would most want to pass on to future generations, his response was, "Get in the habit of practicing courage. Usually, we associate courage with situations involving physical danger. In fact, courage is valuable in all sorts of situations involving actions we want to do, but that involve risk of suffering some kind of pain. It takes courage to speak your mind. It takes courage to put yourself forward. It takes courage to ask someone to dance. It takes courage to keep working when you are tired. It takes a lot of courage to apologize.

"Being courageous in many arenas helps you develop more courage. The thing is, the more you do things that require courage, you'll find that doing them requires less courage. Courage that isn't used becomes inactive. But as courage is used, it becomes replaced by confidence, which is, at bottom, self-knowledge. And with that attribute, we are empowered to handle hard things. We know what we are capable of doing, and we know how to evaluate whether the pain we might suffer is worth the investment. Sometimes it isn't."

He continues, "Practicing courage is more than something we do for ourselves. Practicing courage means setting an example for others. And it means encouraging others — helping them be courageous.

"I was once employed in a job that was very demanding. We had to work on complex topics, under tight deadlines, involving high stakes, under high visibility. Our work was constantly scrutinized. Even my most capable colleagues from time to time felt the pain of falling short. Surely, I did. This often led to people being governed by fear. Mostly it was fear of failure, but sometimes that fear metastasized into a fear to act, to initiate, to speak up.

"Over time, I noticed that there were two kinds of leaders: leaders who practiced fear, and leaders who practiced courage. Leaders who practiced fear drove their subordinates hard, with workloads and deadlines and requirements that constantly escalated. With such practices, these leaders burnished their reputation for being tough and hard driving. But as they did so, they

121

sapped the pride and joy and confidence of the people with whom they worked.

"The leaders I admired were the people who practiced courage. With focus, and preparation, and creativity, they met the tasks in front of them. In doing so, they provided colleagues with an example of what it took to succeed. Most importantly, they actively encouraged subordinates, praising them when they were successful, and teaching them how to do better when they fell short. These leaders built confidence. They helped their colleagues to be courageous. Those were the people I respected."

Jamie recognized the wisdom of the Greek philosopher Aristotle, who called courage the first virtue, because it enabled all the others. Jamie elaborated, "That's because all virtues entail behaviors that involve some risk—to our purses, to our feelings, to our health and well-being. Some risks are foolish and should be avoided, but a life spent consistently avoiding risk is a life that is small and stagnant."

Richard Strier

Be True to Your Word

"Keep your commitments to others and to yourself."
Richard Strier

RICHARD STRIER IS the Frank L. Sulzberger Distinguished Service Professor Emeritus in the English Department, the Divinity School, and the College of the University of Chicago. He responded to the question, "What was a mistake that you made from which you learned a valuable lesson?"

"I have only two pieces of "wisdom" to offer. One is interpersonal, the other professional. Both involve recognizing failures.

"I am a city boy born and bred, yet my own favorite source of wisdom is Thoreau's *Walden*, which is about life as much as it is about nature. With typical brilliance, Thoreau wrote that "the finest qualities of our nature, like bloom on fruits, can be preserved only by the most delicate handling. Yet we do not treat ourselves nor one another thus tenderly.

"I have not always treated friends, and especially colleagues, "thus tenderly." I can remember a case where I failed to respond to a book manuscript that a senior colleague of mine had given me for comment. It was on a topic in which I was not especially interested, and I allowed myself simply to ignore it, thinking — and here was the big mistake — that the colleague in question wouldn't notice or would not really care since the person was much more established than I was. When it was tearfully revealed to me that the person did indeed notice and care, it was too late to repair the damage. A message of disrespect and lack of interest had been sent.

"I should have realized that when someone entrusts something to you that they have spent time and lifeblood on, one has an obligation to respond. I allowed my own lack of interest and lack of recognition of the situation to determine my actions. I thereby lost the chance for a lifelong friendship. Colleagueship, of course, remained, but something rarer, and (as Thoreau put it) more "delicate" was lost — not through brutal handling, but through insouciance, lack of mature understanding."

Richard continued: "In the second case, I failed myself. After publishing one's "tenure book," and getting tenure, one is confronted with the Great Question: what next? In my case, I had (I thought) an immediate answer. My

123

tenure book was on a religious poet, George Herbert, yet it was filled with references to Shakespeare. While finishing the Herbert book, I had written an essay on what I thought was a crucial and relatively neglected area of Shakespeare studies — his presentation of situations where a social or political inferior felt conscientiously obliged to resist a command by a superior. I published the essay on this topic and thought it would be the basis for my next book. A publisher immediately manifested interest and sent me a contract.

"Indecorous Will" never got written. I found myself stumped while trying to write a chapter on how Shakespeare broke decorum in formal (not only thematic) ways. It seemed to me that I had nothing to add to what had already been well said about this topic. So, I dropped the whole project. Now, some forty years later, and after two other more general books that include material on Shakespeare, I am finally publishing "my Shakespeare book." It really should have been my second book, but I lacked faith in my own commitment. I did not take seriously the idea that if I said I could do it, that meant that I really could."

David Halberstam, Uncle Whiz Friedberg

Character Counts

"Character matters. Doing the right thing,
even when the right thing is hard to do."
David Halberstam

I WAS fortunate to spend time with journalist David Halberstam at Chicago Bulls basketball games during the 1997 – 1998 season. David was tall, with a large frame, and patrician in appearance. He was researching his book about Michael Jordan. Because he had written numerous books about large institutions, one of my questions to him was what qualities are necessary to be an exceptional leader.

Personal integrity was at the top of his list. David shared with me the following story emphasizing his point:

"In 1954, Big Tobacco paid to publish an advertisement called, "Frank Statement to Cigarette Smokers" in hundreds of U.S. newspapers. The industry pledged that the public's health was its top priority. They promised changes to make cigarettes healthier. There followed many more years of deception and untold millions of deaths. In 1994 the CEOs of the country's seven biggest tobacco companies testified before Congress under oath, denying that nicotine was addictive. They did say cigarettes might cause lung cancer, heart disease and other health problems, but argued that the evidence was not conclusive. Thus, their mixed messages about smoking continued and millions more died or had their quality of life reduced because of emphysema, heart disease, and myriad other conditions. No one went to jail." David then paused, and dramatically stated, "Character counts."

In our discussions, David also emphasized the importance of gaining wisdom through personal experience. He expressed it as learning from crucibles, by which he meant navigating the severe tests and trials that one encounters during a lifetime. He shared with me one of his best-loved stories from his book *The Best and the Brightest*, which explores the American foreign policy decisions related to the Vietnam War: "After attending his first Cabinet meeting as John F. Kennedy's vice president, Lyndon Johnson told his mentor, Speaker of the U.S. House of Representatives Sam Rayburn, how bright and accomplished the members of the Cabinet were – he was impressed that many of them had attended Ivy League colleges and had written books. Sam Rayburn responded, "You may be right, Lyndon, they may be brilliant, but I would feel a whole lot better if at least one of them had run for sheriff.'"

His point was that there was a difference between intelligence and wisdom. Wisdom was the product of hard-won, often bitter, experience, which for some of the Cabinet members didn't come until *after* the war — when for many soldiers and their families it was too late.

Franklin Delano Roosevelt said, "Courage is not the absence of fear but rather the assessment that something else is more important than fear."

My Uncle Whiz Friedberg showed me the true meaning of courage. "Whiz" was short for Isadore. He was always outspoken, particularly when the rights of others were concerned. He was president of the Galveston Philosophical Society. Their motto was "We agree to disagree without being disagreeable," and he was active in the civil rights movement long before others became involved. He stood 5'7" and weighed 145 pounds dripping wet. You might not think he would fit the image of a fearless warrior.

One incident that has become family legend took place in Galveston, Texas, in the early 1960s. Whiz was a young optometrist building a practice one eye exam at a time. One day a big, burly Texan came into his office and found that an African American woman was already waiting. When Whiz asked the woman to come into his office, the man, exuding hostility, interrupted, "Hey, are you going to take *her* before you take me?" His meaning was unmistakable.

Whiz took the woman back into his office and asked her to wait. He then returned to where the big guy was standing in the waiting room. My uncle told the fellow, "Listen, you no good racist, I want you to get the hell out of my office right now, and if you have any friends, tell them to stay out of here too."

The man left, but he returned a week later. When Whiz saw him in the waiting room and realized the man was fully capable of killing him, he saw his life flash before his eyes. Instead, the man apologized for his earlier behavior. He even bought two pairs of glasses!

Inquiring Minds

At a child's birth, the most useful gift
it could be endowed with is curiosity.
Eleanor Roosevelt

In my whole life, I have known no wise people
(over a broad subject matter area)
who didn't read all the time – none, zero.
Charlie Munger

The world will never starve for wonders,
but only for want of wonder.
G. K. Chesterton

John Callaway

Unquenchable Curiosity

***"Get the facts. If your mother says she loves you,
check it out."***
Newspaper axiom

ISIDOR RABI GREW up in the Lower East Side of Manhattan. He said that
when other students got home from school, their parents asked, "Did you have
a good answer to the teacher's questions?" His parents had a different
approach. They asked, "Izzy, did you ask a good question today?" Isidor Rabi
won the Nobel Prize in Physics in 1944 for his discovery of nuclear magnetic
resonance, which is used in MRI machines.

The best scientists, explorers, and presidents of companies all have one
thing in common: they keep asking questions. They are open to new ideas and
have the humility to continually reevaluate their assumptions. The contributors to this chapter have unbounded curiosity.

John Callaway was a man of keen intelligence and unquenchable curiosity. Discussing ideas was important to John. He was interested in the truth,
not in preconceived ideas. John's combination of range and depth was
extraordinary — he was genuinely curious about all aspects of the human
condition. He and I were in a book club together, and for several years he
selected every book we read. The topics included politics, psychology, sociology, economics, artists, and sports figures. I once asked him if there was any
area in which he didn't have a comfortable grasp. He thought for a moment
and modestly, yet seriously, replied, "I am not as on top of the heavy metal or
hip-hop music scene as I should be." John, you could be forgiven for that.

When John was attending Ohio Wesleyan University, his father became
ill and couldn't afford his tuition. In 1956, John had to drop out of college. He
hitchhiked to Chicago and arrived with seventy-one cents in his pocket. He
got a job as a police reporter for the Chicago City News Bureau, and eventually developed the *Chicago Tonight* program for WTTW-TV, Chicago's PBS
channel. He never lost his childlike sense of wonder.

John's peers considered him "the best on-air interviewer on television." Henry Kissinger said John was the best interviewer he had ever encountered. Part of the reason: John's ravenous curiosity and his meticulousness. For

example, to prepare for the Kissinger interview, John read thousands of pages of background material.

John had a great sense of humor, and his Irish tenor laugh would often reverberate off the walls of our book club meeting room. He seemed to have total recall of Chicago politics and to revel in the personalities of that era. One of his favorite stories was when Mayor Richard J. Daley and Cardinal Cody took a secret walk together along the beach. One night a Chicago Tribune reporter hid in the bushes nearby and observed that when Cardinal Cody's hat blew off into Lake Michigan, Mayor Daley walked across the water, retrieved the hat, walked back on the water, and handed it to the cardinal. The Tribune headline the next day was, "Mayor Daley can't swim."

Each of the contributors to this chapter, Cory Franklin, Valerie Lewis, and Stuart Green, are intensely curious and are driven by an ardent desire to understand the world around them.

Writer Luci Swindoll said, "It's daring to be curious about the unknown, to dream big dreams, to live outside prescribed boxes, and above all, daring to investigate the way we live until we discover the deepest treasured purpose of why we are here."

Cory Franklin, M.D.

The Real Fountain of Youth

"Anyone who stops learning is old, whether at twenty or eighty.
Anyone who keeps learning stays young."
Henry Ford

Cory Franklin, M.D., when asked what life lesson he would wish to pass on to future generations, eloquently emphasized the importance of lifelong learning:

"C. Stanley Ogilvy, a well-known mathematician and world-class sailor, once posed this question, "We are not the same people we once were. Would you like to be the same sailor that you were in your youth? Think carefully before you answer that one." The bravado and physical gifts that we possess when we are young, which are sometimes necessary to perform great feats, ultimately yield to the caution that comes with age. But at the same time, the recklessness of youth, in most people, is replaced by wisdom and experience."

Cory continues, "This never changes. But we now live in a completely different age than ever before: one of social media, smartphones, and the internet. In this brave new world, we have instantaneous access to information in ways undreamt of by previous generations.

"We have instant and constant access to information, but information is not necessarily fact, and truth does not necessarily equate to wisdom. Paradoxically, we live in a world of evermore uncertainty. Ubiquitous smartphones and Twitter accounts have become a source of anxiety and stress.

"How to counter the vagaries and vicissitudes of our age? Through optimism, determination, self-reliance, courage, and adaptability. But there is something else: learn things. That means acquiring not just superficial knowledge but genuine understanding. And do it through ways other than the smartphone or Google. Read books, converse, listen, investigate, and constantly ask questions.

To emphasize this point I want to include a passage from *The Once and Future King* by British author T.H. White. It is his retelling of the Arthurian legend, first written in another uncertain age, the early days of World War II and published at the height of the Cold War. The advice is from Merlin, mentor to young Arthur and advisor to Arthur when he becomes King:

131

Michael S. Lewis, M.D.

"The best thing for being sad," replied Merlin, beginning to puff and blow, "is to learn something. That's the only thing that never fails. You may grow old and trembling in your anatomies, you may lie awake at night listening to the disorder of your veins, you may miss your only love, you may see the world about you devastated by evil lunatics, or know your honour trampled in the sewers of baser minds. There is only one thing for it then — to learn. Learn why the world wags and what wags it. That is the only thing which the mind can never exhaust, never alienate, never be tortured by, never fear or distrust, and never dream of regretting. Learning is the only thing for you. Look what a lot of things there are to learn."

Valerie Lewis

A Spirit of Adventure

**"As soon as I saw you,
I knew an adventure was about to happen."
Winnie the Pooh**

AFTER MY MEDICAL TRAINING, I joined the United States Air Force. I was stationed at U. S. Air Force base, R.A.F. Lakenheath, in England. I attended a party at the Officer's Club and met a most extraordinary woman, Valerie Dewar Searle.

She was a teacher, introducing American high school students to British culture and history. For me, it was love at first sight. She was brilliant, unassuming, and dedicated to making the world a better place. Valerie did not only talk the talk; she walked the walk — literally.

Valerie had been an intrepid traveler and explorer. Her spirit of adventure resulted in her having traveled around the world. Valerie had been raised in England and attended the University of Edinburgh, where she played on the varsity golf team. She had served with Voluntary Service Overseas (VSO), the British equivalent of the Peace Corps, in Ghana from 1964 to 1965. Ready to leave Ghana, she decided to hitchhike from West to East Africa via Nigeria and Sudan, traveling across parts of the Sahara Desert to the Nile, and eventually to the Mediterranean. When I asked her why she chose a rather unusual route to return to England, she replied, "It seemed more interesting than simply getting on an airplane and flying home."

Valerie previously had been a nanny in Spain and had taught in Switzerland. After her African adventures, she taught for two years in Argentina and then traveled widely in South America. From there she boarded a cargo ship and was off to Japan, where she spent six months teaching English. She then crossed Russia on the TransSiberian Railway to get back home. As Eckhart Tolle said, "Life is an adventure. It is not a package tour."

Valerie's sophistication and experience as a world traveler overwhelmed me, but what I really fell in love with was her steadiness, humility, and commitment to helping others. She says, "One of the most important attributes each of us should have is reliability. Each word we speak and each action we take touches others." She never focuses attention on herself. She is proactive and doesn't wait to be told what a situation requires. When my 104 year-old mother became ill, for one month she didn't leave her side.

We were married in England and subsequently moved to the Chicago area, where I joined a private practice in orthopedic surgery. I never doubted that she would be able to make the transition. We have now been married for more than 45 years.

While living in the Chicago area, in addition to raising our two talented daughters, she obtained a master's degree in linguistics and has volunteered for several organizations. She taught English as a second language to adults for many years. She is a member of the Woman's Board of the Field Museum and has volunteered in several departments in the museum. She was active in an organization called Chicago Action for Soviet Jewry and made two trips to the former Soviet Union to meet with Refuseniks, Jews who lost their jobs because they wished to emigrate. She has taken classes on Judaism for many years and was a vice president of Moriah Congregation in charge of education.

We have traveled to all seven continents together. Valerie's spirit of adventure has never left her. She has inspired me, by her example, to be more open to new challenges and experiences. Each day, I continue to strive to be worthy of her.

Stuart Green

A Way-Out-of-the-Box Thinker

"The larger the island of knowledge,
the longer the shoreline of wonder."
Ralph W. Sockman

STUART GREEN HAS ALWAYS BEEN a creative thinker. He was one of the first orthopedic surgeons to recognize the importance of a revolutionary method to treat complex fractures and to lengthen the bones in the leg. It was developed by Soviet doctor G.A. Ilizarov. Stuart wrote about the method in 1980, and in 1987 he went to Siberia to visit Ilizarov and learn from him firsthand. He was the first American to do so; he introduced the method to American surgeons and became a world authority on the procedure. By the mid-1980s, Green was developing improvements on the technique that are still in use today.

Comparing the evolution of knee replacements to the evolution of early life forms on our planet is a striking example of Stuart creatively associating two seemingly dissimilar concepts. This resulted in an article, "The Evolution of Medical Technology: Lessons from the Burgess Shale," in the *Journal of Clinical Orthopaedics and Related Research*. His thesis was that the pre-Cambrian Burgess Shale in Canada is full of fossils representing roughly four billion years' worth of experiments in evolution that failed, and that those necessary failures on the way to successful life forms are analogous to the failures encountered along the way in the development of new medical technology, such as a knee prosthesis. "[M]any of the early devices have proven to be failures," he writes. "However, modern knee replacements would not have been developed without them."

Stuart's writing is not limited to medical texts but reflects his wide-ranging interest in other fields. Drawn to the history of medicine in colonial America, he authored *Dear Dr. Franklin: Emails to a Founding Father about Science, Medicine and Technology*, written in anticipation of Franklin's eventual resurrection. That led to an invitation from the *Saturday Evening Post* (founded by Franklin) to write a weekly blog, "What Would Ben Franklin Say?" on the *Post's* website.

Stuart is also a professional photographer with a portfolio of striking images of people, exotic animals, ships, and far-away places he has visited.

Outwardly, he appears understated, with the quiet demeanor of a retired college professor. In fact, he is always hurtling from one project to the next one. As with so many highly successful people, he is quite modest about his achievements. When I asked him what the key to his achievements was, he responded unhesitatingly, "Adrianne, my wife. She manages everything."

Stuart has always felt a responsibility to give back to his community. Ever since he began practicing orthopedic surgery, he has volunteered one-third of his time at public hospitals. When I asked what the best new idea that he has had in the last few years, his answer was, "Quit working for money; being a volunteer."

Giving More Than Expected

When you have a job to do, it's a little like wrestling a gorilla.
You don't quit when you're tired –
you quit when the gorilla is tired.
Robert Strauss

Play the way you should live your life –
with your whole heart and soul.
Phil Jackson

John Foley, Nathan Lewis

Aiming Too Low and Hitting the Mark

"Be a self-starter. Nobody is going to wind you up in the morning and give you a pep talk and push you out."
Lew Holtz

IN THE LATE 1970S, I was one of the first orthopedic surgeons in the Chicago area to perform arthroscopic knee surgery. I wrote articles and gave lectures on the subject and treated patients from all over the Midwest. I even invented an instrument that became a standard piece of equipment for performing such operations.

Believing that this was the new normal, I thought that my elevated status would continue indefinitely. In fact, other surgeons quickly learned the technique and my competitive advantage rapidly dissolved.

The following statement is attributed to the artist Michelangelo: "The greatest danger for most of us is not that our aim is too high, and we miss it, but that it is too low, and we reach it."

I thought I was giving a 100-percent effort, but in retrospect I was aiming too low. For example, I could have found other creative ways to move forward in the field by organizing orthopedic conferences or instituting a clinical study. Setting a higher standard for my thinking and actions could have allowed me to make a greater contribution to the field. I aimed too low and reached my goal.

John Foley, a former Marine and later a Sloan Fellow at Stanford University Graduate School of Business, is today one of the nation's most successful inspirational speakers. He developed the Glad to Be Here® leadership program, which emphasizes gratitude and giving. We met at a conference, and later I was interviewed on his podcast. He told me the following story:

When John joined the Navy, he desperately wanted to play football. His goal was just to make the team. He did not even aspire to be a starter. So that is exactly what he did — he made the team. Even though as a defensive back for the Midshipmen, he was able to play in two bowl games, he has always wondered what he could have done had he tried for more. He was limited, he explained, purely by his mental outlook, not by his physical ability.

John, like me, resolved never again to set his goals too low, but always to reach higher. Later, John became the lead solo pilot for the Blue Angels, the Navy's most elite flying team, and as a public speaker he has taught thousands how to set and achieve their highest goals.

My father Nathan Lewis had the intelligence, discipline, and stamina to run his own business for more than 50 years. He never missed a day of work. By observing him, I saw how important it was to be your own boss, to make your own decisions and take the consequences.

From his example, I also learned the importance of being dependable. He was rock solid reliable. People knew they could count on him. He was a super-star salesman, always upbeat, who would use humor effectively. One of his favorite lines to family and friends was, "I wish I had one hundred customers like you. Unfortunately, I have five hundred!"

In addition, my father was an outstanding athlete. He was a nationally ranked tennis player while a member of the tennis team at Tulane University. He taught me how much dedication was necessary to be a serious athlete.

Each of the contributors to this chapter, Goldie Miller, Jack Miller, and Marc Silverman aimed high and gave people more than they expected.

Coach Vince Lombardi said, "The quality of a person's life is in direct proportion to their commitment to excellence, regardless of their chosen field of endeavor."

Goldie Miller

Solid Goldie Words

"Hard work, persistence, and determination:
very simple, very boring, very obvious."
Goldie Miller

DURING HER FIVE decades as an entrepreneur in the real estate industry, Goldie Miller has given hundreds of speeches. She says, "My storyline hasn't changed. Success isn't achieved overnight. Hard work, persistence and determination have been my mantra, and I think that's true across all endeavors... not just real estate."

Goldie said, "When I started my career, I remember making more calls in the office than anyone else. No magic. The more calls I made, the more appointments I got. *Hard Work*. When I couldn't get in to see the CEO through the receptionist, I just kept calling. Wouldn't give up. Wouldn't accept 'no.'"

Persistence and determination go hand-in-hand," she said. "I was so determined to be successful, because it was the difference between eating and not eating. As brokers, we were all on commission. So, on January 1st of every year, we had zero income on the books. The more calls I made, the more appointments I obtained, the more leases were signed, and so on. Those successes translated directly into income."

Goldie, always energetic and animated, has put as much commitment into giving back to her profession and her community as she has into her own real estate career. Audrey Hepburn said, "As you grow older, you will discover that you have two hands: one for helping yourself, the other for helping others."

In 2007, Goldie founded the Goldie B. Wolfe Miller Women Leaders in Real Estate Initiative ("The Goldie Initiative") at Roosevelt University. The program is designed to educate, encourage, and promote women in Chicago's real estate industry, and it has built alliances with more than 16 universities, including Northwestern, Georgetown, Cornell, and the University of Chicago. Goldie said, "The Initiative financially supports graduate female students majoring in real estate, as well as mentoring and networking with them. The goal is for them to achieve the highest levels of executive-managers.

We now have more than 150 Goldie Scholars from 16 major universities in the country working at top real estate firms. Some are even successful entrepreneurs themselves."

Now Goldie is president of Millbrook Corporate Real Estate Services. She is on the board of directors of the Jack Miller Family Foundation and its philanthropic arm, the Jack and Goldie Wolfe Miller Fund, a grant-making organization supporting education, Jewish initiatives, and medical research.

Patience, persistence, and perspiration: essential ingredients in Goldie Wolfe Miller's extraordinary success.

Jack Miller

The Skills that Became Quill

"Actions have consequences,
and we are each responsible for our own actions."
Jack Miller

ONE OF JACK MILLER's mantras is that each of us is responsible for our own life. He started putting that principle into practice at a young age. Specifically, he began earning money in grammar school, delivering dry cleaning on his bicycle, setting pins in a bowling alley, ushering at a movie theater and modeling at an art institute. He worked his way through college modeling, washing dishes, and performing acrobatics in clubs and county fairs, but when he graduated from the University of Illinois with a degree in Journalism, he had no idea what he wanted to do.

After a few months working in his dad's poultry store, an uncle offered him a sales job in his food manufacturing company. Jack spent the next five years on the road covering the entire United States east of the Mississippi. He called on distributors of all types, including wholesale grocers and anyone attempting to sell to restaurants and hospitals. It was this experience, much more than college, that gave him the education needed to start his own business as a distributor of office products. He began with a phone in his dad's store and $2,000 borrowed from his father-in-law.

Jack, who always carefully measures his words, said, "I had no grand visions of what I could achieve. I was married to my late wife and had bought a home and just wanted to make a living. I had no fears about being able to do so. I just started out knocking on (business) doors day after day, and slowly began to gain customers. I made my first mailing, a penny postcard sent to about 150 companies with sale pricing on five items."

Jack said, "My brother joined the business a year and a half later, and after 43 years, that first mailing evolved into several million mailings a year, and those original 150 accounts grew to over 800,000 customers nationwide. All because we just kept working hard, focusing all our efforts on running a good business, providing fantastic service and very good prices."

That business was Quill Corporation. Quill became the nation's largest independent direct marketer of office products. The company employed more than 1,300 people and had annual sales of more than $630 million. Quill was sold to Staples in 1998 for three-quarters of a billion dollars.

As well as a brilliant businessman, Jack is a devoted philanthropist. He is president of the Jack Miller Family Foundation, which supports a wide variety of community improvement efforts.

He is also chairman of the Jack Miller Center, which teaches America's founding principles and history. He said, "We started at the university level and now have over 1,000 professors on over 300 campuses nationwide. More recently, we began working with high school teachers in six states and are expanding into more. At the Jack Miller Center, we believe that 'the battle for the soul of our nation will be won or lost in our classrooms.' I am doing it with the same focus and hard work with which I have lived the rest of my life and I am confident we will achieve the same kind of success."

Jack eventually put his journalism degree to good use. He is the author of two books: *Simply Success: How to Start, Build and Grow a Multimillion-Dollar Business the Old-Fashioned Way*, and *Born to Be Free*.

Jack Miller, tall with the wiry, athletic frame of an ex-handball player, is now in his tenth decade. He looks back on his life with great satisfaction and feels tremendous excitement and pleasure in what he is doing now. He said he has lived his life with integrity and has taken advantage of the freedom America has given him to pursue his happiness, his way.

Jack's life lesson is that actions have consequences, and it is up to each of us to make the most of whatever abilities and talents we have been given.

Marc Silverman

A Worthy Work Ethic

**"Don't be afraid to get your hands dirty
with good old-fashioned work."
Marc Silverman**

MARC SILVERMAN IS co-host of one of the most popular talk radio shows in Chicago, the *Waddle and Silvy Show on ESPN,* with former Chicago Bears wide receiver Tom Waddle. But Marc didn't just fall into one of the best sports talk shows in the country.

Marc, who has a gentle demeanor and an infectious smile, explained how he got his start in his career: "When I was in the seventh grade, our career education teacher wanted us to shadow a professional in the field we thought we wanted to be in. Instead of finding someone who knew someone, I cold called each local Chicago TV switchboard and asked to be connected to people in the sports department. It wasn't hard — the TV guide had each station's phone listed at the front.

"Well-known Chicago sports personalities Jack Brickhouse, Johnny Morris, and Tim Weigal were all nice, but they politely told me no. A young sportscaster, Mark Giangreco, said yes, and that was my first lesson in networking. In college, I interned for Giangreco, and several years later he was a regular guest on my own show."

The advice he offers young people just starting out is: "Throughout my career, I would rely on my networking ability to get me in front of important people, whether it was for a job interview, or a one-on-one sit-down with Magic Johnson shortly after he retired from the NBA, or finding mentors who would later become friends. The ability to reach out and create your OWN 'who you know' is vital. In my business, you may have to talk to twenty people just to get put in front of someone you were hoping to talk to. There is never a direct path. But if you're willing to get your hands dirty with good old-fashioned work, your 'job' could be something you love and are passionate about."

Marc credits his upbringing for his unrelenting dedication to his work: "My dad would leave for work at 5 a.m. and return after I got home from school. He was a union electrician, and the work was hard on him. Hot days. Frigid days. He had to work through it all, outdoors, overtime, and weekends.

It was very physical, and it took a toll on him. He didn't get to make a living doing what he loved, but he wasn't scared to get his hands dirty in order to support his family. When he got home, he would spend well over ten minutes getting his hands clean with Lava soap. I took two lessons from that as a child: I was going to make a career out of something that I loved and was truly passionate about, but even with that said, I would NOT be scared to get my hands dirty."

In 2020, Silverman was diagnosed with Stage 3 diffuse large B-cell lymphoma, a form of non-Hodgkin's lymphoma. A year later he was again broadcasting live after having undergone chemotherapy during a pandemic. Marc applied the same determination, and willingness "to get his hands dirty," to doing whatever was necessary to treat his cancer. He is an inspiring example of how the lesson that he learned from his father has paid off in his personal and professional life.

Calvin Coolidge stated, "Nothing in this world can take the place of persistence. Talent will not, genius will not, education will not. Persistence and determination together will solve our problems."

Focusing On Excellence

*We succeed only as we identify in life a single overriding
objective, and make all other considerations
bend to that one objective.*
Dwight Eisenhower

*I only write when inspiration strikes.
Fortunately, it strikes every morning at 9 o'clock sharp.*
W. Somerset Maugham

Bruno Bettelheim, Harold Baines

Actions Do Speak Louder than Words

"Well done is better than well said."
Benjamin Franklin

A SPANISH PROVERB STATES, "It's not the same to talk of bulls as to be in the bullring." The importance of action, not just words, was a lesson I first learned when I was an undergraduate, and it was reinforced many years later by a 21-year-old rookie Major League baseball player.

Psychologist Bruno Bettelheim was a guest speaker when I attended Brandeis University. Although much of his work subsequently was disputed, at the time he was a respected professor at the University of Chicago.

I attended his lecture in 1962, just as the Freedom Riders were traveling by bus into the South to protest segregated public buses. During the question-and-answer period, a student asked the professor why he himself wasn't with the Freedom Riders.

The student received more of an answer than he had anticipated. Professor Bettelheim became red in the face and charged off the stage. He was short and elfin in appearance, but suddenly seemed to be ten feet tall. He then stood over the student, pointed a finger in his face and shouted, "Don't you tell me what to do. I'm doing what I think is important in this world. Instead of making suggestions to others, why aren't *you* on a Freedom Ride right now?"

What a powerful lesson: Just act. It was one of the most unforgettable and transformational moments in my college career.

Fast forward to 1980. I met a 21-year-old Chicago White Sox baseball player named Harold Baines when I was with the team. He was a humble man who remained quiet and unassuming throughout his 22-year baseball career.

A six-time All-Star, he let his actions on the baseball field do his talking. He was famous for one-word responses to questions. When a 25-inning game, one of the longest in the history of major league baseball, ended with Harold hitting the winning home run, a reporter approached him and suggested, "You got all of that one." Baines' classic reply: "Evidently."

In his Hall of Fame acceptance speech in 2019, Baines quoted his father:

149

"Words are easy, deeds are hard. Words can be empty. Deeds speak louder, and sometimes they can echo forever."

The other contributors to this chapter, Michael Jordan, Geoffrey Tabin, and Jerry Krause, illustrate the importance both of being in the arena and being able to focus intensely while there.

Michael Jordan

It Takes More than Talent

**"Michael was first in the batting cage in the morning
and last to leave at night. He is the hardest-working
and most dedicated athlete I have ever known."**
Walter Hriniak

THE MOST SUCCESSFUL people in our highly competitive world give people
more than they expect. Take, for example, Chicago Bulls player Michael
Jordan.

Michael's intense competitiveness and work ethic are legendary. When
Michael first retired from basketball in 1993, he signed a contract to play
minor league baseball in the spring of 1994. Chicago White Sox hitting
coach, Walter Hriniak, initially refused to coach Michael, because he thought
that his playing baseball was just a publicity stunt. But Michael was first in
the batting cage in the morning and last to leave at night. He kept hitting and
hitting until his hands were bleeding. Eventually Hriniak was convinced
Michael was serious. Subsequently he said, "Michael Jordan is the hardest-
working and most dedicated athlete I have ever known."

An essential aspect of Michael's dedication to the game was an unwa-
vering sense of obligation to his teammates, to the league, and to his fans.
Once, only a few minutes before a game, he had such severe pain in his neck
that he was unable to move his head in any direction. I suggested he not play
that night. He told me, in no uncertain terms, that he knew people had come
from hundreds, sometimes thousands, of miles away just to see him play. He
was not going to disappoint them.

Michael's ability to focus and to compartmentalize was also well-known.
He was devoted to his father, and told me, "My dad was my best friend, and
he knew everything about me." James Jordan was murdered in 1993,
allegedly by two teenagers who had hijacked his car. One time when I was
alone with Michael in the training room before a game, his father's accused
killers appeared on TV. Michael simply shrugged his shoulders. I interpreted
that as his superior ability to compartmentalize his emotions. Why waste
energy on them, because, regardless of what happened to them, his father
wasn't coming back?

Michael's trainer Tim Grover, in his book *Relentless,* said, "If one thing separated Michael from every other player, it was his stunning ability to block out everything and everyone else. Nothing got to him; he was ice. No matter what else was going on -- the crowds, the media, the death of his father -- when he stepped onto that basketball court, he was able to shut out everything except his mission to attack and conquer."

Michael's self-control was remarkable. Day after day, year after year, he was bombarded with questions – some thoughtful, many inane, and some mean-spirited – and he had the intelligence and self-discipline never to say anything, even in the heat of the moment, that he would later regret.

Michael was a leader much more by action than words. Even though he was the most talented athlete on the court, he worked harder than anyone else. Michael said, "The minute you get away from fundamentals – whether it's proper technique, work ethic, or mental preparation – the bottom can fall out of your game, your schoolwork, your job, whatever you are doing."

My favorite Michael Jordan leading-by-example story about him was told to me by Neil Funk, the Bulls' play-by-play TV announcer. It was in 1993, when the Bulls were playing the Phoenix Suns in the NBA finals. Unexpectedly, the Bulls lost game five at home and had to return to Phoenix, where they would possibly have to play two games. On the charter flight to Phoenix, everyone had big suitcases for the trip, packed in anticipation of playing the first game, followed by a day off, and then a second game. Michael, however, boarded the plane with a valise – and a small one, at that.

"Gentlemen," he announced, lifting his bag, "these are *all* the clothes I brought. We are *not* going to be in Phoenix long enough for me to have to change into *anything*." The mood of the team dramatically shifted, and they won game six in Phoenix — the famous "three-peat," their third championship in a row.

Dedication, focus, preparation, and leadership by example: traits that have led to Michael's reputation as the greatest player and competitor, not just in basketball, but also *in the history of sports.*

Geoffrey Tabin

Going with the Flow

"The best moments in our lives occur when a person's body or mind is stretched to its limit to accomplish something difficult and worthwhile."
Mihaly Czikszentmihalyi

OPHTHALMOLOGIST GEOFF TABIN, co-founder of the Himalayan Cataract Project, knows how to attain a flow state. That term was coined by Mihaly Csikszentmihalyi in his book *Finding Flow: The Psychology of Engagement with Everyday Life,* which he describes as follows: "The flow state renews one's energy rather than draining it. In a flow state, you are so focused on what you're doing that time flies by or seems to stand still. Concentration is utterly focused on the task at hand. Sense perceptions are heightened; for example, colors are sharper and brighter. Your body and mind are completely attuned and connected. Nothing distracts you. Some people describe the feeling as being "in the zone."

When my wife, Valerie, and I visited Geoff in Ghana in 2007, we watched him, day after day, operate continuously from morning until night without a break. It was an extraordinary setup: The operating room contained three beds, with three surgeons working simultaneously. Each surgery took approximately nine minutes. Not a moment was wasted. As one patient was taken out of the operating room, the next patient would already be on the operating table. All the while, Chicago blues singer Howlin' Wolf was blaring away on Geoff's iPhone.

Geoff said, "I am absolutely in a flow state at those times, and I am as excited about the 75th surgery of the day as I am about the first. When I am operating on an eye, and a mistake could result in permanent blindness, my mind and body are forced into harmony. There are no extraneous thoughts. I *am* what I am doing."

I assumed that at the end of the day, Geoff would collapse in exhaustion. Quite the opposite. He is a firm believer in painting the evening with laughter. At dinner, along with his ready smile and infectious laugh, he would regale all assembled with stories of his exploits, such as when he invented bungee jumping with his buddies at the Oxford University Dangerous Sports

Club, and his adventures with the Dani tribe while climbing the highest mountain on the island of New Guinea.

How does one attain a flow state? Mihaly Csikszentmihalyi instructs us that it is necessary to have clear goals, receive immediate feedback, and have a balance between the challenge of the task and your skill set. The activity should be one you love.

Flow state is accessible to everyone, and can occur during a variety of activities, such as physical activity, listening to music, working in the garden, holding a deep and meaningful conversation with a friend, or even simple day-to-day tasks. I feel fortunate to have achieved a flow state while performing surgery, teaching, playing tennis, and writing this book.

Geoff Tabin is an inspiring example on how to be completely absorbed in the task at hand. Because, as he says, "I *am* what I am doing," he has been able to restore sight to thousands of his patients.

Jerry Krause

A Talent for Scouting

"There are no traffic jams along the extra mile highway."
Roger Staubach

JERRY KRAUSE BECAME general manager of the Chicago Bulls in 1985 and was the mastermind behind the team's six championships. Jerry was as good at scouting as Michael Jordan was at playing the game. Jerry possessed unique skills. He was one of the few evaluators with a world-class ability to recognize talent in two sports, baseball and basketball. He had previously been a pro scout for the Chicago White Sox. I was chosen by Jerry to be an orthopedic consultant for the Chicago Bulls in 1996, and both of us were with the team until 2003.

When he was the Bulls general manager, he had a knack for finding players who may not have been exceptional on other teams, but who had skills that would make them excel with the Bulls. But more than anything else, Jerry was prepared.

Here's one example: One morning Jerry and I were sitting in the stands watching a three-hour Bulls practice session together. We were watching Robert Parish, who had just signed with the team as a free agent. Jerry leaned forward to make sure no one could overhear what we were saying. He told me about scouting reports he had on Robert, which went as far back as 20 years. Jerry knew Parrish so well that he could visualize exactly what role he would fill to fit with this Bulls team.

Another example of Jerry's focus and dedication to researching players: One night after a playoff game I saw him leaving Chicago's United Center with a packed suitcase. When I inquired where he was going, he said that he was flying to Europe to scout a player. Surprised, I responded, "But Jerry, since we are in the middle of the playoffs, couldn't you just look at a video of him?" He said, "Yeah, but I want to see other things." Jerry felt it was critical to observe the athlete's body language to see how he handled himself on the bench with his teammates when he wasn't playing. This extra insight was worth squeezing in an overseas trip between playoff games. In that case, Jerry literally went the extra mile.

Leaders come in a variety of shapes and sizes. Jerry was short, heavyset, and often disheveled in appearance. I would be hard-pressed to find three more dissimilar characters, in appearance and personality, than Michael Jordan, Phil Jackson, and Jerry Krause, yet each was crucial in the championship run of the Chicago Bulls. As Bulls seven-foot center Bill Wennington said, "It takes all kinds of people to make things work."

Professional football player Ray Lewis once said, "There's not a person on my team in sixteen years that has consistently beat me to the ball every play. That ain't got nothing to do with talent. That's just got everything to do with effort, and nothing else."

Serving Others

I expect to pass through this world but once.
Any good thing therefore that I can do,
or any kindness that I can show to any fellow creature,
let me do it now for I shall not pass this way again.
Steven Griellet

The best way to find yourself
is to lose yourself in the service of others.
Mahatma Gandhi

Michael Lewis

Teaching: An Honor, A Privilege, A Calling

"People don't care how much you know
until they know how much you care."
Theodore Roosevelt

BEING DEDICATED to a cause greater than oneself is an essential ingredient for leading a rewarding life, a life of meaning. The medical profession is an ideal opportunity to serve others. Using my head, hands, and heart to heal illness and injury is often exhilarating, and, at the same time, challenging and humbling.

I have always felt that being a physician and surgeon is an honor, and teaching is a privilege and a calling. For physicians-in-training, I attempt to create indelible learning experiences and to foster a protected, safe environment that allows mistakes in diagnosis or treatment recommendations to be quickly corrected without negative consequences. Optimal learning comes from trial and error, and receiving immediate feedback. It does not come simply from watching someone else.

No matter which problems bring the patient to the office, they should leave feeling better than when they arrived. It is essential for the physician to be fully present. Words are important, and a substantial part of communication is nonverbal, so the way a diagnosis is communicated, including body language, is critical. Also, I try to show students the elegance of the science when discussing principles of anatomy, physiology, and bioengineering.

A recent multi-institutional study demonstrated that the characteristics most strongly associated with being an outstanding surgical resident, in addition to the obvious qualities of surgical judgment and medical knowledge, is leadership. Facets of leadership include vision, confidence, accountability, integrity, humility, and effective communication. I would like to think that these skills can be taught by proper instructional techniques as well as by example.

Cross-cultural communication is a critical skill for doctors. I have trained resident physicians from Asia and the Middle East, Europe, Africa, and South America. They have included Muslims, Sikhs, Hindus, Copts, Orthodox Jews, Catholics, and evangelical Christians. I assign topics for the residents to discuss, such as the history, culture, religions, and politics of different countries. The goal is to expand their (and my) horizons, by learning how much we have in common and exploring our different perspectives, in order to help make future encounters with patients from different cultures more meaningful.

For me, the joy of seeing a generation of students grow in knowledge, judgment, maturity, and empathy is unrivaled. Although I am no longer treating patients or teaching, I am gratified that I am still in touch with many of the physicians whom I have taught.

Each of the people in this chapter, Geoffrey Tabin, Dolores Kohl, Elizabeth Glassman, Michael McCaskey, Peter Christopher, and Raymond Kalmans, also have found meaning and purpose in working for causes which benefit others.

For many years, I was intimidated by Geoffrey Tabin and the other contributors to this chapter and the scale of their achievements. Eventually I realized that I wasn't competing with others but only with myself, and that, at least, I could positively impact one person at a time.

Oscar Wilde said, "Be yourself. Everyone else is already taken."

Geoff Tabin

Reaching the Summit of Service

"The ones who are crazy enough to think they can change the world are the ones who do."
John McAfee

AS A MOUNTAIN CLIMBER, Geoff has scaled the Seven Summits, the highest mountains on each of the seven continents, including the East Face of Mt. Everest.

Descending Everest, Geoff came across a team of Dutch doctors who were performing cataract surgery on several people who had been blind for years. Geoff saw his first cataract surgery on a woman who could barely tell light from dark. After the surgery, he watched as she saw the faces of her grandchildren for the first time. "As I looked at the tears of joy running down her face, I knew exactly what I wanted to do with my life. I wanted to restore sight."

Geoffrey was so inspired that he decided to make a career change. At that time, he was in an orthopedic surgery residency but felt he could make a bigger impact in the field of ophthalmology. He took a big risk. Ophthalmology residencies were extremely competitive, but he managed to secure one.

Geoffrey always has reached higher. He subsequently returned to Nepal and with Dr. Sanduk Ruit co-founded the Himalayan Cataract Project. Their objective is to eliminate all preventable and treatable blindness in their lifetime by providing practical, sustainable, high-quality, low-cost eye care to underserved blind people. The project's mission, as Tabin has acknowledged, is "more audacious than setting out to make the first assent of the East Face of Mount Everest."

Geoff has more stamina than anyone I know. He will perform eighty-five cataract surgeries in a day. He says, "It's the single most effective medical intervention on earth. A little miracle. Tomorrow the patient will see 20/20." How does he do it? He credits his achievements with an obsessive focus on self-improvement. He always worked harder than anyone else. He said, "As a mountaineer, I always climbed more pitches than others and came in after dark."

In Geoff's book, *Blind Corners; Adventures on Seven Continents,* he quotes Theodore Roosevelt, who said, "The credit belongs to the man who is in the arena; who strives valiantly; who errs and comes up short again; who, at the best, knows in the end the triumph of high achievement and who, at the worst, if he fails, at least fails while daring greatly, so that his place will never be with those timid souls who know neither victory nor defeat." I think this best explains his philosophy.

Geoffrey Tabin is applying the lessons of the Himalayan Cataract Project across the globe. Now a professor of Ophthalmology and Global Medicine at Stanford University, he spends much of his year leading teams of doctors in Ghana, Ethiopia, South Sudan, Kenya, Ruanda, the Philippines, and Nepal.

To date, the Himalayan Cataract Project has screened and provided basic exams to more than 13 million people and trained 19,000 eye care professionals. It has directly — and indirectly, through local medical personnel trained in cataract surgery — saved or restored the sight of more than 1,000,000 people!

Anne Frank said, "How wonderful it is that no one need wait a single moment before starting to improve the world."

Dolores Kohl

A Visionary Educator

"Tell me and I forget. Teach me and I remember.
Involve me and I learn."
Benjamin Franklin

DOLORES KOHL IS A VISIONARY, deeply committed to supporting early learning through paradigm-shifting, experimental programming, and through awarding outstanding educators.

Dolores and I attended Brandeis University, and Dolores was on the Board of Trustees for many years. Together with her late husband Morrie Kaplan, she has made significant contributions to Northwestern University and many other Chicago-area organizations, but her approach to improving education for young children is her own.

Dolores says, "Early childhood education is my passion. Serendipity lured me into the classroom, and after the first day, I knew teaching was my calling. We all know that the most important time for brain development happens from birth to eight years old."

Dolores designed an interactive, hands-on, traveling art exhibit, *Van Gogh for All*, which was produced by the Dolores Kohl Education Foundation. It uses modern technology and participatory learning to engage children in the arts. Visitors can step into projections of some of Van Gogh's most famous paintings, including "Starry Night" (1889) and "The Yellow House" (1888).

The exhibit includes a scale-model of Van Gogh's bedroom, as he depicted it in his painting, "The Bedroom" (1889), and a recreation of his studio. But it is designed for children of all ages. I will always remember my 104-year-old mother's delight, when she sat on the bed with the red bedspread when we saw the exhibit at the Museum of Fine Arts in Houston, Texas.

Dolores wrote the storybook *Vincent and Me*, illustrated by Caroline Bonne Muller. It tells the fictional tale of Van Gogh for children. Dolores tells me that she fell in love with Vincent at a young age, and when she was sad, she remembered his sunflowers, and the world looked brighter!

The Dolores Kohl Education Foundation, created to enhance education in the U.S. and abroad, has been honoring outstanding educators since 1985,

163

first with the Kohl International Teaching Awards, and later with the Kohl McCormick Early Childhood Teaching Awards.

The Kohl Children's Museum of Greater Chicago, founded in 1985, is a hands-on learning laboratory for children under the age of eight. It includes a 46,000-square-foot museum building and a 2-acre outdoor exhibit area. Dolores says, "I see our children's museum as a 'playground for the mind,' sparking learning, curiosity, and imagination."

The StoryBus is a children's museum on wheels, created by master teachers and the Kohl Children's Museum designers for preschool and kindergarten students. StoryBus brings play-based learning to more than 15,000 children in the Chicago area annually.

Dolores eloquently states, "Children are the messages we send to generations that we will never see. Igniting children's imaginations is what we early childhood educators do."

Elizabeth Glassman

Championing American Art

"When you have a vision, give it a try.
If it doesn't work out, find another way to reach your goals."
Elizabeth Glassman

ELIZABETH GLASSMAN HAS BEEN a major influence in the art world for almost half a century. She has held positions at the Metropolitan Museum of Art, the Menil Foundation in Houston, the National Gallery of Art, and the Georgia O'Keeffe Foundation. In 2001, she became president and CEO of the Chicago-based Terra Foundation for American Art, where her bold vision transformed a museum enterprise into an international ambassador of American art.

Liz and I spoke about what lessons she had learned about art and life during her stellar career.

Her parents, she said, were very spontaneous (they eloped after knowing each other for only six weeks), and their fearless attitude of "Why not give it a try?" gave her permission to take risks and to try new ventures.

Liz told me she has always been very visual. "I look at the world in visual terms, and even as a child I enjoyed exploring the Museum of Fine Arts in Houston. It's like a high, almost an addiction. When I see amazing works of art, I feel such joy that I just want to see more."

Earlier in her career, she enjoyed the role of curator, putting on exhibitions, researching and writing about artists, and bringing several shows to life, including an exhibition on camera-less photography at the Detroit Institute of Art and the Museum of fine Arts Houston. But she found her true calling when she went to business school and earned an MBA. Liz said, "I really liked the action of the business world. It involves strategic planning, creative problem-solving, identifying what people need and providing it."

The Terra Foundation for American Art held an extensive collection of American art. Its donor, Daniel Terra, wanted to expand knowledge, understanding, and enjoyment of American art. Inspired by his vision, Liz made it her mission to be a kind of museum without walls. She wanted to bring American art to other countries, to support projects on American art, and to give it a worthy place in the canon. She was given wide latitude in carrying out her vision for the foundation. "It was incredibly freeing," she said.

It was a powerful mission, one to which she brought her intrepid spirit. "The world is a big place," she said. If one institution did not want to partner with Terra, surely another would. Under Liz's watch, the Terra Foundation closed its small art museum in Chicago, sold its museum in Giverny, and turned itself into a grant-making institution with the mission of promoting American art globally.

She boldly approached the most prestigious museums in the world – the Louvre, London's National Gallery, Shanghai Art Museum, the Musée d'Orsay, and Oxford's Ashmolean Museum. Under her direction, the Terra Foundation master-minded and funded the first-ever exhibitions of American art at the Louvre and in China. According to the foundation, more than 40 million people have seen exhibitions Terra has helped to organize.

In 2018, the Terra Foundation funded most of the $7.8 million it took to present Art Design Chicago, a year-long extravaganza of 46 exhibitions involving 95 cultural institutions. The endeavor led to 29 new publications, including *Art in Chicago: A History from the Fire to Now,* published by the University of Chicago Press, which is now said to be the standard text on art history for the region.

Professionally, Liz was able to have a significant impact in making people throughout the world more aware of American art. She was never afraid to approach the biggest players in the field with her imaginative ideas. This helped to make the Terra Foundation such a powerful force in the art world.

When I asked Liz how she would define personal success, she responded, "Having the respect of my colleagues and the love of my family and friends."

The professional life lesson Elizabeth Glassman said she would like to share is this: "When you have a vision, do not stop at 'no.' If something doesn't work out, don't dwell on it. Instead, move on to something else and find another way to reach your goals."

Michael McCaskey

Teaching was in His Bones

"To whom much is given, much is required."
The Bible

MICHAEL MCCASKEY TOOK over leadership of the Chicago Bears football team in 1983 from his grandfather, George S. Halas, founder and owner of the franchise. In 1986, Michael led the team to a Super Bowl victory. However, Michael's life was devoted to serving others, and teaching was always his first love.

When I asked Michael why he was so passionate about teaching, this was his response: "In 1965, after I graduated from university, I joined the Peace Corps, and taught science and English to junior high school students in Fiche, an isolated rural village in Ethiopia. Fiche had no electricity or running water. It had a two-room schoolhouse. No one from Fiche had ever gone to college. My students were astounding. My days as a teacher in Ethiopia broadened my perspective on the rest of the world, for which I am very grateful."

Educating and training students from Ethiopia was always a priority. He continued, "Beginning in 1984, as a financial supporter and adviser for the Ethiopian Community Association of Chicago, I helped to raise funds to create a state-of-the-art Destiny Computer Training Center for Ethiopians in the city. I created a nine-week entrepreneurship training program for Ethiopian immigrants, and I felt great satisfaction that, as a result, many of its graduates started small businesses in the city."

In 1999, Michael and four other Peace Corps volunteers went to Ethiopia to try to help facilitate a peaceful settlement of the long-running Ethiopia-Eritrea war. (It took another 20 years before the conflict ended). At the beginning of the visit, they met in Addis Ababa with the Ethiopian foreign minister. Michael didn't recognize him, but he recognized Michael. He was one of the students Michael had taught back in the sixties!

This official was just one of many of Michael's pupils who had gone on to achieve never-before-dreamed-of success. Other students that Michael had previously taught included a university professor, grade-school teachers, a pilot for Ethiopian Airlines, a lawyer, an entrepreneur, and a conservation director for the World Wildlife Fund.

Michael S. Lewis, M.D.

Michael was a true servant leader. He focused on empowering and uplifting others. After he left as Chairman of the Board of the Chicago Bears in 2011, Michael worked on health care, education, and leadership training in Ethiopia. He started a McCaskey Safe Surgery Fellowship program for Ethiopian healthcare workers, associated with Atul Gawande's Lifebox program to improve quality and safety in operating rooms. During the last few months of his life, he devoted his energy, creativity, and entrepreneurial skills to developing a system to teach English in rural areas in Ethiopia.

Michael had many passions, including photography. He produced a book on the city of Paris and photographic essays of his projects in Ethiopia. He was passionate about birds. We spent time birdwatching together, and he helped me design and write a book about birds. It was his idea to title the book *Invitation to Joy*. But aside from his family, which was his first priority, he was dedicated to improving educational opportunities in Ethiopia.

He always wore the mantle of being George Halas's grandson with dignity and pride. At the same time, he emphasized that George Halas was the unassuming son of immigrants. He told me, "In addition to owning and coaching the team, my grandfather did their laundry, folded their socks, wrote and mimeographed seven publicity sheets for the seven Chicago newspapers, and even drove the team bus." An essential part of Michael's personality was his innate unpretentiousness and humility. He avoided the spotlight.

Serving others gave meaning to Michael McCaskey's life. His contributions to the Chicago Bears football franchise may have been most visible to the public, but his quiet, behind-the-scenes contributions in Ethiopia have the potential to improve the lives of untold thousands.

Peter Christopher

Lessons from the Headmaster

"What is a headmaster? Above all, he must like young people,
take an interest in the things that interest them, and guide
them towards things that would challenge their abilities."
Peter Christopher

PETER CHRISTOPHER WAS headmaster of King Edward VI Aston school near Birmingham, England, from 1992 to 2004. It is a selective school for approximately 950 boys aged 11 to 18.

Peter was the first person in his family to attend university. As a result, he had great empathy for the challenges his students would face.

I asked Peter about teachers who were important influences in his life. He described Geoffrey Elton, later Sir Geoffrey, who, at the time, was the world's most important scholar of English Tudor history. Peter studied with him while at Cambridge University. Encouragement from such a noted scholar resulted in a powerful boost to Peter's confidence. This gave Peter insight into how important a teacher and mentor could be, which was a decisive factor in his later decision to become a headmaster.

When I asked Peter to describe the challenges and rewards of being a headmaster, this was his response:

"What is a headmaster? He is, by turns, an academic, an administrator, a politician, an accountant, a counsellor, a confidante, a role model, a salesman and a fundraiser. Above all, he must like young people, take an interest in the things that interest them, and guide them towards things that would challenge their abilities.

"He must also have the patience of Job, and at least tolerate his staff and colleagues, most of whom probably think they could do his job far better than he does - which is probably true - especially for the deputy headmaster (otherwise he is a poor appointment). He must keep on the right side of the caretaker (janitor), the cook (kitchen supervisor) and his personal assistant, without whose support the school would not function, and his life would be impossible.

"Hints as to your success or failure come from time to time from the most unlikely of sources, often in tribute to your qualities long after you have

169

moved onwards in your career. For example, I received an invitation from the Lord Mayor of London to go to the Lord Mayor's Banquet, because I had taught him some twenty-five years earlier. Other former students have written to me stating that I had changed their lives. Also, I remember the bus driver whose son gained admission to the University of Cambridge, and who brought me a box of chocolates to thank me for helping the young man when he was my student.

"This makes worthwhile the effort of attending school plays in rehearsal and performance, school concerts and beginners' violin groups, early Saturday morning junior rugby and cricket matches, as well as marking essays on Louis XIV's foreign policy or Shakespeare's *Macbeth*, not to mention the tedium of exam invigilation or Governing Body Board meetings.

"Will it all be the same in twenty years? It is not the same now. Specialization and compartmentalization have moved apace and led to each of the many roles a headmaster fills being subject to individual scrutiny and assessment. Sometimes these days, people seem less important than vision statements and political correctness.

"And yet.... the new headmaster recently showed me around the school with the pride I still harbour for it, and his personal assistant said he was asking her to do more and more, and it was all challenging and fun. She liked him, as did the cook I met, and the one or two members of staff we spoke to well after the school day had ended.

"Perhaps headteachers are born, not manufactured. People do still matter. There *is* hope for mankind."

Winston Churchill said, "Headmasters have powers at their disposal with which Prime Ministers have never yet been invested." Peter Christopher, the first person in his family to attend university, understood his potential impact on a generation of young scholars.

Raymond Kalmans

Community Service from
Generation to Generation

*"My parents made it clear to me that it was my obligation to
give back to the community of which I was a part."*
Raymond Kalmans

WHEN I ASKED RAYMOND KALMANS, recipient of the prestigious Houston
Jewish Community Center David H. White Award for Outstanding Leadership, why he is so committed to charitable causes, this is his response: "As a
young child, I watched as my mother participated in a variety of community
organizations, both religious and secular, where she served on boards and
committees. My father supported and encouraged her work.

"My parents made it clear to me that it was my obligation to give back to
the community. My wife's parents were of the same mindset. So, like my
parents, my wife, Barbara, and I became full partners in our service work."

Following in his mother's footsteps, Raymond served on various allocation
committees for the United Way. "I probably picked this organization because
Mother was involved on the main allocation committee of United Way and
found it very rewarding, as did I," he said.

Raymond was asked by a friend of his parents to be on the board of Seven
Acres Jewish Senior Care Services, a non-profit home for the aged. He
continues to be involved. He also has served on the Administrative and
Personnel Committee of his synagogue, Congregation Emanu El of Houston,
which led to a term as president. In addition, he is a past board member of the
Jewish Community Center of Houston.

Raymond recounts, "I began in my late 20s, and as I enter my 9th decade,
I continue volunteering. Barbara and I are very proud of our two sons, both of
whom along with their wives, have carried on the family tradition of a significant involvement in community affairs."

"And from what we see so far, community service is carrying on through
our grandchildren. When our oldest grandchild reached the age of twenty-
one last year, her parents and both sets of grandparents contributed to a
donor-advised fund, so that she could begin to make meaningful donations in
her own name. She recently advised us that she made her first donation for

the benefit of the Ukrainian refugees. We are very proud of her and plan to do the same for the other four grandchildren when they reach their twenty-first birthday."

This four-generation family tradition of community service looks as if it will continue to be strong for many years to come. I cannot imagine a more thoughtful, far-reaching twenty-first birthday gift.

The Challenge And Honor
Of Public Service

*There is no greater challenge
and there is no greater honor than to be in public service.*
Condoleezza Rice

*Never doubt that a small group of thoughtful,
committed citizens can change the world.
Indeed, it's the only thing that ever has.*
Margaret Mead

Nancy Stevenson

Building Something Better for Future Generations

"Perhaps the first quality for a politician is caring about the condition of others and having the energy and determination to find the root causes of problems and to legislate change."
Nancy Stevenson

WHAT MOTIVATES someone to spend their life working for the common good, often in arduous and perhaps confrontational circumstances? What vision and personal traits compel them to persevere? Five distinguished public servants give their answers to those questions.

Nancy Stevenson is president of the Adlai Stevenson Center on Democracy, a Trustee Emeritus at the University of Chicago, and has served as CEO for Voices for Illinois Children. We met many years ago when my wife was on a committee chaired by Nancy, which was concerned with Day Care Accreditation in Chicago. We have remained in contact.

Government is an important part of Stevenson's life. Her husband of 67 years was Adlai Stevenson III, who represented Illinois in the U.S. Senate from 1970 through 1981. He was the son of Adlai Stevenson II, who served as Illinois' 31st governor, and in 1952 and 1956 ran as the Democratic nominee for president against Dwight D. Eisenhower.

I asked Nancy, based on her decades of experience in state and national politics, what qualities must a good politician possess. This was her response:

"It has been told that a mourner watching the funeral train carrying Franklin Delano Roosevelt's body from Warm Springs, Georgia, to Washington, D.C., asked a man with tears cascading down his face, "Did you know him?"

"No," came the reply, "I didn't know him, but he knew me."

Nancy continued, "Perhaps the first quality for a politician is caring about the condition of others. He/she also must have the curiosity to see wrongs, plus the energy and determination to find the root causes of problems and legislate change.

"To make these attributes real, I've tried to think about the qualities required for local office, such as that of alderman: She should be an observer,

175

should explore her entire district looking for the things that need improvement from garbage collection to redlining. On discovering the root causes, she then would begin to formulate legislation for change. Controversy goes hand in hand with change. Truth-telling, often unpopular, is part of the process. If these changes fly in the face of other leaders who have prospered by neglect, a willingness to be persistent (sometimes called stubborn) may be required, along with a gift for sharing goals with a diverse network. A sense of history can bolster the process. The requirements remain the same as the district expands to a state or a nation."

For Nancy Stevenson, politicians who keep their promises, solve problems, are respectful of their colleagues and staff, and represent the interests of their constituents, especially the most vulnerable, can be a vital force for positive change.

Each of the other contributors to this chapter, including Eli Segal, Michael Moskow, Stephen Jones commenting on Congressman Paul Findley, Michael Golden discussing Melissa Bean, and Cameron Davis, consider the sacrifices and rewards of public service.

Eli Segal

Turning a Vision into Reality

**"Eli Segal is the best person I know who can take a vision and
turn it into a tangible reality."
President Bill Clinton**

ELI SEGAL, a classmate of mine at Brandeis University in the 1960s, was extraordinarily charismatic and, by the first day of classes, he had memorized the names and hometowns of all four hundred of our fellow classmates. Upon meeting someone for the first time, a typical Eli greeting would be, "Nice to meet you, Ellen. How is life in Utica, New York?" He ran for president of the freshman class. I attached myself to his coattails and ran for class vice president, and both of us were elected.

My political career abruptly ended after that sojourn, but Eli took his talent all the way to the White House. He was chief of staff for Bill Clinton's 1992 presidential campaign, and then, as Clinton's assistant, he led two major social reform programs, AmeriCorps and Welfare-to-Work.

AmeriCorps allowed hundreds of thousands of students to pay for college by performing community service. The Welfare-to-Work Partnership encouraged businesses to hire people so they could end their dependence on welfare. Both programs were so effective that President George W. Bush kept them when he was elected and sent AmeriCorps volunteers to help with the Hurricane Katrina clean-up.

Eli was exceedingly inventive in finding ways to help people support his ideas. True story: It was Eli's task to convince Congress to support the bill that established AmeriCorps. He needed West Virginia Sen. Robert Byrd's vote but couldn't even get an appointment to talk with him. He told the other senator from West Virginia, Jay Rockefeller, that he needed a favor — he needed an appointment to see Senator Byrd. Rockefeller told him, "You know I love you, Eli, but I've already used up all my political capital with Sen. Byrd."

Eli grew up in Brooklyn. He was a fanatic about baseball and noticed photographs of baseball players on the walls of Rockefeller's office. Eli said, "I'll make a deal with you. You ask me any question about baseball in the

1950s. If I get the answer right, you'll find a way for me to see Senator Byrd. If not, I won't bother you anymore."

"Who was the organist at Ebbets Field?" Rockefeller asked.

"Gladys Gooding," replied Eli, "but that's too easy. Give me another question."

Rockefeller tried again. "Who were the principles in the trade when the New York Giants acquired Alvin Dark?"

"The Boston Braves traded Eddie Stanky along with Alvin Dark to the New York Giants in exchange for Sid Gordon, Buddy Kerr, Willard Marshall and Red Webb," answered Eli.

Eli got his meeting. And he got Byrd's vote! President Clinton awarded Segal the Presidential Citizens Medal, stating, "Eli Segal was the best person he knew who could take a vision and turn it into a tangible reality."

However, when in Eli's presence, one would never know about his accomplishments. When he was with you, he genuinely wanted to know about *you* and *your* family. He made you feel as if you were the only person in the room.

Eli died after a battle with cancer in 2006. His life was an unfinished symphony. Fortunately, his legacy continues through the Eli J. & Phyllis N. Segal Citizen Leadership Program at Brandeis University, which is fostering the next generation of community leaders.

Barack Obama said, "That's when America soars, when we look out for one another, and we take care of each other, and we try to build something better for generations to come. That's why we do what we do. That's the whole point of public service."

Michael Moskow

The Right Place at the Right Time

"I always tried to pick the best people and was conscientious
about helping my associates develop and improve."
Michael Moskow

MICHAEL MOSKOW HELD fourteen different positions during his professional career, but it wasn't because he had trouble keeping a steady job!

He taught at several universities, worked in government and in private industry, and was confirmed by the senate for five government positions. These included deputy secretary at the Dept. of Labor under Sec. George Shultz, director of the Council on Wage and Price Stability, assistant secretary at HUD, and senior staff economist with the Council of Economic Advisors.

In 1991, President George H.W. Bush appointed Moskow Deputy U.S. Trade Representative, responsible for negotiations with Japan, China, and Southeast Asian countries. He had the rank of ambassador, which gave him sufficient gravitas and stature to be taken seriously in high-level international trade negotiations.

Meeting Carla Hills, head of the Department of U.S. Trade Representatives, led to this appointment.

Michael negotiated an excellent trade agreement with Japan. He negotiated all night, and the agreement was not finished until President George H. W. Bush and the prime minister of Japan walked into the room for the press conference the next morning to announce the results. Working as a trade representative was one of the best jobs in D.C., he said. "It was a small agency with little bureaucracy, and by negotiating with other countries, you could help set U. S. policy." For example, he negotiated with the European Union to reduce subsidies on the Airbus.

From 1994 to 2007, Moskow was president and CEO of the Federal Reserve Bank of Chicago. He is currently vice chairman and distinguished fellow on the global economy at the Chicago Council on Global Affairs, and he serves on the board of directors of several financial institutions.

So how did he manage all of this? He told me that being in the right place at the right time had a lot to do with it. For example, he taught high school for a year, then went to the University of Pennsylvania where he got a PhD specializing in labor economics. While a graduate student, he took courses from George Taylor, an expert in labor relations and advisor to five presidents. Moskow, realizing that collective bargaining rights among public school teachers would be a rapidly emerging field, wrote his thesis on this topic. This led to meeting John Dunlop, a labor relations expert, who would be appointed Secretary of Labor by President Gerald Ford. Dunlop subsequently recommended Moskow for the Council of Economic Advisors. That was the first of his many government jobs.

Two of Michael's heroes are Carla Hills and Don Kelly, former head of Esmark. They had extremely different management styles. Hills, Moskow said, was brilliant, hardworking and a very hands-on manager. Kelly, who didn't have a college degree, was street smart, read people extremely well, and was at the other end of the management spectrum, a "huge delegator."

At the Federal Reserve, Michael utilized both management styles. When he arrived, the structure was hierarchical. Michael set a different tone and worked hard to change the working environment. For example, he asked people to call him by his first name and welcomed suggestions from colleagues, regardless of their position. Also, he got all the senior executives actively involved in the effort to change the culture.

I asked Michael what personal qualities had served him well. He said, "I am not the smartest guy or the most technically proficient, but I am a good listener and a good team player. I always tried to pick the best people, and I was conscientious about helping my associates develop and improve." His peers, he said, describe him as having integrity, humility, a high drive to succeed, and an especially high Emotional Quotient (he was good at reading the room).

When I asked Michael to contribute to this book, he quite seriously said, "I'm not sure there'll be interest in my modest contribution." I suspect that Michael is wrong, and that his remarkable and distinguished career as a public servant will be an inspiration to many.

Stephen Jones

An Exemplary Public Servant

**"Congressman Findley served the people in his district, heard
them, and acted for them."**
Stephen Jones

STEPHEN JONES HAS HAD a distinguished career practicing law and as a
public servant. When I asked him what qualities are required to be an exem-
plary public servant, he easily could have discussed his own career, but
instead he responded by describing Congressman Paul Findley:

"Elected to congress as a Republican in 1960, Paul Findley held the
congressional district in western Illinois that Abraham Lincoln had represented in the House of Representatives in the 1840s. Findley had been
publisher of a small-town newspaper, which he acquired from the daughter of
John Nicolay, one of President Lincoln's secretaries.

"More than half a century ago, in 1966, when I was twenty-five years old,
Mr. Findley hired me, at the end of a day of interviews and travel with him
throughout the district. I became his administrative assistant to serve as his
speech writer and legislative assistant, and eventually, Chief of Staff. It was
the beginning of a lifelong friendship and collaboration. When he died at age
94 in 2018, I was honored to deliver the eulogy at his funeral. I was also his
attorney.

"When Mr. Findley came to Congress, it was a time when friendship,
good humor, collegiality, and practical politics existed among his House
colleagues. Many of his close friends were Democrats. He looked after the
hard daily business of our democracy. As a public servant, he was honest, and
financially, morally, intellectually, and politically incorruptible. He was not
interested in soundbites, or ideology, or calling attention inappropriately to
himself. He was kind, generous, forgiving, and helpful. Even though he was a
member of the minority party in Congress, because of his own personality,
intellect, and political courage, he managed to have significant influence.

"He secured the appointment of the first African American congressional
page, Frank Mitchell. His disclosure of all those Americans who lost their
lives in the Vietnam conflict became the inspiration for the Vietnam Memorial. Alone, one day on the floor of the House, he blocked a third term for

181

General Earle Wheeler as Chairman of the Joint Chiefs of Staff, believing that the policies being pursued in Vietnam were grossly in error.

"He released the names of all individuals who received more than five thousand dollars a year in agricultural subsidies. He was the first Congressional Republican to urge full normalization of diplomatic relations with the People's Republic of China. When Dr. Martin Luther King was assassinated, Mr. Findley urged that Dr. King should be buried in Arlington National Cemetery.

"He knew his people, farmers, small town businessmen and their families; he knew their kind of life – their kind of problems. He served on the House Committee on Foreign Affairs and the Agriculture Committee. He wrote a book about federal agricultural policies, titled *The Federal Farm Fable*. Much of the research for the book was conducted by Mollie Martin Broussard, the high school debate coach shared by Stephen Jones and me!

"Despite all the awards, honors, and recognition Mr. Findley received, his congressional service was best summarized in an article in *The Washington Post* titled "Representative in Congress." It simply listed Mr. Findley's weekend schedule for the forthcoming Saturday and Sunday in the district, which demonstrated this was a congressman who came close to the people, served them, heard them, and acted for them.

"He was uplifting, an inspiration to many young people. He hired more summer interns than any other Congressman. He was a strong supporter of NATO. He always stood for free enterprise agriculture and believed that the family farm was the bedrock of American civilization. He lifted everyone's spirits when he walked into a room."

Stephen added, "Over half a century later, there are only a few like him in Congress, and they are a dwindling number."

When I asked Stephen what life lessons he learned from Congressman Findley, he replied, "For me, Washington was indeed a City on the Hill; from him I learned that I could be right, and my adversary could be right from our different perspectives; I learned the importance of kindness, that one catches more flies with honey than vinegar. And I learned the importance of courage – not to be cowed or intimidated."

Michael Golden

The Demands of Public Service

"I can assure you, public service is a stimulating, proud and lively enterprise. It is not just a way of life; it is a way to live fully."
Lee H. Hamilton

MICHAEL GOLDEN IS the author of *Unlock Congress: Reform The Rules – Restore The System.* When I asked Michael about the challenges and the rewards of public service, this was his response:

"A typical comment concerning politicians goes something like, "I can't stand any of them! They all go into politics just for themselves. They never leave — buncha grifters!"

Michael continued, "I usually let it go in one ear and out the other. But I do know someone who won't let it go. And she knows what she's talking about because she ran against long odds — and won! And then proceeded to pour her life into the job. Her name is Melissa Bean. She was my boss in 2005-06 when she ran for reelection in the 8th Congressional District of Illinois. Two years earlier, running as a moderate, she defeated a 35-year incumbent — the longest serving member of the U.S. House on the other side of the aisle. I asked Melissa how she would respond if someone told her that she was just another self-interested political hustler? Melissa stated that the question was far from hypothetical. This was her response."

"That literally just happened yesterday! I always challenge them. I was walking out of a restaurant and this couple started talking to us. Somehow it got around to politics and the economy, and the guy says something like: 'Well, it's not like they're doing anything. This president and these members of Congress. All politicians are terrible.'"

"Melissa, who served from 2004-2010, surprised the critic with her reply. 'Well, I just have to challenge you on that as a former member of Congress. I just know that's not true. There are plenty of hardworking members of Congress who are there for the right reasons that want to help you.'"

"The couple was shocked: 'Wait — what? You were in Congress?'"

"Yes. But you've got to pay attention to those members to see if they're representing you, and if they're not, you must get rid of them. But there are real people in Congress. They're all real people."

Michael continued, "Political campaigns are rough. Doing the actual job is grueling in a whole different way. I don't think most folks really understand just what raising money while, at the same time, performing the work does to a person's life. As Melissa's campaign manager, I would literally yell at her to make more fundraising calls (this was 10 years before I wrote a book about draining the "money flood" out of Congress). She'd yell back about everything that being a member of the House demanded. We went at it a lot, but always with respect because we both believed in the goal. That said, the sacrifice is truly brutal. I asked Melissa to describe it."

Melissa responded, "I mean, it's your quality of life. It's a huge challenge, which is why I would never urge anyone to do it lightly. It's not like any other job. It's 24/7 from the minute you pull the trigger. You're running all the time. You're missing your kids' stuff. You do have to say to your family, 'I'm going to be stepping out in a way to do this.'"

"Melissa is far from naive about the hyper-dysfunction on Capitol Hill. But she still takes pride in the big things that Congress passed over her six years. Among them, health care, equal pay for equal work, cracking down on credit card companies for ripping off customers through hidden fees and higher interest rates — even the stimulus packages that were passed under presidents from both parties."

Melissa elaborated, "I had a guy come up to me at a train station and say: 'I just want to thank you so much, because that tax credit made the difference of whether we could send our daughter to college. So, thank you for voting for it!'" Melissa hadn't just voted for it; she was one of the members who had introduced it in the first place. She says it's one of those things that made the whole experience worthwhile."

"I grew up in a family where both of my parents' mantra was: 'Quit bitching; fix it. Just do it.' So, I ran. And I've never had a job where you could make the kind of impact you can being a member of Congress. While it was the most exhausting, demanding, flat out almost breaks you kind of job — it was also the most fulfilling thing I've ever done."

Cameron Davis

An Enlightened Environmentalist

"How we treat our planet is a reflection of how we treat ourselves. And in this age when division and anger seem to be everywhere, water is something that unites us. We all need it to survive and thrive."
Cameron Davis

CAMERON DAVIS IS an advocate for the environment. During the Obama Administration, he served as the president's point person for the $2.2-billion project to clean up, restore and protect the Great Lakes region. From 2018 to the present, he has served as a commissioner on the Metropolitan Water Reclamation District of Greater Chicago (MWRD).

As a public interest clean water attorney, he has served as president and CEO of the Alliance for the Great Lakes, where he successfully led the campaign to ban oil and gas drilling under Lake Michigan, and defeated an attempt by British Petroleum to increase pollution discharges to Lake Michigan. Davis's environmental work began as a volunteer organizer cleaning up the beaches of the Great Lakes region.

His work to preserve the natural resources of the planet is deeply tied to his commitment to other people and to living a worthwhile life. Asked what the most important life lesson that he would want to pass on to future generations, he answers, "I teach my kids to be helpful and kind. These qualities never fail. They're the foundation for family, friendships, business, and living a fulfilling life. And they are good for your soul, helping you to move through life with purpose and peace."

He adds, "Hand-in-hand with this lesson is to think outside of yourself. Especially in our society, it's easy to become self-absorbed, self-centered, and make life all about me, me, me. When you are driven to understand what makes other people tick, it helps you to understand how the world works. It works through the lens of science, politics, psychology, economics, and every other approach. When you push yourself to be curious about life outside of yourself, your inner life becomes more colorful, more adventurous, more worth living."

Cameron says the greatest adversity he faced was "finding my place in the world. I grew up not knowing why I was here and doubting that I mattered. The quality that most helped me overcome adversity was tenacity. Growing up, I looked around and saw people who were smarter than me. Better looking. Wealthy. Athletic. But if you're persistent about the things you believe – living your values – those other things become shadows while you turn into the sunlight."

Cam Davis's commitment to the environment goes back to his teenage years. "In 1979, my family and I were driving to Harrisburg, Pennsylvania, to visit my grandmother for spring break. We heard on the news while driving though Northwest Indiana — at the time a smelly, polluted place—of the nuclear power plant accident at Three Mile Island. The images of Northwest Indiana's steel, oil, and chemical plants, coupled with the threat of nuclear danger, have stuck with me."

"How we treat our planet is a reflection of how we treat ourselves," he adds. "And in this age when division and anger seem to be everywhere, water is something that unites us. We all need it to survive and thrive. It doesn't matter what your age, race, gender identification, physical capabilities, religion...the list goes on...we all have one home. Pick a place and help care for it. Even if it's a small garden, part of the forest preserves, or go big with the Great Lakes, oceans, entire populations of wildlife -- you will be doing your soul a favor."

Asked to name a failure that he experienced from which he learned, Davis says, "Too many to list! I failed to make good grades through most of school, so at school I hung on by my fingernails, barely good enough to get into a decent undergraduate school, then barely good enough to get into law school. Along the way, I figured out later that *how* I learn is different. To learn, I had to *do*. And by nature, *doing* involves failing. Too often, we think of failing as something with finality. You *either* succeed *or* you fail. Failure is embedded within success."

The Value Of Our Relationships

You can make more friends in two months
by becoming really interested in other people,
than you can in two years
by trying to get other people interested in you.
Dale Carnegie

Winter, spring, summer, or fall
All you have to do is call
And I'll be there,
You've got a friend.
Carole King

Friends from College, Book Club

Of Friends and Acquaintances

***"Close relationships — more than money, power, or fame
— lead to a more satisfying life."
The Harvard Study of Adult Development***

THE HARVARD STUDY OF ADULT DEVELOPMENT, which began in 1938, is one of the world's longest studies of adult life, tracking the physical and mental health of 268 Harvard graduates from then until the present. Psychiatrist George Vaillant, who led the study from 1972 until 2004, summed up its findings: "The key to healthy aging is relationships, relationships, relationships."

Close relationships, *more than* money, power, or fame, lead to a more satisfying life. People who are more socially connected to family, friends, and community are happier and physically healthier, and they live longer. The older I get, the more I appreciate the importance of friendship.

I am a member of a group of seven college freshmen, who met in a dormitory at Brandeis University in 1960, and who, remarkably, have remained close friends for more than sixty years. They are listed in the acknowledgments. We have celebrated weddings and other joyous events, gone on vacations together, and sadly, attended the funerals of one of our original group and two spouses.

Developing new friendships requires a commitment of time and energy. Marshaling those resources becomes more difficult as we get older. I have been a member of a book club for more than thirty years, and that has been an excellent way to develop rapport with new acquaintances. We meet once a month to socialize and discuss our book selection. It is no surprise that what began as a shared interest in books has often evolved into deeper personal relationships. Past and present members also are listed in the acknowledgments.

I've been slow to appreciate that there are different types of friendships. For example, having spent days, even years, making life-and-death decisions together with other physicians, I assumed these shared experiences would naturally result in close friendships. This has not always been the case. While

I do have genuine friendships with some of my professional colleagues, many remain simply acquaintances.

Because we have a limited amount of time and emotional energy, there are only so many people to whom we can feel deeply connected. I call this the short list. Although I've touched, in some small way, the lives of thousands of people, my impression is that I have had a significant effect on only a few. The short list is just that — short.

In this chapter, Igor Perica, Johanna Tabin, Brian Williams, Ernest Werlin, Mickey Jaffe, K. C. Hayes and Roberta Rubin, each present different aspects of the value of our relationships.

Marcel Proust said, "Let us be grateful for our friends; they are the charming gardeners who make our souls blossom."

Igor Perica and Irina Kirilova

Acts of Kindness

**"The best portion of a man's life is his little, nameless,
unremembered acts of kindness and of love."
William Wordsworth**

IF I HAD to pick only one piece of advice to pass on to my children, grandchildren, and students, my top pick would be this: to perform acts of kindness without expectation of anything in return.

Igor Perica, a 6-foot, 7-inch power forward, was a professional basketball player from Croatia who had torn his anterior cruciate ligament (ACL). In 1998, he came to the United States for surgery, and I reconstructed his torn ligament.

I wanted to do everything possible to make the experience a positive one for Igor. Not only was he injured, but he was also a stranger in a strange land. I negotiated reduced hospital and medical costs on his behalf, obtained a hotel room for him near the hospital, and visited him each day during his stay, something I had routinely done for several patients who came to the United States for surgery.

Igor and I developed a close relationship. He made an excellent recovery, and subsequently said that because of the surgery his injured knee was stronger than it had ever been. He was able to return to his previous level of skill as a world-class basketball player. An unexpected bonus of coming to the U.S. for his surgery was that he met a woman and fell in love. They were later married in Chicago, and I was thrilled to be part of a festive Croatian wedding celebration.

Igor said that he wanted to do something to repay my kindness to him. My response was that meeting him and his having an excellent recovery were more than enough. I certainly never expected anything else.

However, two months later he said 'thank you' by sending me another patient who lived in Croatia. Irina Kirilova was the best female volleyball player in the world. She had won a gold medal representing the former Soviet Union at the 1988 Olympic games in Seoul. In 1990 she was named by her peers as the world's best female volleyball player. Later, she moved to Croatia to continue her career and afterwards became coach of the Croatian national team. Ivica Dukan, Director of International Scouting for the Chicago Bulls, told me that in Europe, Irina was as famous as Michael Jordan was in the United States.

Like Igor, she had torn her anterior cruciate ligament. He knew that Irina could have chosen from among several surgeons in Europe and in the United States, but he convinced her to consult me. He said to Irina, "You can do what you like, but I feel so good about Dr. Lewis. He was like a friend."

After surgery, she too regained her previous abilities. As with Igor, I did my best to make her experience as positive as possible, including surprising her on her birthday during a postoperative visit by decorating her room with colorful streamers and balloons. When she returned to Europe, she continued to play at the highest professional level for several more years.

Witnessing Irina Kirilova's successful surgical outcome and her subsequent outstanding career as an athlete has been a highlight of my career in sports medicine. We became friends, and several years later, my wife and I visited her in Italy.

I truly did nothing unusual when I treated Igor Perica. In my experience, we often underestimate the potential impact of the smallest acts of thoughtfulness to another person.

Poet Maya Angelou said, "I've learned that people will forget what you said, people will forget what you did, but people will never forget how you made them feel."

Johanna Tabin

Cherished Friend

**"To my mind, having a care and concern for others
is the highest of the human qualities."
Fred Hollows**

WILLIAM GLADSTONE and Benjamin Disraeli were two famous British
prime ministers of the nineteenth century. It was said that after you dined
with Gladstone, you left thinking that he was one of the most intelligent and
interesting people you had ever met. After you had dinner with Disraeli, you
left thinking that *you* were a clever, fascinating person. But Disraeli was no
match for Johanna Tabin. She was full of empathy, understanding, and
wisdom, and knew just how to make everyone around her feel appreciated
and important.

The Buddhist concept of mudita, a pure unselfish joy in the good fortune
of others, applied to her. She had that splendid capacity to feel happy simply
because you were happy.

Johanna Tabin epitomized the characteristics of an intuitive and empa-
thetic friend. She had the ability to choose exactly the right words to soothe
and heal. She overflowed with kindness and compassion. She also had an
extraordinary memory. For example, she would remember each of the activities her friend's grandchildren were involved in and ask about them years
later.

She was a nationally recognized psychoanalyst, and she had a wide diver-
sity of friends and acquaintances. She understood people and their foibles.
She used that knowledge to help them to help themselves. For example, she
would send me patients from time to time. A typical phone call would be,
"Please take good care of my friend. She is a remarkable, generous person who
can sometimes be a little demanding, and is a little down on her luck just
now." She responded to the questions you needed to ask, rather than simply
the ones you verbalized.

A Freudian analyst, Johanna spent uncounted hours to read and critique
a book I had written about Abraham Maslow, a psychologist with a very
different philosophy from Freud's. Even though Johanna didn't agree with

193

many of Maslow's premises, she made numerous insightful suggestions. Even at the end of her life, she never stopped caring for and inspiring others.

Here are two emails Johanna Tabin wrote to me approximately a month before she passed away:

Dear Cherished friend, I hope we can get together in the next couple of days. The results are that this is a Stage 4 lung tumor. I am hoping that the EGF receptor mutation popped up. That treatment is easily tolerated, as well as offering some real hope. Nonetheless, the future is crazily clouded. I am dwelling on my blessings. Your friendship is one of the wonderful things on my mind.

Love, Johanna

Dear Cherished friend, I cannot predict anything except that seeing you and your mother would feel wonderful. I am delighted to hear about your mother recovering so well from her recent surgery and the precious time you had together. Love, Johanna.

Remarkable! Imagine that during her last days on earth, while fighting for her own life, she continued her mission: being concerned about our well-being, taking care of us, comforting us, inspiring us.

I learned many life lessons from Johanna Tabin: Focus on what is important to the other person. Take genuine pleasure in your friend's success. Never take friendship for granted, especially because one never knows what tomorrow delivers.

Brian Williams

A Tale of a Too-Brief Friendship

***True friends are hard to find, difficult to leave, and impossible
to forget.***
G. Randolf

DURING MY TENURE with the Chicago Bulls, I developed many rewarding
relationships. But real friendship was an exception.

Brian Williams was one of those exceptions. He came to the Bulls with
nine games remaining at the end of the 1997 season and was an essential
factor in the team winning its fifth championship. He played all 19 playoff
games, averaging 6.1 points and 3.7 rebounds per game. Steve Kerr said that
the Bulls would not have won without Brian's contribution.

Given his wide-ranging intelligence and many passions, this left-handed
forward clearly marched to the beat of several different drummers. He
had a pilot's license. He had traveled the world extensively, running with the
bulls in Pamplona, Spain, camping in the Australian outback, and going to
Beirut during the Lebanese Civil War.

Brian also composed music and played the saxophone, trumpet, and
violin. He loved Miles Davis and wanted to hear every detail related to when
I had heard him perform live in San Francisco and New York. His philosophy
was to never stop learning, and he had the energy to pursue his all-encom-
passing interests. As writer Annie Dillard said, "Make connections; let rip;
and dance where you can."

One of the things Brian and I bonded over was a book, "*Surely You're
Joking, Mr. Feynman!*" written by Nobel Laureate Richard Feynman, a brilliant theoretical physicist. While other players for the Chicago Bulls were
playing cards or listening to music on the plane to a playoff game in Utah,
Brian was reading Feynman's book.

Brian and I developed an instant friendship. We would talk about music,
travel, and philosophy. We had so many areas of common interest. C. S. Lewis
said, "Friendship is born when one person says to another: 'What! You too? I
thought I was the only one."

Brian was obsessed with exploring the world of ideas. He loved to discuss
Friedrich Nietzsche. He believed in his declaration that he who has a 'why' to

195

live, can bear almost any 'how.' He described the excitement of Formula One racing and was disappointed that at 6 feet 11 inches, he was much too tall to drive one of their cars. It was one of many examples of his wide-ranging interests. My wife and I had met Brian's mother, Patricia, an anthropologist, at the 1997 Bulls championship celebration party. I told her how much I felt connected to Brian, and she said she knew that the feeling was reciprocal.

After Brian moved on to the Detroit Pistons, our friendship continued. That year he officially changed his name to Bison Dele, to reflect his Cherokee and African heritage. He would call out of the blue and say, "Bison here, as you know, I have a pilot's license, so we will go flying together." I looked forward to hearing from him and continuing our friendship.

In 1999, at age 30, Bison decided to quit basketball and sail around the world. No one will ever know for sure what happened the summer of 2002 on his 56-foot-long catamaran, Hakuna Matata. Brian appears to have died under mysterious circumstances. I felt a deep connection with him, so I was devastated.

While Bison's life ended much sooner than it should have, I am thankful for the time we had together. His death emphasizes to us that the wheel of fortune can turn in an instant and how essential it is to never miss an opportunity to let people know how important they are to you.

Mindfulness guru Jon Kabat-Zinn stated, "Share the fullness of your being, your best self, your enthusiasm, your vitality, your spirit, your trust, your openness, and above all your presence."

Ernest "Doc" Werlin, Mickey Jaffe

Honesty, and Integrity: A Winning Combination

**"A person's wealth is the culmination of his relationships with
friends and family."
Ernest "Doc" Werlin**

ERNEST "DOC" Werlin spent his professional career as an investment banker,
and Jay M. ("Mickey") Jaffe has run his own independent consulting business
for almost 50 years. However, neither of them defines wealth in terms of
money. Both define the good life by the quality of their relationships.

Ernest Werlin was educated at the University of Texas Austin and
Oxford University. From there he went directly to Wall Street in 1969. "A
friend of mine noted that coming to Wall Street from Oxford was comparable
to a priest leaving the monastery and walking into a jungle." Ernest himself
says of the start of his career, "I spent most of the next decade trying to
survive." Survive he did, spending 35 years on Wall Street in fixed income as
a trader and eventually head of the corporate bond trading department at
Morgan Stanley. He retired in 2004.

In 2008 he started writing a column, "Doc's Prescription" for the *Sarasota
Herald-Tribune*. It seemed almost a foregone conclusion that he would end up
in the newspaper business. His mother, Rosella Werlin, was an accomplished
journalist, and Ernest was named after the famous World War II correspon-
dent Ernie Pyle.

When I asked Ernest what qualities are essential for success, he
responded, "Truthfulness is fundamental. The importance of honesty is the
cornerstone of all relationships. My having this reputation has been indis-
pensable in forming my relationship with family, lifelong friends, business
associates, and even casual acquaintances. I take great pride in my personal
relationships."

He emphasizes the importance of empathy: "Over time I have learned the
value of walking in another person's shoes for one mile." As a result, Ernest
has been an extremely generous benefactor for many organizations. He says,
"It is indeed better to give than receive. I get so much joy out of my charitable
endeavors." These include creating the Ernest "Doc" and Eloise Werlin Park
in downtown Sarasota, Florida. "I also have been hosting events for non-

profits ranging from Children's First, The Police Foundation, Jack and Jill Late-Stage Cancer Foundation, Coming Together Against Cancer, Moffitt Cancer Center, and Lymphoma and Leukemia Association."

Mickey Jaffe has been president of his own actuarial consulting company for almost half a century. I asked him how he had managed to be successful for so long when many of his colleagues tried independent consulting and ended up going back to more traditional kinds of employment.

Although Mickey is a man with strong ideas, he said, "I try to understand my clients' needs and to provide solutions for them. When they do not accept my recommendations, I don't take those decisions personally."

When I asked Mickey how he defined success, he responded, "Success can't be measured simply in terms of income. My biggest feeling of success has come from compliments from my peers. The satisfaction of being recommended for an assignment by a peer is about as satisfying as it gets."

Mickey continues, "Being a professional requires several attributes, but possibly the most important is integrity. I feel it is my most important persuasion tool. If there's something that I don't believe should be done, I'll explain my position to the client. If these explanations fail, then in a few instances I've had to resort to explaining to a client that if I do what he or she is asking, I could 'lose my license.' So far, this message has always resulted in the client agreeing with my position. Always be true to your beliefs."

For Ernest Werlin and Mickey Jaffe, the basis for successful relationships couldn't be more straightforward: honesty and integrity.

Stephen Covey said, "Trust is the glue of life. It is the foundational principle that holds all relationships."

K.C. Hayes

In Hot Pursuit of Love, Truth, and Beauty

"Love is the only Truth."
K. C. Hayes

K. C. Hayes is Professor Emeritus of Biology and director of the Foster Biomedical Research Laboratories at Brandeis University. He is also a poet, photographer, and philosopher. He frequently sends eCards via email. I find them to be beautiful, thought-provoking, and inspiring.

K. C.'s philosophy behind these eCards follows: "Poet John Keats stated, "Beauty is truth, truth beauty, — that is all ye know on earth, and all ye need to know."

"For the past 20 years, I have been trying to demonstrate this hypothesis by pursuing what I call a SearchForSoul through my weekly eCards. They are a combination of my photography and my verse meant to express Love around Agape (the Greek term for Sharing and Caring). The recurrent theme in these eCards concerns Love, Truth, and Beauty. I'm in hot pursuit of how they are interrelated in real time, in the person-to-person expression I call SoulTalk. It represents the truest expression of Self, a connection of mind and soul that lies beneath the persona that we typically share with each other.

"I try to meld thoughts like these with images from my photo files. Thus, I attempt to capture through the camera lens "Beautiful Truths" (by my own estimation) in nature, often with nurturing aspects of human interaction. Then I attempt to translate that piece of my soul into a word form for you, the recipient interpreter, such that my soul shines through to yours in SoulTalk.

"Maybe you see or feel my soul, maybe you don't, but in the process of that attempted exchange of experiences, you will expose your soul to a new adventure, at the very least, assuming I have done my part correctly, and you are a willing listener.

"Beauty, I sense, is immediately recognized by each of us when we encounter it, based on a uniquely human physiological response. What makes art so interesting...if good and rewarding, is that it evokes the total experience around our connection to another's Soul. Truth is more complex. and not always successful, because it requires assimilation of experiences by individual human beings with different histories and understandings of the world.

"Sharing and Caring, along with the "big six" personality traits of humility, honesty, kindness, an ability to forgive, generosity and gratitude...that's what living as a self-actualized person is all about.

"I see, as my daily calling, teaching others how to Share and Care. This is best done when those being taught are learning by choice to perfect a personal skill set that they can one day use for the benefit of all. The most critical time for this exchange to occur is during adolescence.

"Love means so many different things to different people. We may never really know what love is, but it does not matter, really, because in its pursuit, through soulful exchanges, is the secret to joyous living, or so I believe."

To be part of K. C. Hayes's search for truth, love, and beauty through photography, philosophy, and poetry, you may request his eCards by emailing kchayes@brandeis.edu and asking to be put on his mailing list.

K. C. Hayes concludes, "For me the bottom line is that Love (agape, or empathic caring) is the only Truth....mine for you, yours for me through Soul-Talk in an intimate exchange that is beyond romance (Eros). It is through this honest and open empathic SoulTalk that one learns to identify and nurture feelings of connectedness through our lifetimes. This is what I believe makes life worth living."

Roberta Rubin

Be Here Now

"Continue to educate yourself, to listen and express kindness, and to stay involved."
Roberta Rubin

WHEN I recently asked Roberta Rubin to share a life lesson from her experiences, she responded, "I have been listening to Peter, Paul, and Mary singing "Blowin' in the Wind." I really feel the words and emotions as I sing along. The song, written by Bob Dylan, really resonates with me right now. It seems to embody much of what Dylan believes. "I feel his pain, his sensitivities, and his goals for our future. The song asks: How many roads must a man walk down, Before you call him a man? How many seas must a white dove sail, Before she sleeps in the sand? ... And how many ears must one man have before he can hear people cry? Yes, and how many deaths will it take 'til he knows, that too many people have died? The answer my friend is, blowin' in the wind, the answer is blowin' in the wind."

Roberta said she wishes she had a simple life lesson to impart to readers. "I wish I could say, *"The answers are blowin' in the wind."* But life is more complicated than that.

"The lesson I have learned throughout a lifetime is that there is no simple answer to Dylan's questions: *How many roads, how many deaths,* and so on." She has concluded that she must continue to educate herself, to be there, to listen and express her kindness as frequently as possible. Furthermore, it was necessary to stay involved with old friends from the past and new ones from her present, and to try to make the world a better place to live."

She said, "I was fortunate to have been in the book business because my shop afforded many opportunities each day to connect with people. But now, with so much information coming at us through social media, or just our cellphones, life is more complicated than ever before. As I am getting older, I have to work harder on *hearing people cry* and *not to turn my head and pretend that I just don't see.*"

Abraham Maslow describes people on the path to self-actualization as having the capacity to appreciate life's daily activities as fresh experiences. He says, "The present moment is filled with joy and happiness. If you're attentive, you will see it." Roberta highlights the importance of being in the moment. She says, "As American spiritual teacher Baba Ram Dass wrote in his brilliant book *Be Here Now,* I try to *Be Here Now*. I try not to be too busy, too overwhelmed, too scheduled, so that I am *Here Now*. That is the lesson I want to offer for others, and for myself."

The poet Rumi said, "This is now. Now is. Don't postpone till then. Spend the spark of iron on stone. Sit at the head of the table. Dip your spoon in the bowl. Seat yourself next to your joy and have your awakened soul pour joy."

Parents, Siblings, And Children

How to live forever: Plant some new seeds.
Give away what you have learned.
The real fountain of youth is – the fountain with youth.
Marc Freedman

Sisters and brothers are the truest,
purest forms of love, family, and friendship,
knowing when to hold you and when to challenge you,
but always being a part of you.
Carol Ann Albright Eastman

Beatrice, Melanie, Hadley Lewis

The Love of Family

"I am grateful that I can be grateful."
Beatrice Lewis

MAYA ANGELOU SAID, "I sustain myself with the love of family."

The following are among the countless lessons I have learned from my parents and children:

My mother, Beatrice Lewis, understood that gratitude is necessary for leading a satisfying life. Every self-help book on the market emphasizes the importance of appreciating one's gifts. My mother was decades ahead of them all. She frequently stated, "I'm grateful that I can be grateful." As writer William Arthur Ward stated, "Feeling gratitude and not expressing it is like wrapping a present and not giving it." For all her 104 years, she was an optimist. She woke up each morning with the disposition that something perfectly wonderful was going to happen that day.

Fortunately, each of us can increase our capacity for gratitude. In her book *The How of Happiness: A Scientific Approach to Getting the Life You Want,* Sonja Lyubomirsky advises keeping a gratitude journal. She suggests making a weekly entry, recording three to five things for which you're thankful. My personal variation on this theme is finding three new things to be grateful for each day.

A dramatic example of being grateful for what we have, and taking nothing for granted, was Superman actor Christopher Reeve, paralyzed from the shoulders down when he was thrown from a horse, who said, "When I see someone get out of a chair, I want to point out to them how lucky they are to be able to do that."

Another insight my mother taught, by her example, is the importance of listening. She would always ask the most thoughtful questions. It was clear that she deeply cared about you and what you had to say. Everyone in her presence could feel her aura, a spiritual energy, when she would focus her attention on you. My daughter Melanie captured it best: "It really does feel Buddha-like to be around my grandmother. Your blood pressure drops, you get closer to enlightenment, and your chances of getting into heaven increase just by proximity, like being nice to this angel makes all the deities happy."

Michael S. Lewis, M.D.

I have acquired as many life lessons from my two daughters as from anyone else. They are filled with passion, creativity, and enthusiasm. My daughter Melanie is inventive and resourceful. She has always been an original thinker. She teaches intuitive organizational skills. My daughter Hadley is a master teacher, accomplished school administrator, and wise counselor.

Fathers and daughters have a mysterious bond. I feel so fortunate that there is such a climate of trust and openness between us. They own my heart.

My daughter Melanie, age three at the time, taught me a valuable lesson about how we can prompt an immediate change in someone else's attitude. One year my family and I were at spring training for the Chicago White Sox in Florida. On a beach in Sarasota, a woman was shuffling along the sand and appeared to be carrying the weight of the world on her stooped shoulders. Melanie, whose head was filled with fairy stories, had never seen her before but spontaneously asked, "Are you a princess?" The woman thought it over, and suddenly her posture became more upright. "Why, yes, I am!" she responded, and continued her walk along the beach with a much livelier step. Her perception of herself immediately changed.

My daughter Hadley is a talented editor. She helped to crystallize many of the ideas for this book. With great effort, she is thrusting me into the 21st century. She has scrupulously edited each contribution, always gently suggesting a simpler and clearer way for me to say more in fewer words. The book has been dramatically improved because of her invaluable insights.

Several of the many life lessons I learned from my father are part of this book, including the chapter on Inspiring Teachers and Mentors. The other contributors to this chapter, Cecilia Conrad, Wayne Goldstein, and Dennis Connolly, write about their relationship with their parents and siblings.

Winston Churchill said, "There is no doubt that it is around the family and the home that all the greatest virtues are created, strengthened and maintained."

Cecilia Conrad

A Duty to Step Up and Speak Up

*"My parents taught me not to let hatred from others cause me
to lose sight of my goals, and 'it's a poor dog that doesn't wag
its own tail.'"*
Cecilia Conrad

ECONOMIST CECILIA CONRAD is a formidable change agent, from her work at the Federal Trade Commission to her responsibilities as an associate dean and vice president at Pomona College, to her current position as managing director at the John D. and Catherine T. MacArthur Foundation.

The MacArthur Foundation's unrestricted grants are among the most prestigious in the United States. Conrad also directs MacArthur Foundation's Lever for Change, an affiliate of the foundation, and 100&Change, a competition for a single $100-million grant for work that will solve a current critical problem.

Cecilia's work in the field of philanthropy is as creative and innovative as that of the MacArthur Fellows. Her ability to "think big" and create new models of giving has improved the lives of millions. In her work, Cecilia honors the contributions and potential of people of all nationalities, races, genders, and religions. She shared some aspects of her family background that engendered her profound commitment to inclusiveness:

"My father taught me never to hate. When I was a pre-teen, my father became the first Black person elected to the Dallas Independent School District Board and the first Black elected to a city-wide office. I had not wanted him to run for public office. I had seen what had happened to other Black fathers who challenged the power structure of the segregated South, and I was scared. However, my father explained that he was one of the few community members whose well-being was independent of that power structure, and therefore it was his duty to step up and speak out. Indeed, he said that it was our duty to stand up and speak out. So, I buried my fear even when I answered threatening and vile phone calls or picked up flyers depicting him in racist caricatures.

"He won the election, but the harassment continued. On the day that he was sworn in, and for the next five or six years, a woman I'll call Dixie Carter attended every board meeting in full Ku Klux Klan regalia and sat in the front row. I never heard my father say a word against her. Eventually, Dixie Carter stopped wearing the Klan regalia, but she continued to attend the meetings. On the day my father retired from the board, after 10 years of service, she came up to him and said, 'Dr. Conrad, I know that I was rough on you when you were elected, but, after watching you all these years, I've decided that you were the one always focused on what was good for the children.'

"By his example, my father taught me not to let hatred from others cause me to lose sight of my goals. He taught me to believe in the human potential for redemption (a lesson that I sometimes forget)."

Cecilia describes an example of how her mother influenced her: "My mother fought alongside my father in the battle for equal opportunity. From her, I learned the courage to stand up for myself. One of her favorite sayings was, 'It's a poor dog that doesn't wag its own tail.' A story told over and over when I was young involved a trip to the local Sears & Roebuck when I was about three years old. Mom was at the sales counter. I decided to get a drink from the closest water fountain. (It must have had child steps because I was tiny.) The salesclerk, looking over my mother's shoulder, became agitated and he exclaimed, 'She's drinking from the white-only fountain!' My mother calmly replied, 'It's okay. She can't read yet.' And we quickly left the store. My mother guessed that a salesclerk who had just made a commissioned sale of a major appliance was not going to have the customer arrested. He also probably never forgot that encounter. The key lesson here is to 'assess the risks and decide when, where and how to take a stand.'"

Wayne M. Goldstein, M.D.

Father Did Know Best

"My father didn't tell me how to live; he lived and let me watch him do it."
Clarence Budington Kelland

ORTHOPEDIC SURGEON WAYNE M. GOLDSTEIN'S vision was to create a musculoskeletal healthcare organization with dedicated teams of highly trained professionals. As the founder and president of Illinois Bone and Joint Institute, he implemented his vision in 1990.

Prior to this, orthopedic surgeons, who often had solo practices or were members of a small group, were known to be independent, competitive, and territorial. Remarkably, Wayne convinced them that it was better to work together. IBJI now has more than 150 physicians and is the largest orthopedic group practice in Illinois. This enables a patient to have access to all the subspecialties within orthopedic surgery, such as hip and knee replacement, hand and upper extremity, sports medicine, trauma, and pediatric orthopedics.

Wayne, a specialist in hip and knee reconstruction and revision surgery, is an innovator in minimum incision total hip replacement.

I asked Wayne what qualities he possesses that have resulted in his success.

He responded, "I was fortunate to have parents who guided me towards leadership and creativity. My mother was a musician, a playwright, and an organizer of clubs in which everyone performed, whether talented or not. She made me do theater at the age of 12 along with another young boy, Merrick Garland, (who happens currently to be attorney general of the United States).

"My father and his brothers grew up with a mother who was a single parent. He was an excellent student. He subsequently was in WWII in the Pacific. When he returned home, he met my mother and became a CPA.

"He was a gentle and affectionate man who taught me qualities that have persisted my entire life. He would tell me to be kind, to be generous with time and money, and to be honest. He told me to work hard because any task worth doing is worth doing well. He reminded me as I succeeded in my life and career to always be humble, for success can vanish in a second.

209

"My father was a person who would never tolerate cheating and made sure that respect must be at the forefront, because words and behavior are powerful tools that can hurt. He also instructed me to never fight with a weaker person, since victory would be meaningless and could come back to hurt me.

"I have attempted to live like this my entire life. When building Illinois Bone and Joint Institute, I never stated that any person worked for me but rather worked with me. As you build a family or a business, it is never just because of you alone as an individual, but also the people that help you grow. When you are met with people or organizations that may have treated you unfairly, you must still respond with kindness and respect. This eventually may cause these people to follow your ideas.

"My father was an excellent son, husband, father, and friend. He and my mother were married for 71 years.

"He always told me to never confuse spirituality with rituals. Finally, he would tell me to keep learning. Although one has many experiences in life, there is always something new to learn. He laid down a blueprint of life for me that I always wanted to emulate."

Wayne concludes, "Success never is how much wealth you can have, but instead is leaving a legacy of improving the lives of family, friends, patients and acquaintances and asking nothing in return, besides seeing it all come together."

Dennis Connolly

My Brother, My Inspiration

"Some of what life throws at us may be interpreted as a heavy burden or welcomed as an exceptional gift."
Dennis Connolly

I RECENTLY ASKED pediatric dentist Dennis Connolly who has been an important teacher in his life. What follows is his response:

"At age eight, a wonderful gift arrived in my life when my mother gave birth to a baby boy, named George, soon to be nicknamed 'Judgie.' Without his conscious knowledge, he profoundly affected every individual in my family, as well as our family dynamic.

"Some of what life throws at us may be interpreted as a heavy burden or welcomed as an exceptional gift. I vividly remember working in our yard when my dad (a hard-working ex-marine with a high level of expectations for himself and his children) came home from visiting my mom in the hospital. I rushed toward him in expectation of news about our new baby, but sensed anxiety and curtness in my dad's manner. I dropped my rake and greeted him, 'Dad, a boy or a girl?' He answered with redness in his face, 'Your brother has some problems; I expect twice as much out of you now.'

"At that time, I had no idea what he meant. The next day my mom and new brother came home and instead of witnessing excitement and happiness, an aura of sullenness and darkness occupied our house. Depression overcame my mom. Tension prevailed between my parents. My brother was a beautiful, red-headed boy with Down's Syndrome, a chromosomal development presenting a variety of characteristics which frequently include slow and diminished mental development.

"In our family, my parents were striving and accomplished, and expectations for my siblings and me were high. The birth of a child with special needs and lesser potential seemed to put a wedge in my parents' relationship. They both somehow felt guilty for this genetic random occurrence.

"The first impact that my brother had on me was feeling love and a wish to help this innocent child. He had been slower to demonstrate those things that we take for granted in babies: crawling and walking and speech, and reaction to tactile, visual. and auditory stimuli. Somehow at my pre-adolescent

211

age, I wanted to protect and help him. I developed *patience* that I previously had not identified in myself.

"When the neighbor kids or relatives treated him with uneasiness or avoidance or ridicule, I became more defensive. This evolved into greater *empathy*. As I grew into teen years, my only brother continued to need assistance but seemed happy. That observation led to my personal *appreciation* for all the abilities that I could tap and utilize that he did not possess.

"Judgie passed away at age seven from congenital cardiac disease.

"As my life and education progressed, the memory of my brother influenced me to pursue the profession of Pediatric Dentistry where about twenty-five percent of my patients had special needs or were under-served. The *empathy* that developed from my relationship with my brother and the consequential *appreciation* led me to volunteer with health care teams in Central America, in inner city clinics, and in programs that served children with special needs.

"As I've aged, I have been severely restricted because of macular degeneration. The gift of my brother, Judgie, in my life allows me to look at my current situation (though through a blurry view), realize my limitations, and appreciate my opportunities.

"I believe that we can regard many of the people that we meet as teachers if we are open to learning and growing. Judgie taught me generously without realizing that he was teaching, and my life has been more fulfilled because of him."

Spiritual Journeys

*"What way of living is compatible
with the grandeur and mystery of life?"*
Abraham Joshua Heschel

*You are a fragment of God.
Do not be ignorant of your high birth.
Epictetus*

Michael Lewis

What Religion Means to Me

"The root of religion is what to do with our feelings of awe and wonder when confronted with the mystery of living."
Abraham Joshua Heschel

THE CONTRIBUTORS to this chapter on religion, Elie Wiesel, Al Madansky, Kathy Bhartia, Greg Ekbom, Steve Hefter, and Jim Munson, cover a broad spectrum of beliefs. They range from orthodox Judaism and evangelical Christianity to one who does not believe in a supreme being. These thought-provoking essays compelled me to attempt to clarify my own beliefs.

All religions consist of a system of attitudes and beliefs to make sense of life's experiences. My heritage is Judaism. One important perspective toward life it seeks to encourage is simhah, or joy. For me this includes observing Shabbat every Friday night, especially when I can bless my children, grandchildren, nieces, and nephews. At the same time, Judaism teaches humility and empathy. The book of Exodus describes how we were slaves in Egypt. This enables us easily to identify with others who are "strangers in a strange land."

Judaism, like all religions, offers values that allow one to live a meaningful and fulfilling life. I appreciate Judaism's emphasis on a reverence for learning, critical thinking and questioning, and on one's deeds, on Tikkun 'Olam, which is acting in a way to improve the world. As the Dalai Lama stated, "My religion is kindness."

All religions can become a framework for celebrating life cycles. An example in Judaism is shiva, one of the prescribed Jewish rituals surrounding death. It is a structured period of mourning, which recommends a specific set of actions. I have always found it to be comforting, because by requiring specified activities, it removes the need for decision making in one's daily activities, and allows the mourner to focus on dealing with his or her grief.

Two twentieth century leaders in Jewish thought are Abraham Joshua Heschel and Elie Wiesel. Samuel Dresner, the founding rabbi of my congregation in the Chicago area, was a student and biographer of Abraham Joshua Heschel. As a result, we studied Heschel extensively. Elie Wiesel has previously been introduced in the chapter on Profiles in Heroism.

Regarding the emphasis on deeds, both Abraham Joshua Heschel and Elie Wiesel were activists. Heschel stated, "I have learned from the prophets that we must be involved in the affairs of man." He marched next to Martin Luther King in Selma, Alabama, and he stated, "When I marched in Selma, my feet were praying." He continued, "Every deed counts. Every word has power." Elie Wiesel said, "I swore never to be silent whenever and wherever human beings endure suffering and humiliation."

Heschel lived life in a state of radical amazement. He tells us that the root of religion is our need to figure out what to do with our feelings of awe and wonder engendered by the mystery of living. Recent studies using functional MRI have validated the concept of spirituality. It has been found to be an innate, biological capacity which enables us to increase our connection to others and to expand our awareness of transcendent power. These studies more closely link religion and science.

Abraham Joshua Heschel was an observant Jew, and at the same time, extraordinarily ecumenical. He was a great bridge builder. He believed that God is not limited to one nation or to one people. He stated, "The many religions are like pearls on a string," and "For men of different religious traditions, the fear and trembling is the same." Heschel acknowledged, "The challenge is to combine loyalty to one's own tradition with reverence for different traditions."

When asked the question, "Does the universe have a purpose?" psychiatrist Viktor Frankl replied, "The meaning of your life is to take responsibility for your life and to help others find the meaning of theirs." He also said, "Love is the ultimate and highest goal." Elie Wiesel's response to the question was, "I hope the universe has a purpose, and if it doesn't, it's up to us to give it one."

Elie Wiesel

Embodying the Best of Humanity

"Only a believer could be so angry with God."
Elie Wiesel

As a child, Elie Wiesel was a brilliant student of Torah and Talmud. This was not surprising, since he was descended from a long line of Hasidic rabbis.

In May 1944, when Elie Wiesel was 15 years old, the Nazis deported him, his parents, and his sisters to Auschwitz-Birkenau. His mother and 7-year-old sister were sent to the gas chamber. Later, he and his father were transferred to Buchenwald, which the Americans liberated in April 1945. His father did not live to see his only son freed. Elie and his older sisters, Hilda and Beatrice, subsequently emigrated to the United States.

His faith was strongly challenged in the concentration camps. In 1956, he published *Night,* an account of his time there: "Blessed be God's name? Why, but why would I bless Him? Every fiber in me rebelled. Because He caused thousands of children to burn in His mass graves? Because he kept six crematoria working day and night, including Shabbat and the Holy Days? Because in His great might, He had created Auschwitz, Birkenau, Buna, and so many other factories of death? How could I say to Him: Blessed be Thou, Almighty, Master of the Universe, who chose us among all nations to be tortured day and night, to watch as our fathers, our mothers, our brothers, end up in the furnaces? Praised be Thy Holy Name, for having chosen us to be slaughtered on Thine altar?"

"Why bring children into a world in which God and man betrayed their trust in one another?" he wrote in *Night.* Fortunately, he changed his mind and fathered his son Elisha, who became one of the great joys in his life. Elie Wiesel was tormented by God's silence, but he did not lose his faith. He stated, "I never gave up on my faith in God, but I have a wounded faith. I am a God-intoxicated man. Only a believer could be so angry with God."

Every year for twenty-five years, Elie Wiesel visited our synagogue in the Chicago area. During that time, he often discussed his profound love of Judaism. For example, he would describe Shabbat dinners during his early life in Sighet. He imagined angels fluttering around his grandfather's shoulders. When he would sing a Nigun from his childhood, we could feel the mystical power of his musical prayer. Every Shabbat my own family sings a nigun taught to us by Elie Wiesel.

Despite his torment, he felt how important it was to celebrate. He said, "It is so strange, because we live in tragic times, in turbulent times, yet every fiber of my being wants to celebrate. Even in the death camps they danced on Simchat Torah, and we must dance today because of so much sadness." Elie continued, "Let your friends' good fortune be as dear to you as your own."

Elie has been an inspiration to me and to so many others. He had experienced the worst of humanity and yet he came to embody the best, teaching us never to be silent whenever and wherever human beings endure suffering.

Elie Wiesel stated, "How was I saved? I was the wrong candidate for survival. Since I don't find a meaning for my own survival, I must infer a meaning from it. That's why I teach and write. That's why I am involved in all kinds of human rights activities – to justify my existence."

Albert Madansky

Reconciling Science and Religion

**"Religion makes me feel good, science makes me feel smart. I
need both to preserve my balance in life."**
Al Madansky

ALBERT MADANSKY IS a scientist and a devout Jew. "I know it's a
contradiction," he said.

I asked him how he reconciles science and religion. This was his response:
"First I distinguish between what one would see looking at the earth from a
spaceship – lots of different species doing what they normally do — and
what's actually going on. All one will see are the activities and the results of
thinking. But humans think about what it is that makes up the world, physically and biologically. They think about how individuals form aggregates,
politically, sociologically, and economically. They think about how individuals make decisions. They think about how people communicate. They create
art, literature, music, and mathematics.

"Humans think about the big questions: How and why did our physical,
biological, social, political, economic, psychological, communicative, creative
world evolve? Though we seek rational non-mystical answers to all of this, no
matter how much progress we make in getting to such answers, we are left
somewhat empty-handed. We are less empty-handed today than we were
centuries ago, but we still don't have all the answers."

"It is religion," Al said, "that allows us to fill in the gaps in our empty
hands. Not the kind of religion that says here are all the answers, but one that
says you can use me to fill in the gaps, and adjust me as you learn other ways
of filling in the gaps.

"All societies have invented religions, so the one to be adopted is the one
from the society you are born into. Each society's religion has its myths, developed to fill in the gaps when there were lots of gaps to be filled. Being born
Jewish, I adopt the Jewish religion's mantle, modifying its original structure to
reflect what we know today. We don't know enough to shuck it all, so I look to
the notion of God as the ultimate filler.

"I strived to instill in my children, and hope they have instilled in my
grandchildren, a connection to Judaism and the Jewish people. I chose to put

all my children into Jewish day schools so they could have a better Judaic education. I wanted them to have an intellectual connection to Judaism, along with the social, familial, gastronomic connection that they were sure to get from our household."

Al Madansky said he uses religion as his "vehicle for thinking outside the box of my senses and my studies. If I don't think imaginatively, then I am behaving equivalently to the unthinking animals, doing things either instinctively or merely for self and societal gratification."

For Al, a belief in God postulates that there is some transcendent external force that instills in humans the desire to do good. Al says, "The notion of prayer gives me the ability to connect affectively, not cognitively, with this force, along with a language to do so as honed by my Jewish predecessors." For Al, the notion of God is more powerful than philosophical concepts based on pure reason, such as Immanuel Kant's categorical imperative. This concept holds that one must always act in a way that your actions should become universal law. Do only what all others should do under similar circumstances.

Al cites Rabbi Dr. Norman Lamm, former chancellor of Yeshiva University, to support this perspective. The rabbi states, "Grasping a differential equation or a concept in quantum mechanics can let us perceive and reveal Godliness in the abstract governance of the universe. An insight into molecular biology can inspire in us a fascination with God's creation that Maimonides identifies as the love of God. A new appreciation of a Beethoven symphony, a Cezanne painting, or the poetry of Mary Oliver can move us to a greater sensitivity to the infinite possibilities of the creative imagination with which the Creator endowed His human creatures, all created in the divine image."

Carl Sagan said, "Science is not only compatible with spirituality; it is a profound source of spirituality."

Greg Ekbon

The Enduring Power of Faith

"Faith is unseen but felt. Faith is strength when we feel we have none. Faith is hope when all seems lost."
Catherine Pulsifer

FOR SOME PEOPLE, a strong religious faith sustains them in unimaginably difficult times. And some, like Greg Ekbon, are even able to find in their faith the strength to transform personal pain into a mission that brings untold benefits to other people.

Greg was a successful surgeon, with a good marriage and wonderful friends and colleagues, and he was looking forward to retirement. By his own assessment, he had a good life.

Unexpectedly, everything changed. In 2011, his wife Eva died suddenly from a ruptured brain aneurysm. His son began to struggle with alcohol and drugs, and had a near-fatal motor vehicle accident. A second marriage ended in divorce.

A devout Christian, Greg, by his own acknowledgement, nevertheless entered a prolonged time of darkness. God seemed very distant. Yet Greg believed in the promise God made in Deuteronomy that He would never leave him, nor forsake him. (Deut. 31:6)

Greg cried out to God. He pleaded for wisdom and discernment regarding his son, for strength to endure each day, for guidance in career decisions, for relief from the terrible pain of grief and the feeling of being alone and isolated. But God didn't seem to be helping the way Greg expected. Greg questioned the depth of his faith, wondering if he was being sufficiently obedient to God's will.

Greg said, "I turned to Scripture and came to realize that both Moses and Caleb had been called by God to immense tasks. Moses had obeyed reluctantly, and Caleb wholeheartedly. Still God was able to use them both to carry out His plan. I understood that even with my weaknesses and fears and doubts, God, in His grace, could still use me for his purposes."

Canadian author Ann Voskamp stated, "Sometimes we want greater clarity when what we need is deeper trust."

With renewed dedication, Greg worked in Africa, providing surgical education and resident training in Chogoria, Kenya, and Goma, Democratic Republic of Congo. In 2018, while he was in Chogoria, his 32- year-old son, Doug, was hospitalized back in St. Paul, Minnesota, with a blockage in his abdominal aorta. Greg stated, "By God's grace he survived, but eventually required bilateral below-knee amputations. He was discharged and eventually fitted for prostheses."

In 2019, Greg was headed back to Africa, and he was immensely proud when Doug asked to go with him to help in the work, one part of which was to fit amputees with prosthetic limbs that had been provided by the LN-4 Hand Project. They only had 25 protheses, but 170 people turned up at the clinic seeking help. It was clear more needed to be done. Father and son sensed God was "calling them to encourage and support the amputee patients in developing countries."

However, Doug subsequently passed away from an accidental overdose in July 2019. Having lost his wife and only child in the space of eight years, Greg says, "I have personally known darkness and brokenness and pain. I can see how, in a way, the suffering I went through prepared the way for me to give others some hope. Every day is a chance to begin again."

Greg, therefore, started a non-profit called Dignity for the Amputee International in Doug's memory. Greg reached out to Samaritan's Purse and partnered with local hospitals in Chogoria, Kenya and Goma, Democratic Republic of Congo. LimbFit is Powered by Dignity for the Amputee International, a 501(c)(3) nonprofit started in December 2019.

Greg says, "One of the great opportunities I have as a healthcare provider is to be a purveyor of hope, even when things feel hopeless. That's the assignment God has given me – and I'm not finished yet."

Kathy Bhatia

Seeing with the Eyes of Faith

"In the life of faith, sometimes we long for our eyes to see what our spirit believes: that God is deeply at work in the world and that there is more to life than we can fully grasp with our finite minds."
Kathy Bhatia

KATHY RICHARDS BHATIA is a board-certified chaplain who focuses on trauma and resilience. Since 2014, she has served with She Is Safe, a non-profit international ministry.

When I asked Kathy for her life lessons, she discussed the importance of recognizing that faith is not a way to accept the unseen, but is instead a way of seeing. She states, "In the life of faith, it is true that sometimes we long for our eyes to see what our spirit believes: that God is deeply at work in this world, that there is more to this life than we can fully grasp with our finite minds."

She illustrates this idea with a quote from scripture and one from a hymn written in 1876:

"Now faith is the assurance of what we hope for and the certainty of what we do not see." Hebrews 11:1

"and Lord, haste the day when my faith becomes sight..." "It Is Well With My Soul" (hymn by Horatio Spafford)

Kathy continues, "In some miraculous and truly indefinable way, my faith has become sight, which has given me the ability to persevere during dramatic, traumatic circumstances. For example, my call to ministry came to me during the chaos and pain of a messy, devastating divorce. The call required me to see with the eyes of faith. How could a woman, deep in the conservative Christian evangelical tradition, who believed that women should not preach or teach, and who was divorcing her husband, how could she be called to be a minister of the Gospel? Yet, my faith has now become sight. After much wrestling with my faith and my call, I have watched in awe as the various threads of my life have revealed an unexpected sight — my serving in full-time ministry!

"On the heels of my divorce and my graduation from seminary, I found that the work of a chaplain fits my personality, experience, and gifts. Part of my ministry involves deep work around co-dependency and engagement with angry men. I learned to recognize my own responses to anger and fear. This has enabled me to hold my sense of self with most of the angry men I encounter. I have developed a paradigm for rehabilitation called The Three Healing Friends: Laughter, Tears, and Silence.

"I meet and minister to people from many faiths and cultures. Part of my ministry deals with trauma and resilience healing. I work with women and girls through She Is Safe, which rescues and restores women and girls who have suffered from abuse and slavery in high-risk communities across the world, including South Sudan, Myanmar, India, Nepal, the Middle East, Mali, and Indonesia. It equips them to build lives of freedom and faith for a strong future. For example, teaching them how to use a sewing machine nurtures their creativity and skills.

"I have seen deep life changes in the participants in our programs. Rates of child marriage, one of the most egregious forms of human trafficking, have fallen. Individual girls have found a safe community in which to learn and grow. Resilience is growing and hope is alive and well, even during extremely challenging life circumstances.

"This world is a broken place, filled with broken people. Despite the knowledge that we will sometimes be pulled into discouragement and despair, that we will lose heart from time to time, our faith says "I remain confident of this: *I will see the goodness of the Lord in the land of the living. Wait for the Lord: Be strong and take heart and wait for the Lord.*"

"Almost every day, I have the privilege of watching my faith become sight."

Steve Hefter

A Spiritual Path

**"Rather than trusting my ego and giving into fear,
I put my trust and faith in my higher self and in God."
Steve Hefter**

STEVE HEFTER, a partner and lead investment strategist at HLM Capital Management Group, faced a critical situation: he and his business partner parted ways after being together for 16 years at leading investment institutions, because the latter decided to move to another part of the country. The split was amicable, but Steve felt some fear and anxiety at the thought of running a large business on his own.

Steve said, "My initial reaction was that this was a depressing development. It was my wise old friend Everett who reminded me that one can choose how to react to external circumstances. He advised me to think positively, to expect good things, and to have faith and trust in God that things would work out."

Everett told him that the mere act of asking God for help in any situation was a great way to start. "Just ask for strength and guidance," Everett said. Acting on Everett's good counsel, Steve made a paradigm shift in his thinking, including becoming more spiritual.

Then he reinvented his business as a three-person team, bringing in two outstanding colleagues. Steve said, "The chemistry between us, our assistants and future team members was like magic. We not only created a great business, but we also enjoy each other's company and love our jobs."

Within a few years, Steve began a 12-year run as a Barron's number-one-ranked financial advisor in Illinois. Steve once feared that parting with his old partner would be the end of the world. Instead, splitting up turned out to be a positive and important change.

"I try to focus on gratitude for what I have, rather than on resentments for what my ego thinks I should have. With this clarity of thinking, I have come to understand that the greatest reward in life is the ability and desire to help others," he said.

He and his wife have paid college tuition for more than a dozen young adults who don't have the financial resources needed on their own. They have also served on the boards and contributed to organizations such as the Simon Wiesenthal Center, StandWithUs, the African Middle Eastern Leadership Program, and the International Fellowship of Christians and Jews. Each of these organizations promotes tolerance, truth, and understanding between faiths. They also support the 30 Birds Foundation, which helped more than 400 people who have left Afghanistan.

Steve also tries to help friends and family who experience fear-oriented thinking. Steve said, "We all have a choice in how and what to think about. By choosing to concentrate on the solution (ways to make things better through faith and strength) rather than on adversity, we can be more at peace, make better decisions and live a more productive and satisfying life."

Jim Munson

Seeking Moral Excellence

**"It is in our lives, and not from our words, that our religion
must be read."
Thomas Jefferson**

JIM MUNSON COMES from a deeply religious background. One of his
grandfathers was president of Asheville Normal, a Presbyterian women's
teachers' college, and his other grandfather taught at the Presbyterian College
of Wooster in Ohio. Both of Jim's parents grew up on religious college
campuses and attended mandatory daily chapel services. Jim attended
Sunday school and church youth fellowship services and programs through
high school. Nevertheless, Jim describes himself as a person who never has
believed in a supreme being at any point in his life. He says that he is not
against religion at all, but simply is not religious himself. At the same time, he
says that he places an extremely high priority on living ethically.

Jim was a litigation partner of the Kirkland & Ellis law firm in Chicago for
many years. After retiring, he has appeared in numerous plays and films. He
discusses living a moral and meaningful life outside of a religious framework:

"The vast majority of the world is religious. Only 25% are non-religious
and a mere 9% are confirmed atheists. Where does this minority find meaning
in life without divine inspiration and spiritual succor? It is a real question for
families with generations of non-believers who continue to be challenged by
life's inevitable troubles and crises.

"William Shakespeare frames the issue when Macbeth concludes:
Life's but a walking shadow; a poor player,
That struts and frets this hour upon the stage,
And then is heard no more: it is a tale
Told by an idiot, full of sound and fury
Signifying nothing.

"For some, an alternative to spirituality comes from a representative of
Stoic philosophy, Roman emperor Marcus Aurelius, who advises in *Meditations*:

If you discover in human life something better than justice, truth, self-
control, courage...then turn to it with all your heart and enjoy this prime good

227

you have found. But if nothing is shown to be better...if you find all else by comparison with this small and paltry, then give no room to anything else...

"A nice goal, but it leaves the daunting question of how in the real world to achieve such lofty enlightenment without religious training, guidance, and observation. Fortunately, it has become clear that morality is inherent in humans and exists before any instruction in values or ethics. Yale psychology professor Paul Bloom has done ground-breaking research showing that six- to nine-month-olds, before they can walk or talk, judge the goodness of others' actions, feel empathy and compassion, act to soothe those in distress, and even have a rudimentary sense of justice. All of this is inherent, not learned.

Jim also points to Frans de Waal's observations in *The Bonobo and the Atheist*. "Each of our primate relatives, including bonobos, chimpanzees, gorillas, and baboons, has a system of morality that '...arises from ingrained values that have been there since the beginning of time.' Simply put, morality predates religion.

"As encouraging as all this is to the atheist, it still requires great effort by individual human beings even to approach Marcus Aurelius' aspirational encouragement. Winston Churchill, that great pragmatist, provides an answer for some in his 1941 Harrow School speech:

'Never give in, never give in, *never, never, never, never* — in nothing, great or small, large, or petty — never give in except to convictions of honor and good sense.'"

Jim Munson summarizes, "Life can be a tough path for non-believers,but seeking moral excellence in one's own life and relentlessly pursuing it can be its own non-eternal reward."

The Fragility Of Our Lives

Your whole life can be turned upside down overnight.
Life is short.
It can come and go like a feather in the wind.
Shania Twain

Time is a very precious gift of God,
so precious that it is only given to us moment by moment.
Amelia Barr

Ted Bloch, Jim Schroeder, M.D.

Profiles in Living and Dying with Dignity

"The dignity we seek in dying must be found in the dignity with which we have lived our lives."
Sherwin B. Newland

TED BLOCH and Jim Schroeder had much in common. Both were extremely successful in their chosen careers. Both cherished their families and their faith. Both lived their lives with grace and gratitude.

Both men taught me and many others the art of living and the art of dying with dignity.

Ted was a successful commodities consultant. He had a lifelong commitment to education. He spearheaded attempts to enrich the lives of inner-city students at the elementary school that he had attended.

When I asked him what he planned to read during his impending retirement, he responded, "I can't wait to dive into Thucydides: History of the Peloponnesian War." Obviously, Ted, that's everyone's first choice.

Ted set a high standard in many arenas. In addition to his business acumen and his involvement in community action, he had an outstanding art collection in his home designed by Frank Lloyd Wright. He had an exceptional marriage, and a profound devotion to his Judaism. I once asked Ted how important his faith was to him. His response: "My Judaism is extremely important to me. I am a believer."

When Ted became ill, this is how he shared the news with me: "I have Stage IV lung cancer. It's not what I wanted to hear, but it is what it is. Having been a businessman, I am a realist. I'm not afraid to die. I have had a wonderful life. Judaism has taught me how to live and how to die. But let's talk about something more important. Since we are reading *Siddhartha* in our book club this month, let's discuss how Judaism compares to Buddhism."

Jim Schroeder burned with enthusiasm seemingly about everything in life. In our book club, every subject completely engaged his attention. Professionally, as CEO of the Northwestern Medical Faculty Foundation, he championed the digitizing of medical records and improving patient access to them. He was a mentor to numerous colleagues and a superb rheumatologist. Some people have excellent careers and sacrifice their family life, but Jim treasured his family. In all areas of his life, he was a profile of wisdom, humor, enthusiasm, and, especially during his last two years, courage.

One day I was checking in with him on the phone, and, completely out of the blue, he matter-of-factly stated, "I was feeling a little short of breath yesterday, so I got some tests today and found out that I have acute leukemia." He spoke with the tone of a scientist who was curious to find out how an interesting problem will be resolved. His wife, Carol, said he took a very thoughtful approach to his illness and that he was not afraid of dying.

Ted Bloch and Jim Schroeder met life, and death, with dignity and courage. Both lived a life to make their descendants proud.

The other contributors to this chapter, Chip Conley, Rita Wyant Herskovits, Abraham Maslow, and Bill Wennington, share how they have responded to some of life's major challenges.

August Wilson said, "There are always, and only, two trains running. There is life and there is death. Each of us rides them both. To live life with dignity, to celebrate and accept responsibility for your presence in the world, is all that can be asked of anyone."

Chip Conley

Getting our Mojo from Maslow

"The older you are, the more you want to put your lifetime of experience and perspective to work to positively impact future generations."
Chip Conley

CHIP CONLEY FOUNDED the Modern Elder Academy in 2018, which strives to "reframe midlife from a crisis to a calling." It is dedicated to life-long learning, helping its attendees find a renewed sense of purpose, and building a community of "inspired and empowered midlifers." Chip believes that at all ages our potential is unlimited.

Chip's concept of being a wisdom worker is to cultivate and harvest as much wisdom as possible to pass it on to others. Research psychiatrist George Vaillant reports that those who invest in caring for and developing the next generation are three times more likely to lead a satisfying life than those who fail to do so.

Chip points out that the older we get, the ability to use knowledge acquired through past experiences increases. This is known as crystallized intelligence. As Robert Pirsig, in *Zen and the Art of Motorcycle Maintenance*, says, "You look at where you're going and where you are and it never makes sense, but then you look back at where you've been, and a pattern seems to emerge."

Chip wrote *Peak: How Great Companies Get Their Mojo from Maslow*. It was based on applying Abraham Maslow's theories to key business relationships. I had also published a book about Maslow, titled *Seeing More Colors, A Guide to a Richer Life*, concerning Maslow's concept of self-actualization. Chip and I connected because of our mutual admiration of Maslow.

Maslow emphasizes that the essence of being human lies in searching for meaning and purpose. Other ideas Maslow underscores include the importance of making every moment count, being curious and self-aware, having loving relationships and an attitude of gratitude.

Chip says, "We habitually want about twice as much as we have, which is the tyranny of the unnecessary." Chip quotes Rabbi Hyman Judah Schachtel. "Happiness is not having what you want, but wanting what you have."

233

How do we describe those of us who have lived for several decades? What should we be called? Chip likes the terms, "wisdom worker" and "modern elder." In the Hawaiian tradition, elders are called Kapunas, keepers of ancestral knowledge. There is respect for elders, not just members of your family, but all elders. In most indigenous cultures, the tradition is that kapunas carry the wisdom of the past, and from them one learns how to deal with the future as it unfolds.

Chip Conley's Modern Elder Academy is making a difference in helping people to navigate midlife and beyond. Already there are more than 2,500 alumni from 40 countries.

Our generation has been the beneficiary of creative and spiritual capital given to us by others. This has strengthened and ennobled our lives. Chip Conley appreciates that we must, as best we can, replenish and increase that capital.

Rita Herskovits

The Sound of the Wind

"I thought I knew a lot about the loss of a loved one."
Rita Herskovits

RITA HERSKOVITS IS one of the most upbeat, positive people I have ever met. She has always been filled with energy and enthusiasm for her family, friends, and numerous charitable causes in her life. When I asked her how she is coping with one of the most formidable challenges one could face, this was her response:

"'Making the best of it!' has been a guiding principle in my life. I have always benefited from trying to make the best of every challenge and every opportunity.

"Being the child of deaf adults (CODA), I always welcomed the opportunity to educate and explain deaf culture. I wanted to share that 'the deaf can do anything anyone else can do, except hear.' I did not have the luxury of being shy. Growing up before closed captioning and sign language interpreters were widely available, I understood that my normal was unique to others. Often, I needed to communicate and clarify information for my parents. I had to interact with the world in very grown-up ways. This taught me to connect with all kinds of people easily and comfortably.

"I thought I knew a lot about the loss of a loved one. I have experienced the death of my parents, my in-laws, and my grandparents, all of whom lived relatively long lives and were a big part of my life, as well as my family's. We often speak of them with love and laughter, and we honor their memory every chance we get. Losing a close family member or friend can be sad and difficult, but celebrating their lives made the best of it for all of us. I thought I knew and understood that, until we tragically and suddenly lost our son at the age of 38. Nothing prepared me for burying our son.

"David was the definition of life itself! He made an impact on almost everything he did and on everyone he met. He was passionate about creating solutions for the planet through his work in solar energy. His thoughtfulness is legendary. He carried his grandfather in a wheelchair up and down the steps at the Cincinnati Reds Great American Ball Park so that he could meet some of the players on the field while they warmed up. He loved to connect with

235

people and do things to make them happy. He was beautiful in many ways, not just physically. A son, who while not perfect, anyone could be very proud of.

"One might wonder why my lifetime of 'Making the Best of It' does not work as well for me since my son's passing. I say I am putting one foot in front of the other. I am quick to remember and speak of the good times and the plethora of meaningful memories of David that I have. My brain is working overtime to 'make the best of it' but my heart is devastated and in pieces. I am very grateful for my amazing life partner, Tom, our incredible daughter, Kathryn, my daughter-in-law, Kascey, and the best extended family one could ever hope for. Friends and acquaintances of ours, and of David, have been wonderful. Maybe The David M. Herskovits Foundation, which is a nonprofit started by Kascey, dedicated to providing mentorship, scholarships, and grants for STEM education, may be a beginning.

"It may appear to others that I am making the best of it. But it is unfathomable that HE will be frozen in time and not able to share in a conventional way the life adventures ahead. But I will continue to look for him in the reflection of the moon and in the sound of the wind on the golf course, and to feel his presence while I continue to put one foot in front of the other. It may not be possible to 'make the best' of this situation, but eventually accepting that fact may be the best I can do."

Tara Watkins Anderson said, "The strongest person in the world is a grieving mother who wakes up and keeps going every morning."

Abraham Maslow, Bill Wennington

The Transformative Power of Escaping Calamity

"As my fathers planted for me before I was born,
I now plant for those who will come after me."
The Talmud

ON JUNE 8, 1970, my mentor at Brandeis University, Abraham Maslow, collapsed and died suddenly from a massive heart attack. He'd had a cardiac event 19 months earlier and knew that his risk for another heart attack was considerable. Earlier that year, in an interview published in *Psychology Today*, Maslow expressed gratitude for the time he had been given: "My attitude toward life changed. The word I use for it now is postmortem life. I could just as easily have died, so my living constitutes a kind of extra, a bonus.... I may just as well live as if I had already died...every single moment of every single day is transformed."

On September 8, 1994, Chicago Bulls basketball player Bill Wennington was booked on a flight which he missed -- USAir flight 427 – which crashed on landing in Pittsburgh, killing all 132 people on board. He told me that he was transformed by the experience. He developed more humility, put even more energy into being a better husband, father, and teammate, devoted more time to his charities, and became less bent out of shape by the "small stuff."

I had my own brush-with-death experience. Soon after my 71st birthday, I developed stomach pains. An initial test demonstrated cancer of the pancreas. I was devastated. An acquaintance of mine who was my age had recently died a painful death from the same disease.

Suddenly, the angel of death was resting, not so gently, on my shoulder. I was terrified but thought that I needed to make the best of it. I asked my wife to bring to the hospital several books on death and dying. I thought about the things I would never see or do again. Fortunately, subsequent tests did not reveal the presence of a serious condition.

The experience was a wakeup call. It produced life-altering changes in my attitude and behavior. Never again would I see life as anything except a great gift. Having been granted a reprieve, I promised myself that from that day forward, I would live life from the deepest part of my being. I would help others and perform frequent acts of kindness. I would wish for those around me to be filled with passion and to experience delight and laughter. I would be acutely aware of the joy of being alive — to think, to create, to serve, and to love.

As we get older, it is impossible not to be more deeply aware of the fragility of life. As a result, we get better at savoring, whether appreciating small pleasures or at holding onto joyful experiences. We know our time is limited, so we spend it more wisely. We want to acquire as much wisdom as we can and pass it on to those we have loved and nurtured.

Thirteenth century Persian poet Rumi stated, "Travelers, it is late. Life's sun is going to set. During these brief days that you have the strength, be quick and spare no effort of your wings."

Himalayan Cataract Project

All profits from this book will be donated to the Himalayan Cataract Project, an organization co-founded by Geoffrey Tabin, M.D. Its goal is to cure preventable blindness in the world. Responsible for restoring sight to more than one million people so far, the project is well on its way to achieving its goal. The cost is $25 per eye to completely restore sight to a blind person. It is hard to imagine a better investment. Himalayan Cataract Project is a 501(c)(3) nonprofit organization. One of the contributors to this book, Tom Broussard, has generously pledged to match the profits from the sale of this book up to $10,000.00

Himalayan Cataract Project website: cureblindness.org

The Remarkable People Whose
Wisdom Created this Book

Harold **Baines** is a former MLB right fielder and designated hitter; he played for the Chicago White Sox, Texas Rangers, Oakland Athletics, Baltimore Orioles and Cleveland Indians. Harold is a six-time All-Star and was elected to the Baseball Hall of Fame in 2019. We met when he played for the Chicago White Sox, and I was an orthopedic consultant with the team.

Melissa **Bean** served as the U.S. representative for Illinois's 8th congressional district from 2005 to 2011. She served as chair of Midwest operations for JPMorgan Chase. She is CEO of Mesirow Wealth Advisors. She received a B.A. from Roosevelt University.

Steve **Bennett** is a photographer and president of website design and hosting company AuthorBytes. His photographs include both traditional subjects ("the world as seen") and abstract composites ("the world reimagined"). Steve earned a BA from the University of Rochester and an MA from Harvard University. He has designed my website: michaelslewismd.com and has been a friend and mentor for many years.

Robert A. **Bensman** is founder and CEO of The Bensman Group, a group of businesses serving the risk management, estate planning, insurance, employee benefits, and personal strategic planning needs of individuals nationally and internationally. Bob earned his BS from the University of Illinois Urbana-Champaign, and the Chartered Life Underwriter (CLU), Chartered Financial Consultant (ChFC), and designations from The American

College, Bryn Mawr, Pennsylvania. He has been a friend and advisor for more than 40 years.

Marjorie **Benton** served as a delegate to the UN Special Sessions on disarmament and as the U.S. Ambassador to UNICEF. She was a delegate to the Special Session on Disarmament and the co-chair of the Americans for SALT (Strategic Arms Limitation Talks). In 1981, she co-founded The Peace Museum in Chicago. She chaired the board of Save the Children Fund and is co-founder of the Chicago Foundation for Women. In 1994, President Clinton appointed her chair of the President's Commission on White House Fellowships. In 2006, she joined the board of Partners in Health, founded by the late Paul Farmer. Today, she continues philanthropic work in Haiti. I met Marjorie's husband, Charles, more than thirty years ago when we were on a committee together at the Field Museum of Natural History. Sadly, Charles passed away several years ago. Marjorie remains a close family friend.

David **Berg** is the founding partner of Berg & Androphy Law Firm. His firm has received the Tier 1 "Best Law Firm" ranking by *U.S. News & World Report*. He is the author of *The Trial Lawyer: What it Takes to Win* and *Run, Brother, Run: A Memoir of a Murder in My Family*. In 2014, he received the Anti-Defamation League Karen H. Susman Jurisprudence award. He has recently donated his legal papers to the Briscoe Center for American History at the University of Texas. He attended Tulane University and graduated from the University of Houston and the University of Houston Law Center. We were on the same high school debate team coached by Mollie Martin.

Bruno **Bettelheim** was a psychologist at the University of Chicago whose work focused on emotionally disturbed children.

Kathy Richards **Bhartia**, MDiv, BCC, is a board-certified chaplain whose work focuses on trauma and resilience. She has developed a paradigm for healing called The Three Healing Friends: Laughter, Tears, and Silence. Today she works with abused and trafficked girls and women through the international organization She Is Safe. Kathy and her husband Amit have been family friends for many years.

Ted **Bloch** was a commodities consultant, the founder of Bloch Lumber, and a philanthropist. He had been president of Moriah Congregation. Educated at the University of Chicago, he held a Ph.D. in economics. Ted and his wife, Sonia, were family friends for more than forty years.

Ronald "Mark" **Booker**, Jr., currently works for the U.S. Forest Service and Bureau of Land Management. He provides aerial supervision for wild-land firefighters. He is a safety officer for all agencies within the fire service. He is a former Plumas Hotshot smokejumper from Venice Beach, California.

He is featured on the podcast "Wildfire Saved My Life." He was a smoke-jumper with my son-in-law, Richie Campas.

Tom **Broussard** was general tax counsel of Atlantic Richfield, vice president and general counsel of Technicolor, Inc., and then principal of Thomas R. Broussard Ltd., a professional law corporation focused on business, corporate and real estate law. He was the late Mollie Martin's husband. He earned a BS from the University of Pennsylvania Wharton School of Finance in 1964 and a JD from Harvard Law School in 1967. We were on the same high school debate team coached by Mollie Martin.

John **Callaway** was a journalist who interviewed luminaries such as John Updike, Helen Hayes, Aaron Copeland, Howard Cosell, and Jonas Salk. He was the original host of *Chicago Tonight* on PBS. Callaway won the Peabody Award and 16 Emmys. Henry Kissinger said John was the best interviewer he had ever met. He attended Ohio Wesleyan University. We were friends for many years and in a book club together.

Richie **Campas** has been a smokejumper in the western United States and Alaska. He has been an arborist, a boat captain, and is now a general contractor. He is founder and president of ARCH Builders, Hawaii. He is my son-in-law.

Sir John **Charnley** was an orthopedic surgeon who pioneered hip and knee replacement technology. He was knighted in 1977. I studied with Sir John Charnley during my orthopedic residency at his surgical and research center at Wrightington Hospital near Manchester, England.

Peter **Christopher** was headmaster for King Edward VI Aston School, Birmingham from 1992 to 2004. It is a selective school for approximately 950 boys aged 11 to 18 and has a staff of more than 100. He was on the board of directors of the Titan Group and helped establish and was chairman of the British Schools Orienteering Association. He graduated from Clare College, University of Cambridge. My wife, Valerie, met Peter and his wife, Jane, in 1967, when the three of them were teaching in Buenos Aires, Argentina. Valerie and I have visited Jane and Peter in Britain on several occasions.

Chip **Conley** was the founder of Joie de Vivre Hospitality which became the second largest boutique hotel brand in the United States. He was Airbnb's head of Global Hospitality & Strategy. In 2018, he founded the Modern Elder Academy, dedicated to life-long learning. He is the author of *Peak: How Great Companies Get Their Mojo from Maslow, The Rebel Rules: Daring to Be Yourself in Business; Emotional Equations: Simple Truths for Creating Happiness + Success in Business + in Life* and *Wisdom@Work: The Making of a Modern Elder.* He earned a BA and an MBA at Stanford University.

Chip and I connected many years ago because each of us has written a book about Abraham Maslow.

Dennis **Connolly**, DDS, is a pediatric dentist in Kenosha, Wisconsin. He has served as Assistant Clinical Professor at Marquette Dental School. He participated in health care teams providing dental care in Central America. In 2009 he was honored as Person of the Year by the Kenosha Achievement Center for his work with and for children both nationally and internationally. Dr. Connolly earned a DDS from Marquette University and a postdoctoral master's from Milwaukee Children's Hospital and Marquette University. Dennis and I met more than fifty years ago when both of us were in the United States Air Force. He was a dentist, and I was an orthopedic surgeon stationed at R.A.F. Lakenheath in England.

Cecilia **Conrad** is managing director at the John D. and Catherine T. MacArthur Foundation and CEO of the Foundation's affiliate Lever for Change. She was Associate Dean and Vice President for Academic Affairs at Pomona College and a faculty member at Barnard College and Duke University. A former economist at the Federal Trade Commission, she earned her BA at Wellesley College and her PhD in labor economics, industrial organization, and public finance at Stanford University in 1982. I met Cecilia Conrad through her husband Lew Miller, who is in my book club.

Cameron **Davis** is a clean water attorney and environmental policy expert. He has served as president and CEO of the Alliance for the Great Lakes. He was appointed by President Obama to oversee the work of the eleven federal agencies coordinating more than $2 billion in investments on Great Lakes restoration. He is a commissioner on the Metropolitan Water Reclamation District of Greater Chicago and a professor at the University of Michigan Law School. We met at a convention a few years ago.

Donald **Duster** was employed by Commonwealth Edison for 25 years in management positions. From 1977 to 1979, he served in Illinois Governor James R. Thompson's cabinet as the director of the Illinois Department of Business and Economic Development and served as assistant executive director of Chicago Commons Association, a community-based not-for-profit social service agency. He held a BS in mathematics from University of Illinois and an MBA from DePaul University. We were in a book club together.

Greg **Ekbom**, M.D., is a retired surgeon who specialized in oncology, general and vascular surgery, and GI endoscopy. He has held teaching positions at the Medical College of Wisconsin and served as director of Clinical Education at Bethel University. He is an active church leader and founder of the organization Dignity for the Amputee International. I met Greg at a conference several years ago and we remain in contact.

Paul A. **Findley** was a writer and politician who served as U.S. Representative from Illinois' 20th District from 1960 to 1982. He was a civil rights supporter and an early opponent of the U.S. war in Vietnam, and he co-authored the War Powers Act of 1973.

John **Foley** is a former lead pilot for the Blue Angels. He is a Sloan Fellow at Stanford School of Business and a top-rated keynote speaker. A former Marine, John played football for the Navy. He earned degrees from the United States Naval Academy and the U.S. Naval War College. He received a master's from the Stanford University Graduate School of Business and an MA from Stanford University. We met at a conference several years ago, and I was a guest on his podcast.

Cory **Franklin**, M.D., is a former director of the medical intensive care unit at Cook County Hospital in Chicago. He is an editorial board contributor to the *Chicago Tribune* op-ed page, and his work has appeared in *The New York Times, The Jerusalem Post,* and *The New York Review of Books.* Cory authored *The Doctor Will See You Now* and *Cook County ICU: 30 Years of Unforgettable Patients and Odd Cases.* He graduated from Northwestern University and received his M.D. degree from Northwestern University Medical School. We are in a book club and movie group together.

O. H. "Bud" **Frazier**, M.D., is a heart surgeon and director of the Cullen Cardiovascular Research Laboratory at the Texas Heart Institute. He is a pioneer in the development of artificial hearts. He has performed more than 1,300 heart transplants, which is more than any other surgeon in the world. He is the subject of the book *Ticker: The Quest to Create an Artificial Heart* by Mimi Swartz. Dr. Frazier earned his undergraduate degree at the University of Texas and his M.D. at Baylor College of Medicine. We have known each other for many years and share a strong interest in literature, as well as in medicine. We met through his wife, Rachel, who was a high school classmate of mine.

Rachel Merriman **Frazier** taught elementary school and Head Start and worked in school administration for 16 years. While teaching in the Houston Independent School district, she received the Outstanding Young Educator's Award. She has served on numerous boards, including the American Festival for the Arts, Society for the Performing Arts, Theatre Under the Stars, and Imprint. She has volunteered for Texas Children's Hospital, Heart Exchange, which benefits heart transplant patients, and St. Luke's United Methodist Church. She received a BS degree from the University of Texas and did graduate work in English at St. Thomas University. Rachel and I were high school classmates. She is married to Bud Frazier.

Isadore "Whiz" **Friedberg** practiced optometry in Galveston Texas. He was the first Life Master in Duplicate Bridge in Galveston. He graduated from Rice University (formerly Rice Institute) and the Chicago College of Optometry. He was my mother's brother.

Elizabeth **Glassman** has held positions at the Metropolitan Museum of Art, the Menil Foundation in Houston, the National Gallery of Art, and the Georgia O'Keeffe Foundation, where she served as president from 1990 through 2000. In 2001 she became president and CEO of the Chicago-based Terra Foundation for American Art. Under her leadership, the foundation has given away more than $100 million to promote American art in the U.S. and globally. Elizabeth studied at the Institute of Art and Archaeology at the Sorbonne and earned a BA in art history at Sweet Briar College and an MA in art history at the University of New Mexico. Elizabeth and I grew up together in Houston, Texas. Our parents were close friends.

Michael **Golden** is a former political strategist, award-winning broadcast journalist and cofounder of the One Million Degrees community college scholarship project. He is the author of *Write Or Die: Negotiating Life – One Column at A Time* and *Unlock Congress: Reform the Rules — Restore the System.* Michael earned his BA from Indiana University and his MS from DePaul University. He has been a family friend for many years.

Wayne M. **Goldstein**, M.D., is an orthopedic surgeon. He is founder and chairman of the Board of Illinois Bone & Joint Institute and a Clinical Professor of Orthopedics at the University of Illinois at Chicago. Dr. Goldstein specializes in hip and knee reconstruction and revision surgery; he has pioneered several new treatments in the field. He received his medical degree at the Abraham Lincoln School of Medicine at the University of Illinois. We have been friends and colleagues for more than 40 years. In 2004, I joined his practice at the Illinois Bone and Joint Institute.

John **Gould** is a former dean of the University of Chicago Booth School of Business, and a former Special Assistant for Economic Affairs in the U.S. Department of Labor during George P. Shultz's term as Secretary of Labor. He was also a consultant for economic affairs to the Office of Management and Budget for the Executive Office of the President. He is Steven G. Rothmeier Distinguished Service Professor of Economics Emeritus at Chicago Booth. We have been in a book club together for many years.

Gordon **Green**, M.D., is Professor Emeritus at the UT Southwestern Medical Center. He served for six years in the National Public Health

Service. He has served as Director of the Dallas County Health Department. His research interests include bioterrorism, dysmorphology, epidemiology of birth defects, HIV/AIDS, and public health. He received his undergraduate degree from Rice University, his medical degree from University of Texas Southwestern Medical School and a graduate degree from the University of California, Berkeley. Gordon and I attended medical school together.

Stuart **Green**, M.D., is an orthopedic surgeon at the University of California, Irvine. He was instrumental in bringing the new methods of reconstructive surgery pioneered by the Soviet doctor G.A. Ilizarov to the United States. He has authored four books and has authored or co-authored more than 150 articles in medical journals. He is a recognized authority on medical ethics and a member of the Committee on Ethics of the American Academy of Orthopedic Surgeons. Dr. Green received his undergraduate degree from Lafayette College and his MD from New York Medical College. We were orthopedic residents together at Hospital for Joint Diseases in New York City.

Gary **Greenberg** is a principal and managing director at the venture capital firm Feldman Advisors. For 32 years, he served as president of Sage Enterprises, a food service distribution company for the airline industry, which he founded at age 24. He was a board member for Cole Taylor Bank, as well as a vice president of business development. Gary earned a BS at the University of Oklahoma. We met several years ago through mutual friends.

In-Hei **Hahn**, M.D., is an emergency medicine physician and medical toxicologist who divides her time between Stanford University and Veteran's Administration hospitals in Palo Alto, and the Regional Medical Center in San Jose. As medical expedition officer for the department of paleontology at the Smithsonian Institute and the American Museum of Natural History, she has provided health care in places such as the Gobi Desert in China and Mongolia and the backcountry of Transylvania. She helped develop the first responder team for Himalayan Cataract Project in Ethiopia. Dr. Hahn received an MD degree from the University of Maryland School of Medicine. We have been friends for many years. She is married to Geoffrey Tabin.

David **Halberstam** was a Pulitzer Prize–winning journalist and author. In 1964 he won a Pulitzer for his coverage of the Vietnam War as a staff reporter for The New York Times. He wrote several books on aspects of American history and culture, including The Fifties, The Coldest Winter: America and the Korean War, The Best and the Brightest: the Kennedy-Johnson Administrations, The Making of a Quagmire: America and Vietnam During the Kennedy Era, The Breaks of the Game, and Playing for Keeps: Michael Jordan and the World He Made. He received an A.B. from Harvard

University. We spent time together when he attended Chicago Bulls games while writing a book about Michael Jordan and I was an orthopedic consultant for the team.

K.C. **Hayes** is Professor Emeritus of Biology and director of the Foster Biomedical Research Laboratories at Brandeis University. He is the recipient of an NIH Research Career Development Award, and co-inventor on 20 patents, including Smart Balance, a transfat-free margarine to help lower cholesterol currently carried in most supermarkets in the U.S. He has authored or co-authored more than 210 reports, 25 chapters, and 200 abstracts. I met him several years ago at a Brandeis University class reunion. He has been generous and helpful in his support of books that I have published.

Steve **Hefter** is a partner and lead investment strategist at HLM Capital Management Group. He has been named #1 Advisor in Illinois by both *Barron's* and *Forbes* magazines, and he has been listed in *Barron's* annual rankings of the Top 100 Independent Wealth Advisors in America since 2004. He has a BA in economics from Stanford University and an MBA in finance from Harvard University. Steve has been a friend and advisor for many years.

Rita Wyant **Herskovits** is director of the David M. Herskovits Foundation. She is an election supervisor for Palm Beach County, Florida. She was a board member of the National Council of Jewish Women. The child of deaf parents, she and her husband, Tom, founded Congregation Bene Shalom in 1972, the only full-service synagogue in the nation dedicated to the deaf. The services are in English, Hebrew, and American Sign Language. She attended Ohio State University and the University of Cincinnati. Rita has been a friend for more than thirty years. She is married to Tom Herskovits.

Tom **Herskovits** immigrated to the U.S. in 1957. He is a member of the board of directors for Franchise Group Inc., and a managing partner at Feldman Enterprises. He served as managing partner of Herskovits Enterprises from 1993–2010, where he started or invested in eight successful entrepreneurial ventures. He is an experienced board member, holding positions on five current and past public boards and six private company boards. Tom holds a BS and an MBA from Syracuse University. Tom has been a friend for more than thirty years. He is married to Rita Herskovits.

Phil **Jackson** played 12 seasons in the NBA and won two NBA championships as a player. He was head coach of the Chicago Bulls from 1989 to 1998, leading them to six NBA championships. He then coached the Los Angeles Lakers from 1999 to 2004 and again from 2005 to 2011, when he retired from coaching. He has authored several books on basketball, including *Eleven Rings: The Soul of Success*, *Sacred Hoops: Spiritual Lessons of a Hardwood Warrior*, *The Last Season: A Team in Search of Its Soul*, and *The Gospel According to Phil: The Words and Wisdom of Chicago Bulls Coach Phil Jackson: An Unauthorized Collection*. He attended the University of North Dakota. We spent time together when he was head coach for the Chicago Bulls, and I was an orthopedic consultant.

Mickey **Jaffe** is president of Actuarial Enterprises, Ltd. He was a vice president of the Society of Actuaries. He received his undergraduate degree from Brown University and a M.S. from the Sloan School of Management at MIT. Mickey and I are in a book club together.

DeWitt **Jones** is a professional photographer, writer, film director and public speaker whose photographs have appeared in *National Geographic*. As a film director, he had two documentaries nominated for Academy Awards. His TEDx Talk "Celebrate What's Right With the World" has garnered 1.3 million views. Jones's publications include *Anasazi World*, *Celebrate What's Right With the World*, *John Muir's America*, *Canyon Country*, and *The Nature of Leadership* (with Stephen Covey). He holds a BA from Dartmouth College and a master's in filmmaking from the University of California at Los Angeles. We met several years ago, and he has been most helpful as a mentor related to my photographs.

Stephen **Jones** is an attorney in Enid, Oklahoma. He took on several high-profile civil rights cases early in his career and in 1995, he was appointed by the state to defend Oklahoma City bomber Timothy McVeigh. He was a member of the U. S. Delegation to NATO and a personal research assistant to Richard Nixon, when Nixon was a practicing attorney in New York. He served as special assistant to Senator Charles Percy and as chief of staff for U.S. Rep. Paul Findley in the 1960s. He was the Republican nominee for Oklahoma Attorney General in 1974 and ran for the U.S. Senate in 1990. He earned a BA and a law degree at the University of Oklahoma. Stephen and I were on the high school debate team coached by Mollie Martin.

Michael **Jordan** played 15 seasons with the NBA and won six championships with the Chicago Bulls. He was the most famous (and best) basketball player in the world during those years. Today Jordan is a successful businessman. He is principal owner and chairman of the Charlotte Hornets professional basketball team. He attended the University of North Carolina at Chapel Hill. I was able to observe Michael at close range for two Chicago Bulls' championship seasons.

Raymond **Kalmans** is a Houston, Texas, attorney specializing in labor and employment law. He serves on the board of Seven Acres Jewish Senior Care Services and is a former board member of the Jewish Community Center of Houston. He received the prestigious Houston Jewish Community Center David H. White Award for Outstanding Leadership. He received an undergraduate degree from the University of Texas and a law degree from the University of Texas Law School. Raymond and I grew up together in Houston, Texas. Our parents were close friends.

Morrie **Kaplan** was chairman, president, and CEO of the Sealy Mattress Company. He was a member of the Board of Trustees of Northwestern University where, with his wife, Dolores Kohl, he established the Kaplan Humanities Scholars Program. He led the Mayer and Morris Kaplan Family Foundation for more than fifty years. The multi-generational family foundation is based on the Jewish tradition of Tzedakah, a dedication to lifelong learning, and a commitment to social justice. He graduated from Northwestern University. Morrie was a friend and mentor, and we were in a book club together for many years. He was married to Dolores Kohl.

Scott Barry **Kaufman** is a cognitive scientist and a professor at Columbia University. He has taught at Yale, NYU, and the University of Pennsylvania. He is the author of *Wired to Create, Ungifted, Twice Exceptional,* and *Transcend: The New Science of Self-Actualization.* He hosts The Psychology Podcast, which has had more than 20 million downloads and is rated the number one psychology podcast in the world. Kaufman holds a BS in psychology and human computer interaction from Carnegie Mellon, an MPhil in experimental psychology from the University of Cambridge, and a Ph.D. in cognitive psychology from Yale University. We met several years ago because each of us has written a book about Abraham Maslow. Also, I have been a guest on Scott's *The Psychology Podcast.*

Irina **Kirilova** is a retired competitive volleyball player. She won Olympic gold for the former Soviet Union in 1988 in Seoul. In 1990 she was named by her peers as the best female volleyball player in the world. Later, she moved to Croatia to continue her career and afterwards became coach of the Croatian national team. She was inducted into the International Volleyball Hall of Fame in 2017. She was my patient when I was an orthopedic consultant for the Chicago Bulls.

Thomas **Kirk** is a retired colonel in the U.S. Air Force. A military fighter pilot for 28 years, he flew bombing missions during the Korean and Vietnam wars. He was shot down over Vietnam and became a prisoner of war at the "Hanoi Hilton" for almost six years. After his release, Kirk became Vice

Commander of all Special Forces in Europe. We met at a conference several years ago and have remained in contact.

Dolores **Kohl** is founder of the Kohl Children's Museum. She initiated the Kohl McCormick Early Childhood Teaching Awards and Story Bus, a traveling pre-literacy skills development exhibit, as well as a hands-on traveling art exhibit centered on Vincent Van Gogh. She is the author of the children's book *Vincent and Me*. Dolores graduated from Brandeis University and for many years served as a member of its Board of Trustees. Dolores and I have been friends for more than forty years. She was married to the late Morrie Kaplan.

Jerry **Krause** was a sports scout who served as general manager for the Chicago Bulls from 1985 to 2003, years that included the Bulls' six NBA championship seasons. Krause received the NBA Executive of the Year Award in 1988 and 1996,and in 2017 was posthumously inducted into the Basketball Hall of Fame. He attended Bradley University in Illinois. Jerry was responsible for choosing my practice to be the orthopedic consultants for the Chicago Bulls.

Ken **Krimstein** is a cartoonist, author, and educator whose work has been published in *The New Yorker, The Wall Street Journal, The New York Times,* and *The Chicago Tribune*. He teaches at DePaul University, The School of the Art Institute of Chicago and the YIVO Institute for Jewish Research. He is the author of *Kvetch as Kvetch Can: Jewish Cartoons, When I Grow Up,* and *The Three Escapes of Hannah Arendt*. He graduated from Grinnell College and earned an MA at Northwestern University. I have known Ken and his family for more than forty years.

Ron **LeFlore** is a former MLB center fielder and author of *One in a Million: The Ron LeFlore Story* (with Jim Hawkins). He played with the Detroit Tigers, the Montreal Expos, and the Chicago White Sox, and he was an American League All-Star selection in 1976. We met when both of us were affiliated with the Chicago White Sox.

Brenda **Langstraat** is president and CEO of the Chicago Public Library Foundation. Previously she served as CEO for Working in the Schools and as the executive director of the Parkways Foundation. She holds a BA from Wheaton College and a master's from the University of Chicago. We met when I participated in a Chicago Public Library Carl Sandburg Literary Awards Dinner. Brenda has helped to place a large number of my books in underserved areas in the library system.

Charles **Levin** is the founder and publisher of The Munn Avenue Press and a world-class poker player. He has authored four thrillers, *Not So Dead,*

Not So Gone, Not So Done, and *Still Not Dead*, and a collection of short stories, *The Last Appointment*. Charles holds a BA from the University of Rochester and attended Boston College Law School. I met Charles through a mutual friend. He has been of great assistance in publishing this book.

William P. **Levine** was a U.S. Army officer who, during World War II, served with the 34th Anti-Aircraft Artillery Group. He participated in the D-Day invasion on Utah Beach in France. He was among the first to enter the Dachau concentration camp when it was liberated by Allied Forces. After he was discharged from active military service, he joined the Army Reserve and was promoted to the rank of Major General. Levine received his undergraduate degree from the University of Minnesota and graduated from the Army's Officer Candidate School in 1943. We attended the same synagogue in the Chicago area. His wife, Rhoda, and my wife, Valerie, worked together for many years for Chicago Action for Soviet Jewry, an organization dedicated to helping Jews in the former Soviet republics.

Beatrice **Lewis**, my mother, was a teacher and was assistant manager of Lewis-Nathans Jewelry Company. She volunteered for several organizations, including Congregations Beth Israel and Emanu-El. She earned her BA at the University of Texas in 1938.

Hadley **Lewis**, my daughter, currently is a teacher and school administrator in Hawaii. Hadley holds a BA from the University of Denver and has a master's degree in education.

Melanie **Lewis**, my daughter, for many years worked in the design departments of film and theatre in Chicago, New York, and Los Angeles. She also has worked on farms in several countries. She now has a business based in New Orleans, Louisiana, that teaches intuitive organizational skills. Melanie earned her undergraduate degree at Barnard College.

Nathan **Lewis**, my father, was the owner of Lewis-Nathan's Jewelry Store in Houston. He played varsity tennis for Tulane University.

Valerie **Lewis**, my wife, has taught English, Geography, and English as a Second Language. She is on the Woman's Board of the Field Museum. She has been on the board of Brushwood Center at Ryerson Woods and Chicago Action for Soviet Jewry and was vice president of Moriah Congregation in charge of education. Valerie graduated from the University of Edinburgh and holds an MA in linguistics from Northeastern Illinois University.

Albert **Madansky** is an emeritus professor at the University of Chicago Booth School of Business, where he served as associate dean for Ph.D. studies and as deputy dean for faculty. He was editor-in-chief of *The Journal of Business of the University of Chicago*. His books include *Foundations of Economet-*

rics and *Prescriptions for Working Statisticians*. He is a consultant to the Department of Defense and the RAND Corporation. He is president of Madansky and Associates, Inc. His undergraduate degree is from the University of Chicago, and he has received advanced degrees from the department of statistics at the University of Chicago. Al and I have been in a book club together for many years.

Jamie **Malanowski** has been an editor at *Time* and *Esquire* and the managing editor of *Playboy*. He has written several books, including *The Coup* and *Commander Will Cushing: Daredevil Hero of the Civil War*, and a screenplay, *The Pentagon Wars*, as well as articles for *The New Yorker* and *The New York Times*. He earned a BA at LaSalle University and an MA at the University of Pennsylvania. Jamie has edited this book as well as my last book, *The Ball's in Your Court*.

Henry **Mankin**, Jr., M.D., was chief of my residency program in orthopedic surgery at the Hospital for Joint Diseases in New York City. He served as Chief of Orthopedic Surgery at Massachusetts General Hospital and taught at Harvard Medical School. He authored more than 600 publications and lectures. Dr. Mankin graduated from The School of Medicine at the University of Pittsburgh and completed his orthopedic surgery residency at the Hospital for Joint Diseases, where he started his career.

Mollie **Martin** was my high school speech and debate coach. She also taught at Purcell High School in Oklahoma and Hunter College in New York City. She was posthumously inducted into the Hall of Fame of the National Speech and Debate Association in 2020.

Abraham **Maslow** was my teacher and mentor when I was an undergraduate at Brandeis University. He is best-known for developing Maslow's hierarchy of needs, and the concept of self-actualization. His books include *A Theory of Human Motivation, Motivation and Personality, Religions, Values, and Peak Experiences, Maslow on Management, Toward a Psychology of Being*, and *The Farther Reaches of Human Nature*. He received his MA and Ph.D. from the University of Wisconsin.

Michael **McCaskey** was chairman of the Chicago Bears franchise from 1999 to 2011. He served in the Peace Corps in Ethiopia, sparking a lifelong interest in developing health care, education and leadership training programs in that country. He was a professor at UCLA and Harvard business schools. He graduated from Yale University and received his Ph.D. from the Weatherhead School of Management at Case Western Reserve University. Michael and I were friends, traveling companions, and in a book club together for many years.

William **Meltzer**, M.D., was an orthopedic surgeon and one of the first physicians in the U.S. to perform hip replacement surgery, having traveled to England to learn the procedure from Sir John Charnley. He was on the faculty at the University of Illinois College of Medicine. He received his B.S. from the University of Illinois and M.D. degree from the University of Illinois Medical School. We were in orthopedic practice together for almost forty years.

Chris **Miller** is an owner and vice president of QMI Security Solutions. The company makes roll shutters, security grilles and screens, and other products to protect residences and businesses. Chris is a graduate of Lewis University. He has become a supporter of my books and a good friend.

Goldie Wolfe **Miller** is president of Millbrook Corporate Real Estate Services and a pioneer in helping women find their place in the real estate industry. In 2007 she created the Goldie Initiative, which is dedicated to redefining the commercial real estate industry by advancing the careers of women. She received an undergraduate degree from Roosevelt University, which awarded her an honorary Doctorate of Humane Letters in 2015. Goldie has been a family friend for many years. She is married to Jack Miller.

Jack **Miller** is the founder and former president/CEO of Quill Corporation, which became the nation's largest independent direct marketer of office projects, employing more than 1,300 people. He is an active philanthropist who serves as chairman of the Jack Miller Center and as president of the Jack Miller Family Foundation. He was inducted into *Philanthropy World Magazine*'s Hall of Fame in 2008. He is the author of *Simply Success: How to Start, Build and Grow a Multimillion-Dollar Business the Old-Fashioned Way* and *Born to Be Free*. He holds a BA from the University of Illinois Urbana-Champaign. Jack has been a family friend for many years. He is married to Goldie Wolfe Miller.

Llewellyn **Miller** is manager of financing and business development at CMF Global, Inc., and the owner of Stochastic Decisions. CMF Global is an international company that supplies equipment for the construction of major infrastructure projects. Stochastic Decisions is an independent consulting firm that provides valuation analysis for bank asset management. He has worked for the Office of Federal Housing Enterprise Oversight and several international investment companies. He was a city council member for Claremont, California. He has volunteered as a board member for the Yale Alumni Association, the Yale Club of Chicago Foundation; and for Crossroads, a nonprofit that provides housing, education, support, counseling, and employment training for previously incarcerated women in the Claremont area. He holds a BA from Yale University and an MS from Stanford. We are in a book club together. He is married to Cecilia Conrad.

Mark **Moffett** is a tropical biologist who studies the ecology of tropical forest canopies and the social behavior of animals (particularly ants) and Homo sapiens. He is also a photographer. He is the author of *Adventures Among Ants: A Global Safari with a Cast of Trillions, The Human Swarm: How Our Societies Arise, Thrive, and Fall, The High Frontier: Exploring the Tropical Rainforest Canopy*, and *Face to Face With Frogs*. He received his Ph.D. from Harvard University. We met at a conference several years ago and have remained in contact. He is married to Melissa Wells.

Michael **Moskow** is vice chairman and Distinguished Fellow on the Global Economy at the Chicago Council on Global Affairs. He is a past president and CEO of the Federal Reserve Bank of Chicago and formerly served at a deputy secretary at the U. S. Department of Labor, assistant secretary at the Department of Housing and Urban Development, and deputy U. S. trade representative with the corresponding rank of ambassador. He is a professor at the Kellogg School of Management at Northwestern University. He holds a BA from Lafayette College and an MA and Ph.D. from the University of Pennsylvania. Michael and I have been in a book club together for many years.

Jim **Munson** is a former partner in the Kirkland & Ellis law firm and a former assistant varsity football coach at Evanston High School. He has acted in numerous plays, commercials, and films. He holds degrees from Yale University and the University of Wisconsin Law School. We have been friends for many years and are in a book club together.

Kimmie **Ouchi**, M.D., is a family medicine practitioner in Hawaii. She is a member of the Alpha Omega Alpha Honor Medical society. She is medical director and clinic chief for Kaiser Permanente Lahaina Clinic and has been recognized on peer-nominated lists of Best Doctors in America. She received her M.D. degree from the University of Hawaii, John A. Burns School of Medicine, and completed her Family Practice Residency at the University of California at Davis. We met through my daughter and son-in-law who live on Maui and have been friends for many years.

Igor **Perica** is a former power forward basketball player from Croatia. He was my patient when I was an orthopedic consultant for the Chicago Bulls.

Jimmy **Piersall** was a baseball center fielder for the Boston Red Sox and author of *Fear Strikes Out: The Jimmy Piersall Story* (with Al Hirshberg). After his career as a player, he became a Chicago White Sox TV announcer. We met when both of us were affiliated with the Chicago White Sox.

Scottie **Pippen** is a former NBA forward. He played 17 seasons in the NBA and won six championships with the Chicago Bulls. He and Michael Jordan were considered to be the two players who transformed the Bulls into a championship team. In 1992 and 1996, Scottie won both an NBA championship and Olympic Gold. He attended the University of Central Arkansas. We met when I was an orthopedic consultant for the Chicago Bulls.

Brian **Ralston**, M.D., is a physician, leader, educator, and author. Dr. Ralston was a physician and president of the MacNeal Hospital Medical Staff for 27 years. He is currently regional director of informatics at Tenet Healthcare and associate chief medical information officer at Loyola Medicine in the Greater Chicago area. He holds a BS from MIT and earned his medical degree at the University of Virginia School of Medicine in 1990. Brian and I have been in a book club together for many years.

Dennis **Rodman** is a former NBA player who played with the Chicago Bulls during the team's 1995-1996 championship season. He also played for the Detroit Pistons, San Antonio Spurs, Los Angeles Lakers, and Dallas Mavericks. Rodman was inducted into the Naismith Memorial Basketball Hall of Fame in 2011 and was named to the NBA 75th Anniversary Team in 2021. His 1996 autobiography is titled *Bad as I Wanna Be*. Rodman attended Cooke County College (now North Central Texas College) and Southeastern Oklahoma State University. We met when I was an orthopedic consultant for the Chicago Bulls.

Alyssa Webb **Royle** is my niece. She has taught Hebrew and elementary school education and now has her own business tutoring K-12 students. Alyssa received a BA degree from Brandeis University and attended the University of St. Thomas in Houston for graduate studies.

Roberta **Rubin** is the former owner of the Bookstall at Chestnut Court on Chicago's North Shore. The Bookstall was named one of the top ten bookstores in America by *USA Today* and bookstore of the year by *Publishers Weekly*. She is on the Board of Crow Canyon Archeological Center, a governing member of the Chicago Symphony Orchestra, and a founding board member of The American Writers Museum. She received her undergraduate degree from the University of Michigan and a Teaching Certificate from Loyola University. Roberta and I have been friends for many years. She was the first non-family member to look at my first book and say that she thought it was good enough to be published. She has been most encouraging and helpful in promoting each of the subsequent books that I have published.

Jim **Schroeder**, M.D., was a professor and physician, and for 10 years CEO of the Northwestern Medical Faculty Foundation. Dr. Schroeder graduated from Yale University and earned his M.D. at the University of Illinois School of Medicine. We were friends for many years and in a book club together.

Eli **Segal** was a businessman, philanthropist, politician and social entrepreneur. During the Clinton administration, he initiated the AmeriCorps and Welfare-to-Work social reform programs. He is the author of *Common Interest, Common Good: Creating Value Through Business and Social Sector Partnerships* (with Shirley Sagawa). He received a BA from Brandeis University and a J.D. from the University of Michigan Law School. Eli and I were classmates at Brandeis University and remained friends until his untimely death in 2006.

Tom **Sewell** is a multi-media artist, designer, photographer, filmmaker, sculptor, environmental visionary, and real estate developer. Sewell received The Annual Award of Excellence by the United Nations Society of Artists and Writers for his "Enigma of the Mill," and for his contribution to the anti-war/peace movement. During a recent trip to Maui, when my wife and I were visiting our family, we stayed on Tom's Art Estate, where he lives.

Art **Shay** was a world-class photographer whose work appeared on the covers of *Life*, *Time*, *Sports Illustrated*, and *Fortune* magazines. His photographs hang in the National Portrait Gallery and The Art Institute of Chicago. He published more than 75 books for children and adults, including *Chicago's Nelson Algren, Album for An Age*, and *My Florence: A 70-Year Love Story*. He was a friend and mentor for more than forty years.

Marc **Silverman** is the co-host of the *Waddle and Silvy Show* on ESPN Chicago, along with former Bears and Bengals wide receiver Tom Waddle. As a reporter, he covered three Bulls championships. Mark graduated from Southern Illinois University. I met Marc when he was a sports reporter covering the Chicago Bulls championship years in the late 1990s and I was affiliated with the team.

Nancy **Stevenson** is president of the Adlai Stevenson Center on Democracy, Trustee Emerita at the University of Chicago, and the former chair of the Illinois Humanities Council and Federation of State Humanities Councils. She served from 1991 to 1998 as CEO for Voices for Illinois Children. She was married to Adlai Stevenson III, who represented Illinois in the U.S. Senate from 1970 through 1981. We met many years ago when my wife was on a committee chaired by Nancy, which was concerned with Day Care Accreditation in Chicago, and we have remained in contact.

Richard **Strier** is Emeritus Frank L. Sulzberger Professor of Civilizations at the University of Chicago. His books include *The Unrepentant Renaissance from Petrarch to Shakespeare to Milton, Resistant Structures, Love Known: Theology* and *Experience in George Herbert's Poetry.* He earned his Ph.D. at Harvard University. During the past several years, I have attended a monthly seminar with Richard in which we have studied several of Shakespeare's plays line by line.

Richard S. **Strong** is the founder and principal of Baraboo Growth, LLC. He earned his BA in history from Baldwin Wallace College in 1963 and his MBA in finance from the University of Wisconsin-Madison in 1966. Several years ago, I was invited to attend a conference sponsored by Richard. Since then, I have attended several lectures he has sponsored in his hometown of Milwaukee, Wisconsin.

Geoffrey **Tabin**, M.D., is Professor of Ophthalmology at Stanford Medical School and a mountaineer who has climbed the highest mountain on seven continents, including Mt. Everest. He is co-founder of the Himalayan Cataract Project, which has been responsible for restoring sight to more than 1 million patients. He has authored *Blind Corners: Adventures on Seven Continents.* He is the subject of the biography *Second Suns: Two Doctors and Their Amazing Quest to Restore Sight and Save* Lives by David Oliver Relin. Geoffrey graduated from Yale, earned an MA in philosophy at Oxford University, and was awarded an M.D. from Harvard Medical School. I have known Geoffrey for more than thirty years. In 2007, my wife and I accompanied Geoffrey on a Himalayan Cataract Project in Ghana where he restored sight to several hundred patients. He is married to In-Hei Hahn.

Johanna **Tabin** was a psychoanalyst who was presented two lifetime achievement awards by the Psychological Association's Division of Psychoanalysis. She studied psychoanalysis under Anna Freud and Edward Glover. She authored *On the Way to Self: Ego and Early Oedipal Development.* She earned a BA from Northwestern University at age 18 and three years later a doctorate from the University of Chicago. She was a family friend for more than thirty years. She was married to the late Julius Tabin and is the mother of Geoffrey Tabin.

Julius **Tabin** was a physicist and a member of the team that developed the world's first atomic bomb during World War II. He witnessed the first-ever detonation of an atomic bomb and then went into the crater left by the explosion to collect samples. After the war he taught physics at MIT and earned a degree at Harvard Law School, later practicing law in Chicago.

Julius was a family friend for more than thirty years. He was married to the late Johanna Tabin and is the father of Geoffrey Tabin.

Carmen **Terzic**, M.D., Ph.D., is a professor and chairman of the Department of Physical Medicine and Rehabilitation at Mayo Clinic. She has published more than 90 manuscripts and textbook chapters on cardiac regeneration and cardiac rehabilitation. She was a member of the Venezuelan National Fencing Team. Dr. Terzic earned her MSci from the Venezuelan National Institute for Research, her M.D. from Universidad Centro Occidental Lisandro Alvarado and her Ph.D. from the Mayo Clinic College of Medicine. We met at a conference several years ago and have remained in contact.

Bill **Veeck** was an MLB franchise owner and promoter who over his career owned the Cleveland Indians, St. Louis Browns, and Chicago White Sox. He was posthumously inducted into the Baseball Hall of Fame in 1991. Veeck wrote three autobiographical works: *Veeck As In Wreck, The Hustler's Handbook*, and *Thirty Tons A Day*, the last recounting the time he spent running the Suffolk Downs race track. He was a mentor to me when I was an orthopedic consultant for the Chicago White Sox and he was the owner of the team.

Melissa **Wells** is Senior Director, Ambulatory Operations at NYU Langone Health in New York City. She also is the videographer on the research expeditions with her husband, Mark Moffett. She received a BA degree from Smith College. We met at a conference several years ago and have remained in contact. She is married to Mark Moffett.

Bill **Wennington** played with the Chicago Bulls during their championship run and then became a radio announcer for the team. He graduated from St. John's University in New York. We met when I was affiliated with the Chicago Bulls as an orthopedic consultant. We have remained in contact. He was most generous in his endorsement of my book, *The Ball's in Your Court*.

Ernest Pyle **Werlin** is a retired investment banker who has taught classes on Modern American History and European History and now writes the column "Doc's Prescription" for the *Sarasota Herald-Tribune*. He has created the Eloise Werlin Park in Sarasota, Florida, as a memorial to his wife of 40 years, and since renamed the Ernest "Doc" and Eloise Werlin Park. He holds degrees from the University of Texas at Austin and Oxford University. My family and the Werlin family have been closely connected for several generations.

Joseph Sidney **Werlin** was a founding faculty member in the department of sociology at the University of Houston. He led educational tours to European and Latin American countries for his students. His professional papers have been donated to the University of Houston Library. A Joseph S. Werlin Faculty Award to Promote Latin American-U.S. Cultural Understanding Endowment was established in his honor by his son, Ernest Pyle Werlin. Joseph and his family were close friends of my parents.

Elie **Wiesel** was a Holocaust survivor, writer, professor, political activist, and Nobel laureate. He wrote 57 books, including *Night*, which was based on his experience as a teenager in the Auschwitz and Buchenwald concentration camps. I was able to spend time with him when he visited our synagogue in the Chicago area for a weekend every year for twenty-five years.

Brian **Williams** was an NBA center who played for the Orlando Magic, Denver Nuggets, Los Angeles Clippers, Chicago Bulls (with whom he won a championship ring in 1997), and Detroit Pistons. He was of African American and Cherokee descent and as an adult changed his name to Bison Dele. Brian attended the University of Maryland and the University of Arizona. We developed a friendship when he joined the Chicago Bulls in 1997.

Wilbur **Wood** is a retired major league baseball pitcher. He was a three-time All-Star and a four-time 20-game winner, American League Relief Pitcher of the Year in 1968, and American League Starting Pitcher of the Year in 1972. He played for the Chicago White Sox, and we worked together when I was an orthopedic consultant for the team. We have continued to remain in contact with each other. He was generous in his endorsement of my book, *The Ball's in Your Court.*

Eldee **Young** was a jazz musician whose international career spanned nearly sixty years. He co-founded the Ramsey Lewis Trio. He was a patient and a friend. I was able to hear him perform on several occasions at local venues, including his own fiftieth wedding anniversary.

Yuan-Qing **Yu** is an international award-winning violinist. She is assistant concertmaster of the Chicago Symphony Orchestra and a professor at Northwestern and Roosevelt Universities. She is a founder and president of Civitas Ensemble, which brings music to people who have limited access to live music. Yu earned her AD at Southern Methodist University. We are in a movie group together.

Acknowledgments

This book has been a labor of love. One of the main reasons has been the privilege of working with Tanya Hayes Lee. She has been with this project every step of the way, from its conception to the writing and editing of every contribution. She is responsible for many of the best parts of the book. This book would not have been possible without her.

Jamie Malanowski has been an editor for *Time* and managing editor for *Playboy* magazine. I was most fortunate that he was willing to edit our second book together. He is extraordinarily talented and brutally frank. When he would deliver his highest praise, "Not bad," I was elated.

My daughter Hadley Lewis helped to originate many of the ideas for this book. It has been dramatically improved because of her continually challenging my assumptions, her candid insights, as well as her detailed correcting of the manuscript.

Katie Chiasson is a gifted editor. She seemed to have perfect pitch concerning moving paragraphs to be in a more logical sequence. She frequently would "kill my darlings" by telling me that a particular quotation or anecdote didn't quite fit where I had placed it, and, invariably, she was right.

Charles Levin has been involved in all phases of this book. His creativity, calmness under fire, humor and continuous encouragement have been invaluable.

I feel extremely fortunate that Jessica Marony was available to contribute her elegant design work to the book.

Carol Lezak, talented and creative, was responsible for many of the chapter titles and helped to add a lighter touch to the book.

Melanie Lewis made numerous valuable suggestions for improving the content of this book. I am immeasurably appreciative of her help and support.

Tom Broussard has added many concepts in this book, greatly enhancing it. Tom also has pledged to donate $10,000.00 to the Himalayan Cataract Project to match the profits from the sale of this book!

Theresa Hennessey Barcy is creative, talented, and responsive. Working with her is a delight. Her ideas have been invaluable in the marketing of this book.

Andrea Gold has been extraordinarily generous with her time and editing expertise in reviewing the manuscript. It has been greatly improved because of her.

Jeff Banowetz, a skilled journalist, was most helpful in the early stages of the book in assisting to conceptualize and flesh out ideas.

Many years ago, it was my good fortune to meet Steve Bennett, who created my website: michaelslewismd.com. He is a constant source of inspiration and has been involved in all phases of this and each of my previous books.

I am grateful to Robert A. Bensman for helping me to flesh out several of the main concepts in this book. He proposed its central ideas several years ago. It took me a while to catch up to his vision.

Special thanks to each of the contributors for sharing their personal experiences and for the lessons I have learned from them.

A special group of close friends have been especially encouraging with their support and ideas. These include Bulbul and Vimal Bahaguna, Laurel and Arthur Feldman, Carol and Arnold Kanter, Gloria and John Levin, Lisa and Billy Oberman, Bonnie and Marty Oberman, Margo and Michael Oberman, Karen and David Sager, Marilyn Susman and Gary Auerbach.

My book club has been in existence for more than 50 years. Ted Bloch, John Callaway, Howard Conant, David Duster, Donald Duster, Cory Franklin, Jack Gould, Mickey Jaffe, Morrie Kaplan, John Levin, Will Levine, Michael McCaskey, Al Madansky, Llewellyn Miller, Jim Munson, Michael Oberman, Brian Ralston, and Jim Schroeder are past or current members. Their wit and wisdom are an essential part of this book.

Mike Freed, Arnold Kanter, John Levin, Michael Oberman, Lenny Oshinsky, Phil Paul, and Eli Segal met in a freshman dormitory at Brandeis University. Tragically, Eli Segal passed away several years ago. Our group continues to vacation together, and along with our significant others, socializes frequently. Their influence is present throughout this book.

Each of the following people read versions of the manuscript and added creative ideas, appreciably improving the book: Marjorie Craig Benton, Joanne Burgess, Richie Campas, Aaron Feldman, Carol and Larry Fradkin, Stephen and Brittany Friedberg, Ted and Sandra Friedberg, Mick Friedberg, Marta and Bill Greenleaf, Eliezer Oberman, Margo and Michael Oberman,

Annie Pinkert, Betsey and Dale Pinkert, Sherri and Josh Plumley, Gloria Schuman, Mopsy Smithers, Nancy and Barry Waldman, Laurie Waldman, Ken and Karen Waldman, Carol Walker, and Rollyn Wyatt.

Special thanks to Greg Aguera, Tai Baxamusa, David Berg, Susan Battelstein, Amit Bhatia, Ben Bicknese, Linda and Nelson Block, Susan and Steve Berdinis, Oliver Butsch, Steve Brodsky, Carol and Gary Brush, Phoebe and Jay Cabanban, Aero and Cove Campas, Mike Carrasco, Keith Christianson, Pam and Sonny Coclrell, Kate and Al Davidson, Gayle and Jo Donsky, Joey Drenik, Andrea and Adam Durante, Elyse Etra, Carol and Larry Fradkin, Tootie and Steve Fradkin, Michael Freed, Andrew Freeley, Greg Friedman, Pete Giangreco, Thomas Gleason, Liz Geist, Jeffrey Goldstein, Alex Gordon, Marc Grossberg, Judye Hartman, C. J. Hoyt, Joe Jovanovich, Leihua Kalawai'a, Anita Kaplan, Andrew Kaplan, Emily and Chris Knight, Jason Koransky, Phyllis and Sydney Kaplan, Rick Kepler, Ami Kothari, Ira Kornblatt, Alex Kostiw, Maia and Howie Labow, Danny Lehrman, Shellie and Jeffry Lewis, Beverly Lerner, Kay Mabie, John Madigan, Gina Maluai, Steve Mardjetko, Lenny Oshinsky, Leslie and Phil Paul, Djuro Petkovic, Peter Philips, Greg Portland, David Raab, Alejandra Rodriguez-Paez, Roddy Roy, Gayle and Stanley Rothschild, Peggy Sanders, Anthony Savino, Larry Sartorius, Jenny and William Searle, Kay and Oliver Searle, Sarah and Simon Searle, Henry Schwenk, Richard Simon, Barry Silberg, Hilary Slingo, Richard Strier, Susan and Orrin Scheff, Phyllis Segal, Sarah and Simon Searle, Ritesh Shah, Richard Shay, Barry Silberg, Troy Toole, Laura Tucker, Jeffery Visotsky, Liliya Webb, Jeffery Weinberg, Susan and Steven Weiss, Sandy and Noel Wilner, and Andrew Young.

My wife, Valerie Lewis, created the space to allow me to work on this project, which she has supported enthusiastically. With unfailing patience and good cheer, she has read the numerous drafts of the book, each time significantly improving it. Her penetrating insights are reflected on each page.

Bibliography

This is a list of the primary sources used in organizing this book. It is not meant to be a complete bibliography.

Creativity

Howard Gardner *Frames of Mind: The Theory of Multiple Intelligences* and *Art, Mind and Brain: A Cognitive Approach to Creativity,* Daniel Goleman *Emotional Intelligence,* Robert J. Sternberg *Successful Intelligence,* Antonio Damasio *Descartes' Error,* Jonah Lehrer *How We Decide.* Books on how to improve creativity: *Whole-Brain Thinking* by Jacquelyn Wonder and Priscilla Donovan, *The Mind Map Book* by Tony Buzan, *The Creative Spirit* by Daniel Goleman, Paul Kaufman, and Michael Ray, *Drawing on the Right Side of the Brain* by Betty Edwards, and *Whose Truth, Whose Creativity? A 21st Century Art Manifesto* by George J. E. Sakkal.

Leadership and Business

The Captain Class: A New Theory of Leadership by Sam Walker, *Leadership in Turbulent Times* by Doris Kearns Goodwin, *Grit: The Power of Passion and Perseverance* by Angela Duckworth, *The Frontiers of Management* by Peter F. Drucker, *On Becoming a Leader* by Warren Bennis, and *Principle-Centered Leadership* by Stephen R. Covey.

265

Bibliography

Shaping Our Own Destiny

The writings of Henry David Thoreau, Ralph Waldo Emerson, and Benjamin Franklin. *Educated: A Memoir* by Tara Westover, *Think Again: The Power of Knowing What You Don't Know* by Adam Grant, *Rescuing Socrates: How the Great Books Changed My Life and Why They Matter for a New Generation* by Roosevelt Montas, *When We Cease to Understand the World* by Labatut Benjamin, *The Biggest Bluff: How I Learned to Pay Attention, Master Myself, and Win* by Maria Konnikova, and *Tribe of Mentors: Short Life Advice from the Best in the World* by Timothy Ferriss, Kaleo Griffith et al.

Medicine

Healing Heart by Norman Cousins, The Puzzle People: Memoirs Of A Transplant Surgeon by Thomas Starzl, Head First: The Biology of Hope and the Healing Power of the Human Spirit by Norman Cousins, The Greatest Benefit to Mankind by Roy Porter, How Doctors Think by Jerome Groopman, The Social Transformation of American Medicine by Paul Starr, The Knife Is Not Enough by Henry Kessler, The Way of the Physician by Jacob Needleman, Anatomy of an Illness as Perceived by the Patient by Norman Cousins, The Doctor with Two Heads: Essays on Art and Science by Gerald Weissman, The Physician in Literature by Norman Cousins, Self-Compassion by Kristin Neff, Healing and the Mind by Bill Moyers, Intoxicated by My Illness and Other Writings on Life and Death by Anatole Broyard, Alexander Broyard et al., The Open Heart Club by Gabriel Brownstein, The Memoir of a Fortunate Man by Jean D. Wilson, Listen to the Patient by Ivan Ciric, The Code Breaker: Jennifer Doudna, Gene Editing, and the Future of the Human Race by Walter Isaacson, Mayo Clinic Strategies to Reduce Burnout: 12 Actions to Create the Ideal Workplace by Stephen J. Swensen and Tait D. Shanafelt.

Sports

Baseball: The *Boys of Summer* by Roger Kahn, *Koufax* by Sandy Koufax with Ed Linn, *The Long Season: The Classic Inside Account of a Baseball Year, 1959* by Jim Brosnan, *White Sox: The Illustrated Story* by Richard Whittingham and Minnie Minoso, *Southside Hitmen: The Story of the 1977 Chicago White Sox* by Dan Helpingstine, *Branch Ricky's Little Blue Book: Wit and Strategy from Baseball's Last Wise Man, One Last Strike* by Tony La Russa, and *Here's the Catch* by Ron Swoboda, *The Hustler's Handbook* by Bill Veeck and Ed Linn; *Veeck—As in Wreck: The Autobiography of Bill Veeck* by

Bibliography

Bill Veeck and Ed Linn; *Bill Veeck: Baseball's Greatest Maverick* by Paul Dixon; and *Bill Veeck: A Baseball Legend* by Gerald Eskenazi.

Basketball: *Beyond Basketball: Coach K's Keywords for Success* by Mike Krzyzewski and Jamie K. Spatola, *The Book of Basketball Wisdom* by Criswell Freeman, *Wooden: A Lifetime of Observations and Reflections On and Off the Court* by John Wooden and Steve Jamison, *Basketball: Multiple Offense and Defense* by Dean Smith, *Traveling: Three Months on the NBA Road* by John Nordahl, *The Dean's List: A Celebration of Tar Heel Basketball and Dean Smith* by Art Chansky, *Full Court: Stories and Poems for Hoop Fans* edited by Dennis Trudell, *A Sense of Where You Are: Bill Bradley at Princeton* by John McPhee, *A Season on the Brink: A Year with Bob Knight and the Indiana Hoosiers* by John Feinstein, and *Bill Russell: A Biography* by Murry R. Nelson. Books about the Chicago Bulls include *Playing for Keeps: Michael Jordan and the World He Made* by David Halberstam, *The Chicago Tribune Book of the Chicago Bulls: A Decade-by-Decade History, Chicago Bulls: The Authorized Pictorial* by Roland Lazenby and photography by Bill Smith, *Jordan: The Man, His Words, His Life* by Mitchell Krugel, *Michael Jordan: The Life* by Roland Lazenby, *Relentless: From Good to Great to Unstoppable* by Tim S. Grover, *Sacred Hoops: Spiritual Lessons of a Hardwood Warrior* by Phil Jackson and Hugh Delehanty, *Eleven Rings: The Soul of Success* by Phil Jackson and Hugh Delehanty, *For the Love of the Game: My Story* by Michael Jordan and Mark Vancil, *Rebound: The Odyssey of Michael Jordan* by Bob Greene, *The Jordan Rules* by Sam Smith, *In the Year of the Bull: Zen, Air and the Pursuit of Sacred and Profane Hoops* by Rick Telandar, *No Bull: The Unauthorized Biography of Dennis Rodman* by Dan Bickley, *The Big Three* by Peter May, *Transition Game: An Inside Look at Life with the Chicago Bulls* by Melissa Isaacson, *Hang Time: Days and Dreams with Michael Jordan* by Bob Greene, *Bad as I Wanna Be* by Dennis Rodman, *Walk On the Wild Side* by Dennis Rodman with Michael Silva, *Talking to the Air: The Rise of Michael Jordan* by Jim Naughton, *Tales from the Chicago Bulls Locker Room* by Bill Wennington and Kent McDill, *Scottie Pippen: Reach Higher* by Scottie Pippen and Doug Keith, *The Triple-Post Offense* by Fred "Tex" Winter, *Trial by Basketball: The Life and Times of Tex Winter* by Mark Bender and Phil Jackson, and *Coach Tex Winter: Triangle Basketball* by Ann Parr.

Politics, History

The Soul of America: The Battle for Our Better Angels by Jon Meacham, *MBS: The Rise to Power of Mohammed bin Salman* by Ben Hubbard, *Work-*

ing, by Robert Caro, *Caste: The Origins of Our Discontents* by Isabel Wilkerson, *The Vanishing Middle Class: Prejudice and Power in a Dual Economy* by Peter Temin, *War: How Conflict Shaped Us* by Margaret MacMillan, *Ida in Her Own Words: The Timeless Writings of Ida B. Wells from 1893* and *Ida from Abroad* by Michelle Duster, *Grant,* by Ron Chernow, *Maverick: A Biography of Thomas Sowell* by Jason Riley, *The Man Who Ran Washington: The Life and Times of James A. Baker III* by Peter Baker and Susan Glasser, *Genius & Anxiety: How Jews Changed the World, 1847-1947* by Norman Lebrecht, *We Have Been Harmonized: Life in China's Surveillance State* by Kai Strittmatter, *The Ages of Globalization: Geography, Technology, and Institutions* by Jeffrey D. Sachs, *Remembering Denny* by Calvin Trillin, *Principles for Dealing with the Changing World Order: Why Nations Succeed and Fail* by Ray Dalio, *The Future of Humanity: Terraforming Mars, Interstellar Travel, Immortality, and Our Destiny Beyond Earth* by Michio Kaku, *The Upswing: How America Came Together a Century Ago and How We Can Do It Again* by Robert D. Putnam, *Red Roulette: An Insider's Story of Wealth, Power, Corruption, and Vengeance in Today's China* by Desmond Shum.

Psychology

The *Interpretation of Dreams, The Ego and The Id,* and *Civilization and its Discontents* by Sigmund Freud, the scientific papers of Harry Harlow; and *Science and Human Behavior* and *Walden Two* by B. F. Skinner, *Man's Search for Meaning,* by Viktor E. Frankl; *Becoming* by Gordon W. Allport, *Love and Will* by Rollo May, *The Art of Loving* by Erich Fromm, *A Way of Being* by Carl R. Rogers, and *Mind Gym: An Athlete's Guide to Inner Excellence* by Gary Mack with David Casstevens, *The Progress Paradox* by Gregg Easterbrook, *Stumbling on Happiness* by Daniel Gilbert, and *How to Live Forever* by Marc Freedman.

Books by Abraham Maslow: *Motivation and Personality: Religions, Values and Peak Experiences; Principles of Abnormal Psychology* by Abraham Maslow and Bela Mittelmann, *The Farther Reaches of Human Nature; Toward a Psychology of Being,* and *Maslow on Management* (with commentary and contributions by Deborah C. Stephens and Cary Heil).

Positive Psychology: Jonathan Haidt *The Happiness Hypothesis,* Martin E. P. Seligman *Authentic Happiness,* Corey L. M. Keyes *Flourishing: Positive Psychology and the Life Well-Lived,* David G. Myers *The Pursuit of Happiness,* Sonja Lyubomirsky *The How of Happiness,* Lisa G. Aspinwall *A Psychology of Human Strengths: Fundamental Questions and Future Direc-*

tions for a Positive Psychology, Ed Diener and Robert Biswas-Diener *Happiness: Unlocking the Mysteries of Psychological Wealth*, Chip Conley *Emotional Equations: Simple Truths for Creating Happiness* and *Wisdom2-Work: The Making of a Modern Elder*, Tal Ben-Shahar *Happier, The Pursuit of Perfect*, and *Even Happier*.

Flow State: Mihaly Csikszentmihalyi *Finding Flow*. Other works on the flow state include *Flourish: A Visionary New Understanding of Happiness and Well-Being* by Martin Seligman, *Learned Optimism: How to Change Your Mind and Your Life* by Martin Seligman, *Winning!* by Michael Lynberg, and *The Transcendentalists and Their World* by Robert A. Gross, *In the Zone: Transcendent Experience in Sports* by Michael Murphy and Rhea A. White.

Mystical and Peak Experiences: William James *The Varieties of Religious Experience*, Arthur Schopenhauer *The World as Will and Representation*.

Other books on psychology: *The Goodness Paradox: The Strange Relationship Between Virtue and Violence in Human Evolution* by Richard Wrangham, *Compassionomics (The Revolutionary Scientific Evidence that Caring Makes a Difference)* by Stephen Trzeciak and Anthony Mazzarelli, *Together: The Healing Power of Human Connection in a Sometimes Lonely World* by Vivek H. Murthy, *The Undefeated Mind: On the Science of Constructing an Indestructible Self* by Alex Lickerman.

Friendship

Thoughts on friendship were influenced by Plato's ideas of universal forms, Aristotle's essays on ethics, Ralph Waldo Emerson Essays on Friendship, Philosophical Explanations by Robert Nozick, The Moral Animal by Robert Wright, and The Club: Johnson, Boswell, and the Friends Who Shaped an Age by Leo Damrosch

Science

Surely You're Joking, Mr. Feynman! by Richard Feynman, *Genome* by Matt Ridley, *Einstein* by Walter Isaacson, *Under a White Sky: The Nature of the Future* by Elizabeth Kolbert, *Speed & Scale: An Action Plan for Solving Our Climate Crisis Now* by John Doerr, *This is Your Mind on Plants* by Michael Pollan, *Tales of a Shaman's Apprentice: An Ethnobotanist Searches for New Medicines in the Amazon Rain Forest* by Mark Plotkin and *Scientist: E. O. Wilson: A Life in Nature* by Richard Rhodes, E.O. Wilson *Naturalist, Biophilia, On Human Nature, Sociobiology,* and *Consilience*.

Bibliography

Religion

The Bible, Abraham Joshua Heschel *Who is Man, Man's Quest for God, The Prophets* and *The Sabbath*, the complete works by Elie Wiesel. My knowledge of Judaism has been further enhanced by Rabbis Hyman Judah Schachtel, Samuel Dresner, Samuel Fraint, Ben Kramer, and David Lyon. Books by Rabbi Schachtel include *The Real Enjoyment of Living* and *The Shadowed Valley*. Books by Samuel Dresner: *Abraham Joshua Heschel* by Edward K. Kaplan and Samuel H. Dresner and *I Asked for Wonder* edited by Samuel H. Dresner. *God of Me: Imagining God throughout Your Lifetime* by Rabbi Lyon. In the 1960s, "Eastern religions" were in vogue, and I read many Hindu, Buddhist, and Zen Buddhist texts, including the *Bhagavad Gita,* and the works of D. T. Suzuki, Alan Watts, and more recently, the writings of Ken Wilbur, Lama Surya Das, and Jon Kabat-Zinn. Books on stoic philosophy have included *Meditations* by Marcus Aurelius, and the writings of Seneca and Epictetus. Books by Paul Tillich, Reinhold Niebuhr, William James, and Marcea Eliade have expanded my awareness of Christianity and other world religions. Books helpful about death and dying are *Kaddish* by Leon Wieseltier, *Lament for a Son* by Nicholas Wolterstorff, *The Tibetan Book of Living and Dying* by Sogyal Rinpoche, *A Grief Observed* by C. S. Lewis, and *Walking Each Other Home: Conversations on Loving and Dying* by Ram Dass and Mirabai Bush. *The Awakened Brain* by Lisa Miller demonstrates scientifically that we have an innate capacity for spirituality.

Travel

Many authors have written enlightening accounts of their travels across America in search of wisdom and themselves. These include *Life on the Mississippi* by Mark Twain, *Blue Highways* by William Least Heat-Moon, *Zen and the Art of Motorcycle Maintenance* by Robert M. Pirsig, and *What Really Matters* by Tony Schwartz. Among many books related to world travel are *The Great Railway Bazaar, Dark Star Safari, and The Old Patagonian Express* by Paul Theroux, *Down and Out in Paris and London* by George Orwell, *Endurance* by Alfred Lansing, In *Patagonia* and *The Songlines* by Bruce Chatwin, *The Places in Between* by Rory Stewart, and *A Journal of a Tour of the Hebrides* by James Boswell.

Writers and Artists

A Writer's Notebook by Somerset Maugham, *An American Childhood* and *The Writing Life* by Annie Dillard, *Bird by Bird* by Annie Lamott, *Jack London: Sailor on Horseback* by Irving Stone, *Genius* by Harold Bloom, *The*

Bibliography

Art Spirit by Robert Henri, *A Life of Picasso* by John Richardson, *My Old Man and the Sea* by David Hayes and Daniel Hayes, *The Book of Delights* by Ross Gay, *Here at the New Yorker* by Brendan Gill, and *A Philosophical Enquiry into the Origin of our Ideas of the Sublime and Beautiful* by Edmund Burke. Books about memoir writing include *The Art of the Memoir* by Mary Karr, *Letters to a Young Writer* by Colum McCann, and *Mastering the Craft of Writing* by Stephen Wilbers. Influential books by and about novelists include *A Portrait of the Artist as a Young Man* by James Joyce, *Hiroshima* by John Hersey, *The Great Gatsby* by F. Scott Fitzgerald, *Jack London: Sailor on Horseback* by Irving Stone, *Beloved* by Toni Morrison, *Homeland Elegies: A Novel* by Akad Akhtar, *A Gentleman in Moscow: A Novel* by Amor Towles, *The Bridge of San Luis Rey* by Thornton Wilder, *Things Fall Apart* by Chinua Achebe, and *The God of Small Things,* by Arundhati Roy.

Books Written by or About the Contributors to this Book

Blind Corners: Adventures on Seven Continents by Geoff Tabin; *Second Suns: Two Trailblazing Doctors and Their Quest to Cure Blindness, One Pair of Eyes at a Time* by David Oliver Relin; *Common Interest Common Good: Creating Value through Business and Social Sector Partnerships* by Shirley Sagawa and Eli Segal; *The Everyday Enneagram* by Lynette Sheppard; *Visions of Wilderness, Celebrate What's Right with the World!,* and *John Muir's America* by DeWitt Jones; *The Three Escapes of Hannah Arendt* and *When I Grow Up* by Ken Krimstein; *The Federal Farm Fable* by Paul Findley; *The Doctor Will See You Now* and *Cook County ICU: 30 Years of Unforgettable Patients and Odd Cases* by Cory Franklin; *Ticker: The Quest to Create an Artificial Heart* by Mimi Swartz; *Write Or Die: Negotiating Life – One Column at A Time* and *Unlock Congress: Reform the Rules — Restore the System* by Michael Golden; *The Fifties, The Coldest Winter: America and the Korean War, The Best and the Brightest: the Kennedy-Johnson Administrations, The Making of a Quagmire: America and Vietnam During the Kennedy Era, The Children, The Powers That Be, The Breaks of the Game,* and *Playing for Keeps: Michael Jordan and the World He Made* by David Halberstam; *One in a Million: The Ron LeFlore Story* by Ron LeFlore (with Jim Hawkins); *Simply Success: How to Start, Build and Grow a Multimillion-Dollar Business the Old-Fashioned Way* and *Born to Be Free* by Jack Miller; *Chicago's Nelson Algren, Album for An Age,* and *My Florence: A 70-Year Love Story,* by Art Shay; and *The General: From Normandy to Dachau to Service in America* by Alex Kershaw and Richard Ernsberger, Jr., *The Trial Lawyer: What it Takes to*

271

Bibliography

Win and *Run, Brother, Run: A Memoir of a Murder in My Family* by David Berg.

I have read collections of the writings of each of the poets quoted in the book, as well as the complete works of Mary Oliver, Pablo Neruda and Rumi. A list of all the works of fiction that have influenced this book is the subject for another project.

I have collected quotations for the past fifty years from reading the primary sources of those who are quoted, and from collections of quotations, including *Bartlett's Familiar Quotations* and the *Yale Book of Quotations*.

Praise for Books by Michael S. Lewis, M.D.

THE BALL'S IN YOUR COURT: A DOCTOR SHARES LIFE LESSONS FROM MICHAEL JORDAN, PHIL JACKSON, ABRAHAM MASLOW AND OTHER INSPIRING TEACHERS

"With insight and humor, Dr. Michael Lewis accurately captured our time together with the Chicago Bulls. I enthusiastically recommend this book."
Bill Wennington, member of the Chicago Bulls championship teams, 1996-1998

"Everyone wants a life filled with passion, adventure, and love! This amazing book will bring you on a joyous journey, with Dr. Michael Lewis as your guide, to the essence of a life well lived."
Geoffrey Tabin, M.D., Professor of Ophthalmology, Stanford University; Director, Himalayan Cataract Project

"Dr. Lewis's book is a perceptive and entertaining account of the Bill Veeck era with the Chicago White Sox. It brought back lots of memories. It's a good read."
Wilbur Wood, Chicago White Sox pitcher, 1967-1978, three-time All-Star

ONE WORLD: A VIEW OF SEVEN CONTINENTS

"Michael Lewis is a gifted artist who was born with a true photographer's eye— a rarity in anyone, much less a celebrated pro in another field."
Art Shay, veteran Time-Life photojournalist and author/photographer of 62 books

"What a powerful and wonderful experience it is to be taken on this fabulous global trip. I felt that I was witness to many 'sacred moments' and I was with you all the way. This book lifted my spirits."
John Callaway, PBS-TV journalist

SEEING MORE COLORS: A GUIDE TO A RICHER LIFE

"Your book is a splendid treatise on Life. Brilliant in thought and execution...perhaps the best focus I've read on how to express Love, both visually and mindfully."
K.C. Hayes, DVM, PhD, Professor of Biology (Nutrition) and Director, Foster Biomedical Lab, Brandeis University; inventor of Smart Balance food products.

"Your book is enlightening and life-affirming. The exquisite photographs, the pointed quotations, the instructive anecdotes, the distillations of Maslow all work so well together. You have captured the rainbows that can be found both outside our visions and inside our souls."
Arnie Reisman, panelist on National Public Radio's Says You! Producer, writer, and director of the film The Powder and the Glory

INVITATION TO JOY: VIEWING BIRDS ON SEVEN CONTINENTS

"Invitation to Joy is a true gem! Michael's photographs are mesmerizing, taking you deep into the heart of each winged friend. The quotes he pairs with the images bestow humor, humanity, and wisdom. This book does more than delight---it soars!"
Dewitt Jones, National Geographic Photographer and Nationally Known Motivational Speaker

The photos are stunning. If they represented a collection from photographers all over the world, it would be valuable for the beauty depicted. But that you took all the pictures is truly amazing.
Joel Greenberg, Research Associate, Field Museum, and coproducer of the PBS special, From Billions to None: The Passenger Pidgeon's Flight to Extinction

About the Author

Michael S. Lewis, M.D., is an orthopedic surgeon and former consultant to the Chicago White Sox Baseball Team, Chicago Wolves Hockey Team, and Chicago Bulls Basketball Team, with whom he won two championship rings. He previously served as chief of staff at NorthShore University Health System's Skokie Hospital and received a best teacher award from Rush Medical School. Dr. Lewis has published six books, including *One World: A View of Seven Continents* (as seen on PBS TV), *Seeing More Colors: A Guide to a Richer Life*, *An Invitation to Joy: Viewing Birds on Seven Continents*, and *The Ball's in Your Court*. His photographs have been shown in several galleries and have been published in numerous books and magazines. An avid tennis player, he has competed successfully in his age group at the national level. He was recently honored as a noted Chicago author at the annual Chicago Public Library Carl Sandburg Literary Awards Dinner. He lives in the Chicago area with his wife, Valerie. His website is michaelslewismd.com

CPSIA information can be obtained
at www.ICGtesting.com
Printed in the USA
LVHW021641270523
747155LV00020B/122